MONEY AND POWER

Third World in Global Politics
Series Editor: Professor Ray Bush (University of Leeds)

The Third World in Global Politics series examines the character of politics and economic transformation in the Global South. It does so by interrogating contemporary theory and practice of policy makers, planners and academics. It offers a radical and innovative insight into theories of development and country case study analysis. The series illustrates the importance of analysing the character of economic and political internationalisation of capital *and* national strategies of capital accumulation in the global South. It highlights the political, social and class forces that are shaped by internationalisation of capital and which in turn help shape the character of uneven and combined capitalist development in the South. The series questions neoliberal theories of development and modernisation and, in highlighting the poverty of the mainstream, offers critical insight into the theoretical perspectives that help explain global injustice and the political and social forces that are available across the globe, providing alternatives to economic and political orthodoxy of the advocates of globalisation.

Also available

The End of Development: Modernity, Post-Modernity and Development
Trevor Parfitt

The Political Economy of Turkey
Zülküf Aydin

Poverty and Neoliberalism: Persistence and Reproduction in the Global South
Ray Bush

Money and Power

Great Predators in the Political Economy of Development

Sarah Bracking

First published 2009 by Pluto Press
345 Archway Road, London N6 5AA and
175 Fifth Avenue, New York, NY 10010

www.plutobooks.com

British Library Cataloguing in Publication Data
A catalogue record for this book is available from the British Library

ISBN-13 978 0 7453 2012 0 (hardback)
ISBN-13 978 0 7453 2011 3 (paperback)

Library of Congress Cataloging in Publication Data applied for.

10 9 8 7 6 5 4 3 2 1

Designed and produced for Pluto Press by
Curran Publishing Services, Norwich, UK
Printed and bound by CPI Group (UK) Ltd, Croydon, CR0 4YY

And for Pascal, Louie and Miles

Contents

Abbreviations

ADB	Asian Development Bank
ACP	African, Caribbean and Pacific (countries)
AEF	African Enterprise Fund
AFD	Agence Française de Développement (formerly CCCE)
AfDB	African Development Bank
AMSCO	Africa Management Services Company
APDF	Africa Project Development Facility
ARDA	Agriculture and Rural Development Authority (Zimbabwe)
ARV	antiretroviral (drugs)
BERR	Department for Business, Enterprise and Regulatory Reform
BIS	Bank of International Settlements
BWI	Bretton Woods Institutions
CAFSL	Crown Agents Financial Services Ltd
CCCE	Caisse Centrale de Coopération Economique
CDC	Commonwealth Development Corporation
CDG	Commonwealth Development Group
CEO	chief executive officer
CPRC	Chronic Poverty Research Centre (Manchester, UK)
CSO	Central Statistical Office (UK)
DAC	Development Assistance Committee (OECD)
DEG	German Finance Company for Investments in Developing Countries
DfID	Department for International Development (UK)
DFI(s)	Development Finance Institution(s)
DGVIII	Directorate General for Development, European Commission
DTI	Department of Trade and Industry (UK) (forerunner of BERR)
EAP	Engineers Against Poverty (UK)
EBRD	European Bank for Reconstruction and Development
EC	European Community
ECA(s)	export credit agency/ies
ECGD	Export Credit Guarantee Department (UK)
EDF	European Development Fund
EDFI	European Development Finance Institutions
EFP	European Financing Partners
EIB	European Investment Bank
EPSA	Enhanced Private Sector Assistance (programme)

ERP	Economic Recovery Programme (Ghana)
ESAF	Enhanced Structural Adjustment Facility (IMF)
ESAP	Economic Structural Adjustment Programme
EU	European Union
FATF	Financial Action Task Force
FCIA	Foreign Credit Insurance Association (US)
FCO	Foreign and Commonwealth Office (UK)
FDI	foreign direct investment
FMO	Netherlands Development Finance Company
FSA	Financial Services Authority (UK)
FSF	Financial Stability Forum
GDA	Global Development Alliance (US)
GDP	gross domestic product
GFATM	Global Fund to Fight AIDS, Tuberculosis and Malaria
GNI	gross national income
GNP	gross national product
GRD	global resources dividend (Pogge's concept)
HC	House of Commons (UK)
HDI	Human Development Index (UN)
HIPC	Highly Indebted Poor Country Initiative
HIV/AIDS	Human Immunodeficiency Virus/Acquired Immune Deficiency Syndrome
HMSO	Her Majesty's Stationery Office (UK)
IADB	Inter-American Development Bank
IBRD	International Bank for Reconstruction and Development
ICE	Institution of Civil Engineers (UK)
ICESCR	International Covenant on Economic, Social and Cultural Rights
ICMA	International Capital Market Association
ICSID	International Centre for the Settlement of Investment Disputes (World Bank Group)
IDA	International Development Association
IDC	International Development Committee (UK)
IFC	International Finance Corporation (World Bank Group)
IFI(s)	international financial institution(s)
IFU	Industrialiseringsfonden for Udviklingslandene (Danish Industrialisation Fund)
IMF	International Monetary Fund (World Bank Group)
ISI	Import Substitution Industrialisation
KfW	Kreditanstalt für Wiederaufbau
MDB	Multinational Development Banks
MDGs	Millennium Development Goals
MDRI	Multilateral Debt Relief Initiative
MIGA	Multilateral Investment Guarantee Authority

MMC	Monopolies and Mergers Commission (UK)
MNCs	multinational corporations
MOU	Memorandum of Understanding
MSCI	Morgan Stanley Capital International (stock market index)
NAO	National Audit Office (UK)
NCM	Nederlandsche Credietverzekering Maatschappij
NEPAD	New Partnership for African Development
NGO	non-governmental organisation
NIB	Nordic Investment Bank
NIEO	New International Economic Order
NIFA	New International Financial Architecture
NPM	New Public Management
NRI	Natural Resources Institute (UK)
ODA	Official Development Assistance
ODA	Overseas Development Administration (UK forerunner of DfID)
ODF	Official Development Finance
ODI	Overseas Development Institute (UK)
OECD	Organisation for Economic Co-operation and Development
ONS	Office for National Statistics (UK)
OOF	other official flows
OPIC	Overseas Private Investment Corporation (US)
PEFCO	Private Export Funding Corporation (US)
PPP(s)	public–private partnership(s)
PRS	poverty reduction strategy
PRSP	Poverty Reduction Strategy Paper
PSD	private sector development
PVOs	private voluntary organisations
RDBs	regional development banks
ROSCs	Reports on the Observance of Standards and Codes
SADC	Southern Africa Development Community
SAP(s)	structural adjustment programme(s)
SBI	Société Belge d'Investissement International
SDCEA	South Durban Community Environmental Alliance
SDRs	special drawing rights (BWI unit of currency)
SIFIDA	Société Internationale Financière pour les Investissements et le Développement en Afrique
SILICs	severely indebted low income countries
SMEs	small- and medium-size enterprises
TINA	'there is no alternative'
TSO	The Stationery Office (the privatised HMSO)
UA	unit of account (currency unit in AfDB)
UK	United Kingdom

UN	United Nations
UNAIDS	Joint United National Programme on HIV/AIDS
UNCITRAL	United Nations Commission on International Trade Law
UNCTAD	United Nations Commission for Trade and Development
UNCTC	United Nations Centre for Transnational Corporations
UNDP	United Nations Development Programme
UNECA	United Nations Economic Commission for Africa
UNESCO	United Nations Educational, Scientific and Cultural Organisation
UNFAO	United Nations Food and Agriculture Organisation
UNHCR	United Nations High Commissioner for Refugees
UNICEF	United Nations Children's Fund
UNIDO	United Nations Industrial Development Organisation
US	United States of America
USAID	United States Agency for International Development
USD	United States' dollars
WAS	World Aid Section (UK)
WB	World Bank
WFDFI	World Federation of Development Finance Institutions
WHO	World Health Organization
WIPO	World Intellectual Property Organization
WTO	World Trade Organization

Preface

This book has taken a long time to write. It was begun in the mid-1990s and then picked up again intermittently until January 2008, when I applied myself to it more properly. This should not detract from its central thesis: it is, instead, a book that has been 'well cooked'. The book is timely because the unwieldy global development machine is moving again to focus on growth and the private sector, just as it did in the early 1980s, as opposed to poverty reduction and national programming with government 'partnership'. A shift in the modus operandi of intervention, or *'modus interventionus'*, is forming around direct aid transfers to private sector development, and this book reviews these in a critical light, over the medium to long term. These medium-term trends in the development industry are normally sufficiently long for a collective myopia to set in around the failures of performance last time around, but because this book evaluates across two of these phases – roughly from the mid-1980s to 2007 – the characteristics of aid to the private sector can be recounted timeously, just as a new phase of similar activity comes to operational capacity. This may allow readers to put the development industry into the context of the global political economy of development, or at least that is the book's aim. In other words, despite all the recent talk of poverty reduction, behind the scenes the whole industry of profitable development in *the private sector*, promoting profitable capitalism, has been going on regardless, and is now getting a whole set of new investments. This book is about this industry.

The argument here is that political economy processes that have made poverty in the present have not done so in the absence of efforts in the area of development 'aid' but in spite of it and alongside it, and systemically with the support of development finance institutions (DFIs). Bearing this in mind, the book examines the proposition that the political economy of development and development finance builds a process in which poverty is, in a counterintuitive sense, not reduced, but embedded and (re)produced. In sum, the book takes what we are used to seeing – aid as a benevolent act of charity – and (re)represents it as a profitable industry fixed in its own political economy. The 'Great Predators' in all of this are the DFIs, whose activities must be brought under democratic popular control in order to eliminate hunger and deprivation. Left unaccountable, as they are now, and they will help to produce more poverty in the foreseeable future.

At first glance, the book might appear packed with noisy numbers and statistics, but I hope, as a reader, that you will see the benefit of this – I have picked those numbers which serve a purpose of illustration, and the text still serves as narrative. I am also trying to arrest the problem found in some similar works of there being few if any empirics, to use a technical term, so allowing stories to be told about development which serve the interests of the story teller but have little correspondence to the experience of the world's poor. Development for many is a chance to create a world in their own image, to use a superego to make for others the (sometimes hellish) world they have made for themselves: development, in short, can say as much about the rich's view of themselves as it does about the poor's quality of life. Numbers are therefore urgently required to sweep away the piles of nonsense that have built up around the unreal benevolence that is the Cinderella tale of global development intervention, and replace it with the materiality of a work in progress of global capitalist expansion and consolidation. This is not to say that there is no room for solidarity, charity and concern, far from it, rather that such activity must be redirected and focused to cooperative, democratic and popular ends.

Many people have helped in the making of the book, although its errors, foibles and eclecticism remain mine. I interviewed a number of people who deserve thanks for their time and patience between 1991 and 1995 in the offices of development agencies in Harare and London as part of my Doctoral research, and some of that formative data is referred to here, although the names of the individuals have not been recorded as originally agreed. Ray Bush then provided reminders and encouragement, so that this data and its transcripts, and the early work on this book, didn't remain locked in my bottom drawer, perhaps forever. I would also like to particularly thank Morris Szeftel who had the onerous job of supervising the original work I did in this area – perhaps now I can tell him that it is finally finished! – and Patrick Bond, Paul Cammack, Lloyd Sachikonye and David Beetham. Thanks to Barry Winter for supporting me, and all of my family and friends, particularly my parents Christine and Colin for their unerring patience. Colleagues and students also need a mention, since intellectual influence is never entirely confined to written sources but is part of the daily inspiration of teaching and learning. Sojin Lim, Mark Langan and Sithembiso Myeni were directly involved in helping me with particular data, while Philip Woodhouse and Tim Jacoby spurred me on to the writing. Other people who helped me access particular statistics are named in notes.

Overall, I would like to dedicate the book to parents and carers everywhere who must bear that most terrible of tragedy: not having food to give to a hungry infant. We can do better – *when the elephants fight, the grass gets trampled* – so we must take the power to control what the elephants are doing!

Sarah Bracking
Manchester
September 2008

1 The political economy of development

Every day tens of thousands of workers and 'beneficiaries' toil to make development happen: to feed hungry children, to vaccinate against disease, to build schools, roads and airports, to promote good governance and civic education, and to do a host of other activities on an ever-increasing list. Development competes with the great religions of our time, motivating and disciplining, providing moral leadership and proving a clarion call against the neglect of the poor, diseased and incapable. As a social project it carries all the great meanings of the modern age, from the Enlightenment to now, of human progress and the civilising mission of human intervention. After the eclipsing of the socialist project in the early 1990s, it has also become a harbour and home for radicals of all persuasions, and has provided activities for well-meaning people more generally, who care about the welfare of others, to work, volunteer or donate their money for the greater human good. In short, the common view of development is of a 'great collective effort to fight poverty, raise standards of living and promote one or other version of progress' (Ferguson 1990: 9). In this view progress and 'modernisation' will be the result of all this human effort, because '"win-win" solutions are available to development problems and an inclusive and globalising market economy contains no intrinsic obstacles to a better life for all' (Mosedale 2008: 21).

But an alternative view also exists, where the collective efforts of the mass of development workers can be blighted by relations of power in society. The privileged and wealthy, in short, may not want to give up their position, or share global resources more equitably. This is particularly the case when it comes to those development interventions which affect the economy directly. That is to say, even the wealthy may support greater childhood vaccinations and pay a charitable contribution to see that happen, but will resist a large-scale rise in their taxes. This confirms the gift as a palliative at most, within a global social and economic system which constantly reproduces marginality and destitution: just as one child is helped, another, or two or more, becomes vulnerable. In this view continued poverty is produced by an imperialistic relation between the centre of the global economy and the edges, or periphery (Ferguson 1990: 13), and this imperialist relation is part and parcel of capitalist development (Bernstein 2005: 118; reviewed in Mosedale 2008: 21). This book is in the second tradition. It goes further than is normal practice, however, in explaining the intimacy between the development industry and the promotion of capitalism, through detailing the interventions made in the private sector.

In other words, it is not just that a virtuous development industry exists which is blighted and confounded by immanent processes of capitalism, thwarted by social forces beyond its control. This in itself is a fairly radical position. It is also that interventions in the private sector in particular have come to reproduce and mirror those of the capitalist global economy. A development bank, in short, does very little that is different in meaning than a generic private bank. And it has the bonus of the charitable label. A development project, like the Chad–Cameroon oil pipeline, looks similar to a private sector initiative, and indeed in this case, takes venture capitalism to new boundaries of the possible in negotiating with authoritarian governance structures in order to 'get things done'. In other words, development is intimately connected and implicated in capitalist process and imperialist logic.

This book explains how the development industry and its institutions such as development banks contribute to the governance and regulation of global capitalism. This in turn affects prospects for political and economic development in the South. It contends that mass poverty is a consequence of the system of regulation that development contributes to. After nearly 70 years of effort to 'do development' at an intergovernmental level, Northern states still help capitalism prosper, while simultaneously claiming to help the victims of the inequalities it produces. And development has failed: there are ever more instances of victimhood and blight. Now there is a subtle point to be made here, to distinguish this book from the many other neoliberal economists and neoconservatives who claim that development is a waste of time because it never works. My purpose is to show why the efforts of so many right-minded people are being wasted in a system that channels them wrongly. At present, they can't work hard enough to keep cleaning up after capitalism, and one way of making their job easier is to stop powerful states making more social and economic inequality in the first instance. The cruel irony being, that development institutions often have a particular place in activities in the private sector which take away people's assets and livelihoods, impoverish them, and then stymie the people's efforts, alongside development workers, to help themselves recover. If this remark strikes you as particularly 'off-message', or suggestive of an indefensible tendency to conspiracy theory, you need only take a look at the evidence that has been recorded, against the odds, from people displaced and abused by development, such as the anguish of the people of the Lesotho Highlands who were made destitute by a dam and hydroelectric complex (at 'Mountain Voices' on the internet).[1]

Thus, contrary to most books on development you may read, 'failure' in development will not be assessed here by looking at the so-called deficiencies and absences of various attributes – skills, money, political will, capacity and so on – within the South. This is the bread and butter, and misguided product, of development studies, and has been critiqued before by authors in the post-development and radical development traditions.[2] Instead, the book will examine bilateral and multilateral political economy relations between states, in order to illustrate the nonsense that is the claim of benevolence in the post-colonial practice of international aid. To clarify, individual acts of charity in terms of food or vaccinations may sometimes be worthy of the term benevolent, but the overall system is not. Not least because the larger picture is dominated by transfers of public funds to private companies, not by bowls of food to children. Who has the 'development dollar', and what they choose to do with it, profoundly matters to people's lives. Therefore, the focus of this book is on this larger, mean sibling of the welfarist public face of aid. It is about the 'Great Predators' in particular, a term used here to refer to the development finance institutions (DFIs) of Europe, North America and elsewhere, who, under the guise of assistance, act as a Trojan horse, transporting the world's biggest companies and local 'Big Men' into a dominant position in the economies of poor countries. But why 'Great Predators'?

The metaphor relates to a classic construction of capitalism proposed by Braudel, which is contrary to the conventional view of capitalism that sees it as synonymous to the market with the state positioned antithetically to both (Arrighi 1994: 10). Braudel, instead, and in a way which turns the classical formulation on its head, saw capitalism as absolutely dependent on state power and as antithetical to the market. For Braudel capitalism is a three-tiered construction, the bottom layer of which is material life, the 'stratum of the non-economy, the soil into which capitalism thrusts its roots' (Braudel 1982: 229). The second tier is the market economy, where a degree of automatic coordination occurs which links supply, demand and price. Most economics roots itself in explaining this level, but there is another, higher level, 'the zone of the anti-market, where the great predators roam and the law of the jungle operates. This ... is the real home of capitalism' (Braudel 1982: 229–30).

This zone is 'on the top floor of the house of trade' (Arrighi 1994: 25), a 'shadowy zone' where financiers operate, using a 'sophisticated art open to only a few initiates at most' to decide where foreign exchange should go (Braudel 1981: 24). Given that capitalism, for Braudel, was absolutely dependent on state power, it is not an abuse of his construction to examine the role of pseudo-public sector financiers in particular, the DFIs, as a sub-group of his class of 'great predators'.

This book has done just that, cognizant that the DFIs work with, and alongside, finance companies operating more fully in the 'private sector'.

The argument of this book is that regulation of markets through the use of public liquidity is central to managing the aspirations of Southern populations in a permanent austerity cycle, and that the people that do this job largely work in DFIs. Others have argued that poverty in the South, and in Africa in particular, is constructed by people from the North, using institutional systems that have been built historically to benefit the rich (Bush 2007; Bond 2006). For example, Bush (2007) wrote a trenchant critique of existing processes of global capital accumulation, and showed how poverty is constantly created and remade daily by processes inherent to the system: privatisation, trade liberalisation and market 'reform'. Bond (2006), following in the footsteps of Walter Rodney's seminal treatise, *How Europe Underdeveloped Africa* (1972), systematically assessed the routes and systems through which Africa is looted of her resources and wealth. He provides empirical data and examples to illustrate the inequities of the trading system, the persistence of unequal exchange, the myths surrounding the benevolence of aid, phantom aid and the degree of capital flight and brain drain afflicting Africa. This book focuses on the institutions that actually move the money around and create the iniquitous flows that Bond (2006) outlines and the poverty that Bush (2007) examines.

The book examines the political economy of global capitalism as it particularly affects the poorest, by examining the mystified institutions of the global concessional financing system (see also Gélinas 2003) and the narratives in political economy which explain what they do. It examines obscure and peripheral parts of the Northern states where large and significant amounts of 'aid' money are vested to be used and circulated in Southern countries for the benefit of the North, although this is rarely said in these terms. We also see how development institutions contribute to regulating the global economy and managing social order and aspiration. The book ends by comparing the political economy of development, as described here, with two predominant narratives concerning development in sub-Saharan Africa. These are, first, the *'crisis but salvation'* narrative found in neoclassical economics and used by the Bretton Woods institutions (BWI) and mainstream development economists, which argues that 'underdeveloped' countries are in a crisis of poverty that needs external intervention in order to transport the poor to their salvation. Second, the *'resistance but subordination'* narrative of radical or heterodox alternatives used in the dependency theory tradition and by social movements, in which workers and peasants in the South nobly resist the encroachments of global capitalism but are nonetheless relatively powerless because they are dependent on it.

In brief, we will see how the *'crisis but salvation'* narrative, the first of these, couples and conflates 'development' with capitalist growth and then misrepresents political economy in sub-Saharan Africa while serving the interests of powerful people well. Meanwhile, the second narrative, *'resistance but subordination'*, reflects the radicalism of the independence and nationalist period but in contemporary terms fails to appreciate the critical role of African elites in negotiating with, and participating in, the processes of power and 'subjectification' ensnaring modern African populations. In other words, Anglophone Africa inherited adverse political economy structures which are maintained by contemporary development practice, with the participation of African elites (see chapter 11). This book examines the empirical bases for these narratives of the political economy of development with reference to Africa primarily and focuses on the economies in which the poorest, or the 'Bottom Billion' as Collier (2007) has recently called them, live.[3]

Institutions of the global economy

So, why has social development failed in large swathes of the South (see Chronic Poverty Research Centre (CPRC) 2004; and chapter 6) and how has the profitability of global market capitalism, represented in ostentatious and incredible wealth accumulated by core institutions, states and privileged individuals within them, been perpetuated in the North? The first contention is that the two phenomena are critically related (see Hickey and Bracking 2005; Green and Hulme 2005; Pogge 2001; Milanovic 2003), and not just by illustration or intuition but by purposive action by institutions in support of particular structures of markets, investment and trade. Power is made everyday by the small and large actions and reactions of individuals, groups, communities and institutions, going about their business within the inherited structures of class struggle. So what are the critical institutions representing the power and interests of the rich?

First, it is important to indicate that the global economy is not an even space of regular economic interactions but has lumpy nodes of multiple exchanges and thin areas where less exchange takes place. The powerful nation states are these lumpy nodes and from them economic transactions spring out and reach for, generally, other critical nodes. Thus, the even coverage of colour of a densely sown flowerbed might look like an even canvass but below the canopy there remain only discrete stalks descending into the soil below. Metaphorically, these stalks are the nation states, emerging from the

everyday life of their citizens in a discrete locality of global capitalism, while the canopy is the apparently ephemeral space of the globalisation age, promising as it does comprehensive connectivity and
inclusion for all. This book has no substantive business with the
finer points of the globalisation debate (which can be reviewed in
Bisley (2007)) or in studying the dizzying technologies and possibilities of the canopy, since the subject here is the soil below. The
methodology of this book is empirical enquiry.[4] It has a similar view
to Ferguson's seminal essay 'Seeing Like an Oil Company' (2005),
where he talks of capital 'hopping over' large swathes of space
to alight only on lucrative hotspots of mineral extraction.
Development finance does that too.

The reader must now meet, face to face and unmasked, the exter-
nally-oriented institutions of the most powerful states, as these are
thrown up and out from the core centres of domestic and territorially
based power and authority. The obvious ones that come to mind are
the generic ministries of foreign affairs, the Foreign and Commonwealth Office (FCO) in the British case; the departments for trade and
investment and/or export such as the Department for Business,
Enterprise and Regulatory Reform (BERR) in the British Blair vernacular; or the ministries of foreign aid like the UK's Department for
International Development (DfID). These are not, however, the ones
which are principally referred to here. These are ministries normally
found in a national state, the 'Whitehall' state in the British case, and
perform the governance spectacle for the domestic public gaze.
Instead, the 'Great Predators', the DFIs, are found on the periphery
of the old imperialist regulatory order. We can metaphorically refer
to these as being part of the 'frontier state',[5] a regulatory space on the
edge of domestic political, social and discursive practice. They are
resident in a grey zone where extra territorial, intergovernmental
and multilateral institutions of the global order overlap and multi-
layer their governance activities; a space dedicated to global regulation and social ordering. The institutions which exercise global
power and distribute 'development' entitlements belong in this zone.

In the British case, the institutions we need to unmask would be
the Commonwealth Development Group plc (CDG),[6] the Export
Credit Guarantee Department (ECGD) and the Crown Agents: the
bilateral institutions of the 'frontier' state. These financing institutions are direct successors to those of the colonial age, which in turn,
for the two latter, had forerunners in service institutions for merchant
capital companies in the pre-colonial era. Their role now remains the
export of capital, some of which is raised on international markets.
Development finance within the capital export regime more generally, is managed on the British 'national' behalf by these bilateral

institutions, which we explore more fully in chapter 5, but here we will pursue the general case and describe a generic 'Great Predator'.

Frontier institutions

Each major creditor state in the global order has a bilateral development finance institution or DFI, which are collectively referred in this book as the 'Great Predators'. The European DFIs are examined in chapter 8, while emerging economies and Asian tigers now also have bodies which lend intra-governmentally. However, our exploration does not end with the sum of the bilateral relationships. Throughout the history of capitalism different critical masses of capital owners, and the state structures of power into which they are embedded, have fought for power and territory against each other. Sometimes this conflict has resulted in one contender being denuded while the other is made victorious. But, more often, the outcome has been a new power formation, a merger or agreement to form a collective 'power-sharing' agreement or, in Marxian vernacular, a committee to manage the common affairs of an (enlarged) bourgeoisie. The history of imperialism, and development, its successor, is no exception, but an important example of this process. The agreements to share power and influence, and opportunities for capital export, are critically and centrally underpinned in the modern age by the World Bank, the International Monetary Fund and by the rules and regulations agreed at the Development Assistance Committee (DAC) of the Organisation for Economic Co-operation and Development (OECD). This latter, in particular, regulates the rules of the spoils game, so that investors do not encroach upon each other's spheres of influence except in anticipated ways: through formal performances of competition. This formalised association and regulated 'competitive' framework critically enables permutations of members to constantly benefit from DFI funding, constantly 'passing the parcel' between each other, most often led in consortia by a Bretton Woods international financial institution (IFI).[7] We explore some examples in chapters 7 and 8, where multilateral institutions head a consortium of bilateral DFIs, private companies and transnational private foundations, 'crowding in' more truly private partners when a concrete development project is underway.

Thus, springing from the richest countries there are webs of related financial institutions, wholly owned or underwritten, authorised or legally sanctioned by the modern state. And then there are the 'joint venture' multilateral equivalents. These can be organised into generic types.[8] There are three major types:

- export credit institutions, which help domestic companies trade by lending them money to insure their exports and investment against the risk of not getting paid;
- development finance institutions (DFIs), which, broadly, lend companies money to buy factories and facilities abroad, most often in the context of Southern countries; and
- jointly held, multilateral financial institutions, which are majority owned by a collection of rich states.

These institutions live in a twilight world, in the shadow of the state,[9] or in the frontier zone. They are generally not part of a state's domestic structure or formally constituted in a public debate. They do not generally have transparent relationships of accountability to the public through the legislature, although the degree of accountability does differ (see Storey and Williams 2006). The first two types are also organised in collective associational bodies, on a global and regional basis, such as the Association of European Development Finance Institutions (EDFI) which coordinates the activities of the 16 European DFIs from Brussels or the Caribbean, Latin American, African and Asian equivalents (see chapter 8).

These institutions greatly expanded from the mid-1970s, when the system of distribution of liquidity in the global economy developed to accommodate the new 'eurodollar' and 'petrodollar' windfalls. In the mid-1980s the DFIs matured into strategic global institutions through their role in managing the 1980s debt crisis. This involved transferring and reorganising private and commercial debt into a liability for the public sector. Debt crises, then as now, can make many more bankrupt companies, banks and states than we know of, as liabilities are transferred over to the frontier institutions of the state, to be re-accounted later. The response to the current financial crisis in the UK in 2008 has repeated this pattern. Overall, the transfer of liability conforms to Chomsky's characterisation of capitalism itself, which works to socialise risk (and loss) and privatise profit (Chomsky 1993). Financial management of bad debt (loss) is transferred to pseudo-state institutions and the general public, as workers and consumers pay the price over time, through rents deducted as taxes from the collective value they produce.

Why is money so important?

There is a point of clarification we need to make first about money in the world order. 'Financial capital', or 'development finance', or 'aid', or even 'commercial credit', are interchangeable in one important respect. They are all forms of liquidity or available money, whose exact term is chosen with reference to the context in which the money is found and its relative price. The word we use in a particular context relies on how much the price is, who is doing the lending and borrowing and where in the world they are doing it. Thus, as a hypothetical example, if the Malawi Government borrows money from the World Bank at 5 per cent interest over 20 years it is called 'aid' or 'development finance', whereas if the British Government borrows money from a Cayman Island offshore bank at, maybe, 6 per cent, it would be called commercial bond borrowing. Thus, even though a generic definition of aid would be 'a transfer of concessional resources, usually from a foreign government or international institution, to a government or an NGO in a recipient country' (Lancaster 1999: 490), it is the critical construction of the meaning of 'concessional' that matters, and this defining falls to those doing the lending. Indeed, the idea that aid is a 'concessional' form of distributing money is based in regulations defined by the lenders. 'Aid' can be just as expensive as commercial borrowing, but is defined as aid because the lender views their own structure as imparting features of 'added value'.[10] Who is allowed money, and on what terms, is a central technology of global governance, and it is mediated in public–private networks ordered by the institutions of the frontier state. The defining or terminology, and control of the overall discourse on 'aid', as in other areas of social life, is strategically controlled by the powerful, in a varying degree of purposive process.[11]

The DFIs regulate liquidity in the world economy: the money which flows through the tributaries and arteries of firms, governments, households and banks (as the nodal gatekeepers). They are the finance institutions closely related to the most powerful nation states. The whole system can be imagined as a tidal marsh area, regulated by Dutch-style water management: windmills, sluice gates, dykes and sinks. Those countries at the edge of the marsh, away from the central routes for liquidity, are most likely to lose access to money as the tide goes out; when recession hits the global economy. They are also subject to the whims of those that control the distribution system, those that open or shut the sluice gates!

Institutions matter

The extension of 'free markets', even in the neoliberal period of the 1980s and 1990s, tended to ever-increasing publicly authored regulation rather than corporate takeover. The importance of institutional regulation emanating from the powerful states grew in the global economy, ironically at just the time that communism had been proved a failure. People largely thought that regulation in the pursuit of social and economic justice was not possible and led to perverse societies such as the old communist states of the Union of Soviet Socialist Republics (USSR). However, the Great Predators were working away regardless, authoring re-regulation and making futures for individual people trapped in post-colonial structures of political and economic development. For example, for an African country 'developing' under structural adjustment from the mid-1980s onward, the two broad types of institution affecting the political economy of development were the bilateral development finance companies, the export credit department and the 'aid' ministries of the old European empires, regional institutions and the international Bretton Woods institutions (BWIs). This would include the BWI-derivative institutions specific to Africa: the Africa Enterprise Fund (AEF), Africa Management Services Company (AMSCO) and Africa Project Development Facility (APDF).

In the global regulatory system of the DFIs, these multilateral and bilateral institutions supported the most fundamental objective of structural adjustment, formally the achievement of balance in external payments by the provision of debt finance, with conditionalities attached in terms of the regulation of a country's political economy. Most poorer countries in Africa and beyond shared similar experiences of structural adjustment during the 1990s, as high international liquidity in the 1970s, followed by decreasing commodity prices and rising world interest rates in the 1980s, led to widespread problems of indebtedness. The arrest of commercial financial lending after 1982 caused the poorer countries to need public external financing in order to pay their obligations on previous debt, and the higher costs of living following the 'Volcker Shock'[12] adjustment. Then, the negotiated settlement of the debt crisis, between the creditor banks, the creditor governments and the international institutions, constitutionalised economic adjustment in more formal structural adjustment policy programmes, with their attendant rules of conditionality. In general, as private liquidity drops and foreign direct investment (FDI) is harder to obtain, as in the credit crunch beginning in 2007 and lasting through 2008, poorer countries are forced to garner liquidity from intergovernmental sources. The Great Predators then lend, with attendant terms of conditionality. But because these Great Predators are captured by firms of Northern states, and because they serve the interests of their owners, the Northern states, borrowing money from them rarely helps the poor, it just deepens the debt cycle and turns the private sector of the developing country into a playground for the rich of the North. In this playground the little fish, the local businesses and enterprises, are often eaten up or crushed.

The withdrawal of FDI, relatedly termed 'loss of business confidence' or 'high political risk', was crucial to the cycle of structural adjustment and its role in restoring dependent development, as presciently discussed in Girvan et al. (1980), and reproduced in Figure 1.1. This figure adeptly illustrates the process a government undertakes to try to escape dependent development or, more broadly, the disciplines of neoliberalism in order to increase workers' share of the social product. First it seeks reforms, it meets reaction and opposition from capital, which justifies the 'necessary' intervention of the international financial institutions (IFIs), which results in a return to

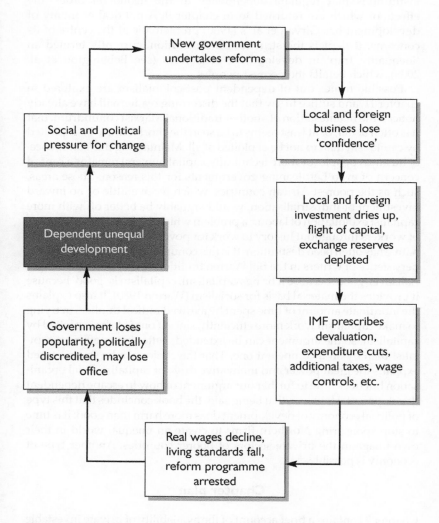

Figure 1.1 The International Monetary Fund and dependent development

dependent unequal development. This process can be traced around the boxes clockwise, starting from the grey box.

Following the global liquidity crisis of 1991, the regulatory institutions of the frontier nation state reformed and expanded again, as part of what has become known as the 'third wave' of institution building in the international financial architecture. In chapter 5, the British state and its 'frontier' institutions are explored as a case study of bilateral institutions that regulate dependency in the neoliberal order, the effects of which are returned to in chapter 9. A political economy of development has Girvan et al.'s (1980) problematic at the centre of its concerns. It depicts the structural incarceration, currently termed an 'inequality trap' in development economics (see Bebbington et al. 2008), which befalls the poorest peoples.

Possible routes out of dependent post-colonialism are explored in chapter 11, and suffice to say that the discerning reader will have already noticed the manifestation of another traditional Marxist conundrum: that it is often better, or at least seems to be so in the short term, to be exploited by capitalism than to not be exploited at all. Maintaining the 'confidence' of business people (or more technically, capital owners) remains a central concern of even Left-leaning governments for this reason. Those areas, such as the poorest African countries, which receive little or no inward investment or industrialisation, would arguably be better off with more capitalist exploitation of labour; a problem which explains the willingness of workers throughout history to work for poverty wages, since the alternative has often been destitution. It is this conundrum which is behind the persistence of writers in the Bill Warren tradition of functionalism: imperialism is 'good' because it brings capitalism; capitalism is 'good' because it provides the material basis for socialism (Warren 1980). It also explains the inordinate amount of time spent by avowed radical thinkers in trying to make capitalism work more efficiently, since if one is to be exploited by capitalism, so the argument can be extended, better by an efficient capitalist then by an incompetent one. That the choice can be so structured explains the great power and innovative drive of capitalist social organisation but does little to further our argument of how to escape dependent development. However, that being said, the book concludes that this type of political economy of development does more harm than good: it is time to stop sponsoring Northern firms to create an unequal world in their own image in the private sectors of poorer countries. Another type of economy is possible.

Chapter plan

Chapter 2 contains a brief account of the availability of private investable funds, liquidity, debt and aid flows for the poorest countries in the last

30 years or so and, by means of this account, introduces the reader to the contours of the political economy of development and the institutional regime within which 'creditor states'[13] compete and co-operate in the extension of markets. The term 'creditor state' is used here to mean a state which manages relationships of institutional lending, debt and liability with another. It outlines the genealogy of DFI-building in the period following the early 1980s debt crisis and the collapse of the former Soviet Union (USSR). In chapter 3, the relational and systemic properties of this institutional regime are examined, by examining further how markets are constructed and the key role of a mathematical risk management regime in proxying for relations of power in the everyday economic transactions within markets. Chapter 3 also looks at how risk regulates markets. In chapter 4 the relationship between international banks and core creditor states is examined in more detail and a model of the 'global Keynesian multiplier' is proposed; a model of the political economy of aid (which shows how money moves) is used and circulates around the system, with implications for countries wanting to gain access to finance.

In chapter 5, the bilateral institutions of British development finance and capital export are examined, as a case study of how a creditor state can generate and sustain unequal political economy relations with the poorest countries. This case study proxies well for the institutional 'type' of similar post-colonial European creditor states, although it is less representative of the newer Asian models of how development finance is used to expand dependent markets. In chapter 6, we return to some elements of the current crisis of poverty in the global South and Africa in particular, and examine how the 'aid industry' is theoretically supposed to assist. A review of the mainstream literature which evaluates the aid system is left for chapter 10, where it is argued that this complex literature mostly measures the wrong things, such as growth, as proxies for development.

In chapters 7, 8 and 9, instead of echoing more mainstream accounts by dwelling on how much is apparently being 'donated' or spent by creditor countries, we look at how aid 'works' to produce inequalities within capitalism. Chapter 7 looks at the direct effects of spending on aid in contracts generated by the IFIs. Chapter 8 looks at the wider effect of aid expenditures on private-sector development and the (re)production of privilege and inequality more generally; and chapter 9 presents an example. We examine the relationships of co-operation and competition within and between the bilateral DFIs and the Bretton Woods system of global regulation, using some case studies of landmark consortia projects such as the Zimbabwean sugar duopoly and Globeleq and the African energy sector. Chapter 7 describes the opportunities for profitable (mis)adventure which arise directly from the expenditures of IFIs, in the form of contracts with firms for the bridges, ports, roads, privatisation plans and technical assistance for public administration and so forth which arise from development projects. It explores the pattern of beneficiaries and how this reflects capitalist competitiveness and collusion more generally.

Chapter 8 begins with an examination of aid instruments designed to assist the private sector and then reviews the scale, scope and profitability of European and North American DFIs. In chapter 9, examples from Kenya, Zimbabwe and Ghana – Anglophone African countries with a close historical relationship to the British frontier state – are then used to evaluate how these instruments have been used in practice. These examples then enable a deeper examination of the Commonwealth Development Corporation's (CDC) portfolio and how it has rendered communities of privilege, enclaves and rentier elites, whose worlds are conditioned and shaped by development finance. These case studies also show how a concessionary business environment can lead to maldevelopment and corruption. The 'concessionary' aspect is related to the public subsidy spent by the DFIs in order to garner private profit for multinational companies. Chapter 9 reviews the bilateral economic relations of the British state. In chapter 10, the literature on aid effectiveness is read and weighed with the evidence from chapters 7, 8 and 9. The point is to show how aid effectiveness is not normally measured around the factors this book explores: it assumes benevolence, whereas aid here is (re)presented as profitable business.

In Chapter 11, which concludes the volume, we return to analyse the importance of the whole network of institutions to a) regulation in the global economy; b) development prospects in Southern countries; and c) relations of power in the interstate system, and look at the relationships between the political economy of development and poverty. We briefly assess how this system distorts the economies and polities of Africa, creating pressure for exclusivist political regimes and exclusionary economies. This chapter argues that post-colonialism is not simply a legacy from a previous historical era, but a constant reinvention of the state-sponsored development system. The oppositionism of the anti-globalisation campaign will be problematised against a renewed call for social democratic control over global financial systems and institutions. We return to our two grand narratives – 'crisis but salvation' and 'resistance but subordination' – and find them both wanting: the failure to account for power in the academic literature of international political economy has allowed neoliberalism to remain the dominant ideology of international development theory and for the Great Predators of the age – the multinational industrial and financial companies and unaccountable national firms – to run amok in the

lives of poor people. While Fanon famously advocated the decolonisation of the mind, this book calls for the decolonisation of DFIs as a first
step to dissembling the invisible yokes of global power which keep
poor people 'in their place'.

Notes

1. On 23 October 2008 this could be found at: www.mountainvoices.net/
    lesotho.asp.html
2. The inadequacy of the development duopoly of the modern and 'other',
    the developed and developing, is well critiqued since the seminal *Culture
    and Imperialism* (Said 1993; see also Benuri 1990; Cowen and Shenton 1995;
    Sachs 1999) and will not be repeated here.
3. Many books with generic titles, which may include 'political economy' or
    'globalisation', pretend global scope and then ignore Africa and concen-
    trate on North America, Europe and Asia. This book upturns this
    relationship, concentrating primarily on Africa. For the countries here,
    dependent as they are on largely arbitrary rules, this is a book which
    focuses on their global political economy.
4. This book follows in the Marxian empirical tradition of *Globalization and
    the Postcolonial World* (Hoogvelt 2001) and *The New Political Economy of
    Development* (Kiely 2006).
5. See Bracking (2003). The word 'frontier' is chosen since, as Palan reminds
    us, 'Geographers distinguish between the concept of boundary and fron-
    tier: boundaries are lines, frontiers are zones' (2000: 1), and, citing Kristof,
    a 'frontier is outer-oriented. Its main attention is directed toward the
    outlying areas which are both a source of danger and a coveted prize ....
    The boundary, on the contrary, is inner-oriented. It is created and
    maintained by the will of the central government' (1969: 126–8).
6. The recently privatised incarnation of the longer-established Common-
    wealth Development Corporation (CDC). To underline the genealogy of
    the institution I will use the acronym 'CDC' throughout, even though
    technically CDG, since 2000, might be more accurate. See chapter 4.
7. An IFI in this book is the international type of Great Predator. Regional
    and bilateral finance institutions are also included in the overall label.
8. An earlier version of this taxonomy appeared in Bracking (2003).
9. I stress, I am using this term 'shadow' here in a metaphorical sense and
    without any relation to the work of William Reno on the 'shadow state' in
    Sierra Leone (2000).
10. The Development Assistance Committee (DAC), 'judge that interest rates
    and payment structure (which determine the "concessionality" of aid) do
    not fully describe multilateral aid. In particular, nonconcessional multilat-
    eral aid is additional to what would be otherwise available at that interest
    rate, is often targeted toward public goods, and may be accompanied by
    valuable technical assistance. It may also serve as a catalyst for other
    funds... For these reasons, it functions more like bilateral ODA than like a
    nonconcessional bilateral flow' (Mellor and Masters 1991: 504).
11. This is not a conspiracy as such, for participants are only partly aware of
    what they do; the consequences of how they talk and act.

12. The 'Volcker Shock' refers to a monetary contraction in the United States that brought a sharp rise in world interest rates and a sustained appreciation of the dollar in 1979. Named after Paul Volcker, then chairman of the Board of Governors of the Federal Reserve.

13. I realise there is a genealogy for this concept, although I don't intend to invoke it here.

2 Money in the political economy of development

Various factors have been included in analysis of the increased impoverishment of the poorer world in the last quarter century or so: declines in commodity prices; negative real interest rates in the mid 1970s changing to high interest rates in 1979 after the Volcker Shock, and even higher in 1981; global recession in the early 1980s and again in the early 1990s; monetary crashes in the late 1980s; the Asian financial crisis of 1998 onward; the excess liquidity of the early 2000s, followed by the sub-prime crash and credit crunch of 2007 to 2008. Over the long period of 30 years or so, commodity prices have generally fallen (although there have been brief upswings), soft currencies have exchanged at worsening values to key currencies, and the constitution-alisation of the neoliberal project has walked hand-in-hand with the greater relative poverty of the people in poor countries (see Bond 2006; Bush 2007). It is worth reviewing the availability of finance over this period from the perspective of the poorer countries, to show how the numbers behind the benevolent rhetoric of debt relief and increased aid just don't add up to a different kind of regulation of the global economy which could help the South. In chapter 9 we test this propo-sition empirically by examining a case study of British bilateral economic relations with Africa over the medium term. The numbers show that the post-colonial system is firmly seated and contributes to keeping the continent poor. Liquidity available to poor countries is generally understood as of three types – private finance, debt and development assistance – although we can understand these as some-what interchangeable. In this chapter we will examine how poorer countries have fared in the market for flows of private finance, debt and development assistance, taken as a whole.

While these three types can be seen as somewhat interchangeable in terms of 'liquidity' as a concept, they can also be related to the mechanics of government and, in particular, to paying sovereign bills and liabilities where money can easily move from one category to another, mostly from 'aid' to 'debt'. What a government has to do, however, is make the books 'balance', using a combination of tools to manage these three categories of money. Their efforts are recorded in the balance of payments accounts. In a previous era, 'structural adjust-ment' was invented as a whole structural approach to achieving external balance in the balance of payments account; in other words, to making the incoming and outgoing expenditures of a nation balance, making sure at a practical level that there is enough foreign exchange in the central bank at any particular moment to meet the needs of citizens and firms. Richer countries have less of an immediate imperative to balance the books. Technically (and it is worth reviewing the position briefly here) five policy choices face a country with a deficit. It can pay the deficit directly from reserves; it can lower the domestic price level and domestic incomes relative to other countries in the world system (if the imbalance is in the current account); it can devalue its currency; it can change domestic interest rates (if the imbalance is in the capital account); or it can suppress the imbalance and directly control current and capital transactions (Scammell 1987: 18, 51–2). But these measures may become exhausted and the reserves of gold and foreign exchange quite literally run out. Private finance, debt and aid can help restore the payments position, balance the books and provide foreign exchange for imports.

A distinction between first- and second-line international liquidity is also useful to understanding how governments manage these three categories: first-line liquidity is international money held in central bank reserves, while second-line international liquidity consists of trade credits, long-term private credit and bank lending for stabilisation purposes and concessionary intergovernmental finance such as development assistance (see Scammell 1987: 10–12). Thus the ability to borrow from other governments or receive aid or trade export credit can greatly stretch a country's workable reserves, since 'beyond a certain threshold of indebtedness there is virtually no possibility of private financing, from banks or other lenders' (Lafay and Lecaillon 1993: 12). From here, second-line liquidity looks very much like a sovereign version of social capital, reciprocal claims or simply goodwill! In an extreme situation where countries can no longer finance their external payments deficit, other options include suspending debt service, borrowing from a foreign country, or seeking financial aid from an international organisation, normally during an acute fiscal crisis (see Lafay and Lecaillon 1993: 41). Thus, it is claimed, debt relief and development assistance make demand adjustment – unavoidable austerity measures – more gradual and bearable, when a country has trouble earning enough to keep itself. IFI 'help' can be sought while medium- and long-term structural reform and productive investments are made. Or at least that is the theory. In practice, earning ability might be permanently too low to meet people's aspirations and they are, in sovereign terms, 'on welfare' in an effort to protect their basic human dignity. Indeed, it is an important principal, but one that is very weak in international terms, that people should receive assistance particularly when they haven't enough money to pay for it, as the various UN human rights instruments, including the 'Right to Food' of

1966 or the recent 'Responsibility to Protect' of 2005, suggest.[1] But that is for another book.

Here, we must go on to note that there is a relationship between a country's access to first-line liquidity held in international money (hard currencies and gold), and its ability to gain access to credit and second-line liquidity. For example, a memorandum from the UK's Export Credit Guarantee Department (ECGD) to the Trade and Industry Committee's deliberations on trade with southern Africa in 1994 (just before the end of apartheid) explained that:

> The international debt crisis of the 1980s, resulted in one country after another, particularly in Africa, becoming unable to convert its currency into the hard currency in which export contracts are denominated. One of the consequences of this was huge claims against ECGD guarantees and those of our overseas counterparts[2].... Since the health of a country's economy, and most particularly its debt position, is a crucial determinant of ability to service export credits, ECGD cover is not now available for most African countries.
>
> (House of Commons (HC) 1994: 11)

So, because these countries had run out of money, they were not seen as worthy enough to be able to borrow any either! Being unable to find first-line liquidity in hard currencies at the particular point of crisis has thus affected African countries' subsequent ability to gain access to second-line liquidity. It seems very like a classic human story, where a person's source of gifts and favours can shrink just as their need for it rises, as other people anticipate a 'burden'. We return to how the British state has managed liabilities held by others in chapter 9.

A short history of development finance

The period where the current debt overhangs of the poorest countries were largely accumulated began in the early 1970s. After the oil shocks and the inflation that ensued, world international liquidity greatly expanded within the private banking sector, spurred on by the large deposits made by the oil exporters (Folkerts-Landau 1985; Lindert and Morton 1989). There followed a concomitant expansion of the external debt of developing countries, accumulated in large part for financing balance of payments deficits. Non-oil-developing countries began to finance their balance of payments deficits on commercial terms from 1973 with loans from banks, banking consortia and, in a eurodollar market swollen with liquid dollar assets, from oil-exporting countries. Their demand for private finance was partly due to the consequences of more expensive imports. The consequences of a swollen supply side and huge demand led to 'large and profligate lending outside the limits of banking probity, inability by borrowers to repay and to service loans; a threat to international banking stability and a frenzied search for ameliorating measures' (Scammell 1987: 122). It also made possible the transfer of $140 billion between 1977 and 1982 (Nelson 1990).[3]

During the 1970s the sovereign debts appeared sustainable with the growth rate of exports expressed in dollars higher than the interest rate (Lafay and Lecaillon 1993: 54). The situation appeared positive, not least because of the 'multiplier effect' of public development finance, where one dollar of World Bank money attracted about four more (Lafay and Lecaillon 1993: 54, citing Laïdi 1989: 210). However, recession hit in 1979 with the second oil shock and the restrictive monetary and fiscal policies which were introduced in the industrial countries, which in turn led to a rise in interest rates and an automatic increase in debt service for Southern countries on that part of the debt contracted at variable interest rates.[4] The recession reduced world trade such that interest rates rose above the growth rate of export earnings in the developing countries (Dornbusch 1989). By 1982 aggregate debt was more than $600 billion, 37 per cent held by US banks of which 34 per cent was attributable to the nine largest banks (Lafay and Lecaillon 1993: 54). Citibank's loans to Latin American countries were 174.5 per cent of the bank's capital. For Bank of America the figure was 158.2, Chase Manhattan 154.0, Morgan Guaranty 140.7, Manufacturers Hanover 262.8 and Chemical 169.7, such that 'all normal criteria of bank-lending security had been surpassed' (Scammell 1987: 123). The result was that in 1982 private bank loans to sovereign borrowers completely dried up (Thomas and Crow 1994). Net transfers of resources (new loans less interest and repayments) were then reversed to the benefit of the creditors, moving from a positive $140 billion between 1977 and 1982, to a negative $5 billion between 1983 and 1987 (World Bank 1988).

From 1982, effectively, sources of external finance reduced for developing countries from four – commercial banks, private foreign direct investment (FDI), governments and international financial institutions (IFIs) – to two: just the public organisations. Moreover, the relationship between the commercial banks and the creditor states was reformulated as the costs of the crisis unravelled, to ensure a long-term strategy for getting the money back. Private finance did not disappear permanently, rather it re-emerged in a more qualified context, secured within institutional garrisons underwritten by the public institutions which in turn were moved into the position of primary lenders. In this sense, a process of socialisation of cost in development finance took place, in lieu of a return to the privatisation of profit. The weight of credit fell to creditor governments, who then issued government bonds and sought export credit reinsurance guarantees from the private capital markets. In the South, future lending became dependent on the conditionality of structural adjustment programmes (SAPs), a constitutionalisation of economic adjustment within a discrete and binding macroeconomic package, in order to better guarantee the profitability of private sector lending. Liabilities were transferred, in turn, to frontier institutions where second-line (il)liquidity could be stored.

It is important, however, not to make an error of teleology here: the effect of the introduction of SAPs may have been to restore profitability in development finance, but the confusion and anarchy of the early 1980s should still not be underestimated. In all financial crises, such as around 'Black Wednesday' in the UK in 1992 when Britain ignominiously left the European Exchange Rate Mechanism, or the 'Asian contagion crisis' of the late 1990s, or the 'sub-prime crisis' of the late 2000s, bankers seem initially shocked, like 'buffalo stilled by the midday sun'.[5] The term 'structural adjustment' was initially coined in association with a quick-dispersing lending window in the World Bank, an on-the-hoof gesture caused by the perceived limitations of project lending in the context of severe balance of payments crises and the need to restore external financial flows (see Williamson 1990; Mosley et al. 1991). It later became synonymous with wholesale structural change at the behest of external powers.

In terms of the International Monetary Fund (IMF) SAPs were the result of a long evolution, with the principle of conditionality implicitly introduced into loan policy in 1952, when 'stand-by' agreements were created to solve balance of payments problems within a three- to five-year pay-back term (Hooke 1982). The stand-by facility rapidly became the method of linking economic policy prescription to financial assistance, with the principle of conditionality explicitly introduced in the IMF Charter in September 1968. The mid-1970s saw further extensions of lending time periods and conditionality: the 'extended fund facility' providing three years financial support was introduced in 1974; stand-by agreements were generally extended to three years in 1979, and the policy of 'enlarged access' was introduced in 1981 (Lafay and Lecaillon 1993: 72; Sidell 1988: 6). The debt crisis of the early 1980s, combined with a neoclassical revival in economic thought (Holloway 1995; Demery 1994: 26–9), which represented austerity as inescapable economic reality, did however allow the IMF to be more transparent and assertive about its prescriptive role: together they provided an overall legitimation for the erosions of national sovereignty inherent in structural adjustment conditionalities. The relationship between 'good' macroeconomic policy measures, the likelihood of attracting incoming FDI and virtuous circles of growth, was taken throughout this time largely as a paradigmatic given.

Twenty-five years on, and the effects of this period are still being felt. The extraordinary ineptitude of international bankers has been forgotten (although the 'credit crunch' might be a reminder) and replaced by a seemingly permanent pathology of poor people's polities as economically inept and in need of assistance. The loss of faith in the ability of African states to manage economic policy, combined with the triumphalism of the pro-market Right, have led to an ideological hegemony in favour of the type of incursions into national economic and political life which the SAPs facilitated (see also Bush and Szeftel 1994). Indeed, the consensus over the need for financial control of Southern states has arguably become ever deeper, as the economic package of the SAP era is periodically rebranded – with the World Bank addition of the Highly Indebted Poor Country Initiative (HIPC) in 1996, with deepened conditionality and partial arrears write-down, and IMF and World Bank encouragement of Poverty Reduction Strategy Papers (PRSPs) from 1999 – with no real change in the economic package but a great deal of enhancement to the legitimation of the intervention through its association with poverty reduction. Legitimacy has also been sought through periodic political initiatives at a regional and global level, the most notable of which would be the New Partnership for African Development (NEPAD) in 2001 and British Prime Minister Tony Blair's Commission for Africa in 2005.

Thus, after just 20 years or so of political independence for most African countries – less in southern Africa – the state was effectively bankrupt in the majority of cases. While the role of public mediation grew from the North, the emphasis placed in discursive terms was on attracting back the private sector. The attraction of FDI was given a prominence in the policy advice of the IFIs throughout the 1980s and 1990s. It became increasingly clear, however, that what can be termed 'free-floating' investment (i.e. capital flows entirely caused by the price indicators within the 'market') was not forthcoming to any degree sufficient for industrial growth. Direct investment as a proportion of net resource flows into sub-Saharan Africa fell from 5 per cent in 1980–82 to 1.3 per cent in 1985–87, a decline from a comparatively low starting level as compared to the average for all developing countries of about 40 per cent (Cockcroft and Riddell 1990: 4). Investment into sub-Saharan Africa also fell during the 1980s as a proportion of the sending countries' total: in the British case from 4 per cent of its total foreign investments in the early 1980s to 0.5 per cent by 1986; from 4.5 per cent to less than 1 per cent in Japan's total worldwide investments; with US investment remaining at less than 1 per cent from 1985 to 1992 (Brown et al. 1992: 139). The picture was bleak, such that in 1994 Bennell wrote that the key issue in the promotion of FDI is 'as much how to keep what foreign investment remains as it is to attract new inflows' (1994: 14–15). Countries had become beholden to the public providers of hard currencies.

The global position for Africa relative to all other countries and areas taken together was of a sudden return to being beholden to external powers for liquidity. Africa's net financial accounts turned negative during the 1990s, despite widely publicised commitments of donors to increase aid and make debt sustainable. Trade liberalisation has cost Africa $272 billion since the early 1980s according to Christian Aid (cited in Bond 2006: 159). Foreign direct investment stagnated for two decades, and then began to rise in the late 1990s, although the bulk of this is accounted for by just two major trends: South African capital's changed domicile and oil investments, especially in Angola and Nigeria (Bond 2006: 159). Meanwhile, and throughout all this time, Africa has 'retired' $255 billion during the 1980s and 1990s, paying back 4.2 times the original 1980 debt (Bond 2006: 39, citing Toussaint 2004: 150). Indeed, since 1980, 'over 50 Marshall Plans worth over $4.6 trillion have been sent by the peoples of the Periphery to their creditors in the Centre' (Toussaint 2004, cited in Bond 2005). In relative terms, 'Third World repayments of $340 billion each year flow northwards to service a $2.2 trillion debt, more than five times the G8's development aid budget' (Manji 2007, citing Dembele 2005).

In sum, Arrighi, in his seminal essay on the 'African Tragedy' noted that from the mid-1970s onward, African economies suffered 'a true collapse – a plunge followed by continuing decline in the 1980s and 1990s' (2002: 16, cited in Ferguson 2006: 9), with 'disastrous consequences not only for the welfare of its people but also for their status in the world at large' (2002: 17, cited in Ferguson 2006: 9). Similarly, van de Walle describes Africa's 'progressive marginalisation from the world economy' (2001: 5), a theme repeated in many current accounts of globalisation which talk only of Africa's exclusion, marginalisation and symbolic defeat. Van de Walle cites figures showing that the average African country's GNP per capita shrank between 1970 and 1998, with GNP in 1998 just 91 per cent of the figure for 1970 (van de Walle 2001: 277, cited in Ferguson 2006: 9). However, the metaphor of 'marginalisation' can be misleading, as Bush has recently argued, preferring 'unevenly incorporated' as a better description, given high volumetric trade, trade barriers and issues of market access (2007: 183–4).

From debt crisis to system stability?

The international payments position of Africa (although not of some countries within it) illustrates the problem that concessionary finance has failed to arrest the debt crisis as a social crisis: its insufficiency has relegated thousands of lives every year to malnutrition and avoidable death, while capitalism proceeds regardless, generating its super profits for companies registered abroad. Not only has the debt crisis not been solved on a social level (we return to this in chapter 6), at a systemic level it remains a problem too. The sheer scale of international private lending on a global level, notwithstanding the small amounts which reached Africa, continues to cause instability. Huge liquidity movements have contributed to the Mexican peso crisis of 1994–95, the Asian financial crisis of 1997–98, the Russian financial crisis of 1998, the long-term capital management collapse, and the 'vulture fund' attacks in Latin America, such as on Argentina in 2001. Each of these country-based attacks set off and was a symptom of a form of contagion where speculative attacks on currencies spread rapidly. These speculative movements on the private capital markets left poorer countries particularly vulnerable to balance of payments crises.

The IMF responded by extending available liquidity, beginning in 1997 with the launch of the Emergency Financing Mechanism (faster response in return for more regular scrutiny), which was followed in 1998 by the Supplementary Reserve Financing Facility (premium rate lending in short-term liquidity crises). The 1995 Halifax Summit also called for 'New Arrangements to Borrow', which doubled previous General Arrangements to Borrow, which when established in 1997 expanded the number of countries to be called upon from 11 to 25. Regulatory reform was also extensively discussed at the Halifax Summit. The Group of Ten accompanied extensions of credit with new regulatory mechanisms in the Core Principles for Effective Banking Supervision of 1998 (see Spero and Hart 2003). However, more public money did not in itself solve the problem and could have contributed to it, such that eventually core countries and regulatory bodies sought to reform the 'financial architecture' in three key policy areas, identified by Payne (2005) as debt, offshore finance and aid.

Responsibility for the stability of the financial system is seen to rest with the G7/8, who, according to Porter and Wood, 'effectively issue directives to the IMF and other international financial institutions', by 'announcing priority initiatives in their communiqués' (2002: 244, cited in Payne 2005: 139). Germain (2002: 21) summarises that following the Asian crisis, the G7/8 were looking to build a New International Financial Architecture (NIFA) to include more countries in decision-making, by extending mechanisms of inclusion to include new institutions, a regulatory initiative and a new IMF committee. The first new institution in response to the Asian financial crisis was the G22, set up to assist in the US-led reform process. This was followed, after the Cologne Summit, by the G20, which was established in response to a G7 desire to 'establish an informal mechanism for dialogue among systemically important countries within the framework of the Bretton Woods institutional system' (Group of Seven, 1999, G7 Communiqué Köln, cited in Payne 2005: 140). It included G7 members, representatives from the World Bank, European Union and IMF, and Argentina, Australia, Brazil, China, India, Mexico, Russia, Saudi Arabia, South Africa, South Korea, Turkey and then, subsequently, Indonesia. Payne summarises that 'systemic importance' is a 'polite way of referring to countries whose financial problems had the potential to become problems for the system as a whole' (2005: 140). Thus, larger, emerging economies were included with the G20 members and, as a whole, represented 87 per cent of world GDP and 65 per cent of world population (Payne 2005: 140). While collective surveillance was extended and more countries were ostensibly brought into financial governance, the step did nothing to include the poorest. It was 'not an attempt to shift the balance of power between the developing and developed world' (Soederberg 2002: 614).

Further regulatory initiatives included the establishment in April 1999 of the Financial Stability Forum (FSF) to prevent financial contagion from emerging market economies, again as a response to perceived instability by G7 members (Andresen 2000), and a New International Monetary and Financial Committee in the IMF. Payne summarises that despite these efforts to encourage emerging economies to join new governance structures – the G20 and the FSF – the G7, IMF, World Bank, Bank of International Settlements (BIS) 'and bodies such as the International Organization of Securities Commissions' remain 'at the centre', such that 'to put it mildly, the "old" architecture still matters hugely' (Payne 2005: 142; see also Best 2003). Additionally, deepened surveillance can be identified in the 2000 Prague initiative for (poorer) members to produce Reports on the Observance of Standards and Codes (ROSCs) in eleven areas where standards have been identified as important for institutional underpinning of macroeconomic and financial stability. Evaluation, performance and governance reviews are now replete in type and coverage of economic performance, financial governance and central audit authorities (see Santiso 2007). Equal disclosure in the G7 has not been forthcoming.

Debt relief and commercial write-downs

Thus we have a problem in the global system as a whole, of contagion and instability caused by large movements of funds caused by speculative trading and 'vulture fund' attacks, which can set in train crashes on particular exchanges. From 2007, this took on historic proportions as the sub-prime crisis in the US housing market, and associated rises in oil and basic commodity prices, set off inflationary pressures, and caused a global recession of a magnitude not seen since the Great Depression of the 1930s. The poorest countries, while not able to join in the feasts of liquidity in the good times, are structurally positioned to pay the burden of inflation and rising food prices when a downturn emerges. Because of their low quality of life indicators (which we explore further in chapter 6), and the sheer impossibility of debt repayment, from 1997 the poverty reduction initiatives from the IFIs have promised that more bad and odious debt be written down or removed from the books. However, progress has been slow, with reluctance on the part of bankers to admit that liquidity problems might be a symptom of insolvency more broadly. Wall Street continues to oppose initiatives, such as Krueger's Sovereign Debt Repayment Mechanism of 2001, which would constitute a more structural resolution of severe indebtedness, preferring instead the profitable business of debt 'work-outs'. The US Treasury, meanwhile, prefers 'collective action clauses'. Needless to say, there continue to be 'geopolitical write-downs' post-2000, such as in Turkey (since 1999), Brazil (2002) and Iraq (2004). The significant write-off of Nigerian national debt by the British in 2005–06 and 2006–07 also seems reactive (but could be a coincidence). As China enters the ring as a major competitor, the UK, as market leader, significantly cheapens the cost of liquidity!

The global figures for debt reduction are less than breathtaking. In policy terms, HIPC I (1998) and HIPC II (1999) were formulated as the current international framework for debt management, and ostensibly focus on sustainability with first 250 per cent then 150 per cent of debt-export ratio triggering the right to action the scheme, which has a decision point and then another period to completion point. Controversially, for some, a PRSP is required to qualify at the former 'point'. By autumn 2004, 27 countries had benefited, with $34 billion involved, marginally more than Iraq's Paris Club deal (Watkins 2004, cited in Payne 2005: 154). These debt write-offs then become re-accounted in changes in Official Development Assistance (ODA). For example, total ODA from the G7 increased from $58 billion in 2004 to $80 billion in 2005, then dropped to $75 billion in 2006, a year-on-year decrease of nearly 6.3 per cent, while non-G7 contributions increased by 6 per cent between 2005 and 2006. However, the Organisation for Economic Co-operation and Development (OECD) reports that much of the increase in ODA in 2005 was attributable to debt relief: if debt relief is excluded from OECD aid figures then ODA from Development Assistance Committee (DAC) members decreased by 1.8 per cent in 2006 (HC Library 2007).

The only caveat to the conclusion that debt relief has so far been a relative disappointment is the predicted increase for the late 2000s. For example, the Multilateral Debt Relief Initiative (MDRI), agreed at Gleneagles in 2005, means that when countries complete HIPC they also receive a 100 per cent cancellation of their remaining African Development Bank (AfDB) debts (AfDB 2008), in addition to cancellation at the World Bank and IMF. By 2008, 30 countries had reached this point, with the AfDB cancelling over $8.3 billion. According to the UK's Department for International Development (DfID), reported in International Development Committee (IDC) minutes, MDRI had provided 'an additional' $33 billion of debt cancellation for African countries from the AfDB, World Bank and IMF since 2006 (HC 2008: 18). It remains to be seen whether this is a book exercise at these banks or whether more funds will be made available as a consequence. It can be reasonably predicted, given the current global recession, that new money will be limited; such that the write-off of antique debts will be without major consequence.

Overall, the figures are less than impressive; as troubling is the macro policy conditionalities which continue to incur wider economic costs in the 'recipient' countries, including those losses to the national accounts of forced privatisation. For example, the PRSP was rolled out to other low income countries, as a 'generalised means of intervention in economic and social policy and political governance'(Cammack 2002: 50, cited in Payne 2005: 154). Despite the good intentions of debt campaigners, increased surveillance of indebted countries has accompanied any small reductions in debt stock that have taken place, a factor singularly contributing to the popularity of Chinese and Indian development finance in Africa, which tends to arrive with much less conditionality.[6] Conversely, and again despite the good intentions of debt campaigners, an absence of surveillance means that debt cancellation can provide a one-off rent for elite consumption: even in Tanzania and Uganda, generally viewed as 'donor darlings', debt cancellation was shortly followed by the purchase of new presidential jet planes (Calderisi 2006: 219). In itself, this does not say much, except that there is no necessary relationship between debt cancellation and increased quality of life for the majority.

What is clear about the overhang of debt accumulated from development finance to private sources (rather than governments), which has not been repaid, is that it becomes highly lucrative business for the international securities market and probably contributes to the speculative trading that makes the financial system as a whole so volatile, with the attendant costs that are born by the most vulnerable countries and people. This market, in its current form, originally grew as a response to a US tax law of 1963, aimed at discouraging foreign issuers from borrowing from US investors and which simultaneously made it difficult for US companies to fund subsidiaries from within the United States. Thus companies wishing to raise debt denominated in US dollars turned to Europe, where tax rates were lower and the Eurobond market began. The debt crisis prompted an extension of innovative financial instruments – such as debt-for-equity swaps and debt-for-environment swaps – while worldwide trading now encompasses all sorts of substitutable financial products denominated in a host of currencies and, as well as warrants, global depository receipts, international floating rate notes and Euro commercial paper. Various forerunners merged in July 2005 to become the International Capital Market Association (ICMA), with a 40-year provenance in regulatory governance, acting as a self-regulatory organisation and trade association in the international debt market, 'providing a stable self-regulatory framework of rules governing market practice' (ICMA 2008). Market size, a measurement of the total number of outstanding international debt issues, was estimated to be over $8 trillion in December 2004 (ibid.) and $11.5 billion (equivalent) in 2007 (ICMA 2008a, citing Xtrakter 2007). The ICMA has a membership which includes regional banks and traders, but its core, what it refers to as its 'market making community', comprises a 'council of reporting dealers', made up of around 40 firms, almost three-quarters of which are based in London, which together account for the 'majority of cross-border business in the international capital market' (ibid.).

Aid: 'much heat and light and signifying nothing'?

From 1992 to 1997, OECD official development assistance decreased by 21 per cent to only $49.6 billion, an ODA to GNI ratio for DAC members of 0.22 per cent, 'a far cry' (Thérien 2002: 458) from the 0.7 per cent agreed at the United Nations some 30 years earlier. Moreover, the ODA to the least-developed countries dropped from $17 billion in 1990 to $12 billion in 1999, and much of this was tied (Payne 2005: 160–162). But from around 1999, a new importance was attached to ODA, codified in the Millennium Development Goals (MDGs) and the 2000 Millennium Declaration. A mood of optimism prevailed as an International Conference on Financing for Development opened in Monterrey in 2002 and the 'Monterrey Consensus' was reached, even though this too ultimately proved disappointing. Some G7 members announced modest rises in ODA, with, for example, the United States launching its Millennium Challenge Account. As the OECD itself calculated, even if Monterrey were fully met, by 2006 the ODA/GNI ratio in DAC countries would have risen by only 0.02 to 0.24 per cent (Payne 2005: 163).

Africa was then accorded a measure of priority in the NEPAD in 2002, to achieve a 7 per cent annual economic growth sufficient to fund the halving of African poverty by 2015. The political strategy was to cost the price of meeting the MDGs and encourage donors to pay more, in return for renewed loyalty to the conditionalities of neoliberalism. However, commitment to poverty reduction remained weak. Even James Wolfensohn, then President of the World Bank, noted in 2004 that $900 billion was spent globally on defence, as compared to $50–60 billion on development, but 'if we spent $900bn on development, we probably would not need to spend more than $50 billion on defence' (reported in the *Financial Times*, 26 April 2004, cited in Payne 2005: 165). Bond, similarly, notes that 'compared to military spending of $642 billion by rich countries in 2003, aid of $69 billion is a pittance' (2006: 33). In terms of just Africa, $25 billion is spent per year (for 600 million people) compared with $200 billion spent in 2003 and 2004 on the war in Iraq, an oil producer with only 25 million people, or compared to $350 billion spent by the European Union to protect its farmers (Calderisi 2006: 218). Viewed comparatively, the overall figures for aid expenditure look miserly. We will return to examine the volumes, scope and value of ODA in more detail in chapter 6.

The current market for development finance

From the above summaries of private finance, debt and aid, we arrive back at our original question: whether the current market for development finance has adequate liquidity, or whether the costs of this money remain normatively unacceptable. A reasonable conclusion would be that however welcome the contemporary (small) increase in funds might be there remain serious problems in the market for development finance from the perspective of developing countries. Spero and Hart (2003) summarise the mainstream position on these as the (in)ability and (un)willingness of debtor governments to implement reform, especially in terms of information provision and disclosure; the (in)ability of IMF to force implementation; continued weaknesses in international bank supervision and regulation, particularly with regard to securities firms and securities markets; and an absence of a restructuring mechanism. More particularly they are concerned with the increased moral hazard associated with country bailouts (Spero and Hart 2003: 58–9), while they anticipate conflicts in governance:

> between globalisation and national sovereignty. Managing globalisation requires the coordination of national economic policies and the imposition of international discipline over policies that traditionally have been the prerogative of national governments.
>
> (Spero and Hart 2003: 59)

This conflict can indeed be anticipated, and the weaknesses in holding private securities markets to account, and the continued absence of a sovereign bankruptcy mechanism, are indeed market weaknesses. However, the strict divide between a sacrosanct sovereignty and an imposition from 'outside' is too simplistic and absolute. Instead, from a political economy perspective we can be concerned about the way that this system affects governance, democracy and development processes.

From our more structuralist perspective there remain two main types of problem: the first is the continued parsimony of assistance per se, despite the acute rhetoric of benevolence. This is not to advocate deepened interventionism by creditor states – far from it – just to recognise that although the numbers might sound large, they are not, and the money can't go very far or buy very much for mass populations, although it is sufficient to tip the balance of power in favour of incumbent governments when used strategically around elections. The second problem is systemic and concerns the compromised and failed legitimacy of sovereign debt when there is so much evidence that:

1. 'Aid-spoilt' local elites have often adopted a particular style of anti-democratic, exclusionary politics, sometimes with the collusion of donors (on Kenya, for example, see Murunga 2007; Bracking 2006).
2. 'Aid' has played a significant role in helping multinational corporations (MNCs) both collude in this exclusionary game, while passing on their investment costs of plant and machinery to their workers through the sovereign debt mechanism
3. Related to point 2, much aid and debt relief – that is, advertised liquidity – is phantom and exists principally as a subsidy or Keynesian injection with which creditor governments assist their own companies, particularly by underwriting and then socialising the costs of risks and investment. This relationship is depicted in Figure 4.1, at the end of chapter 4. We return to the effect of development finance on politics in chapter 11.

These problems with the political economy of development have been noted by writers who point to the apparent incoherence of development policy, ranging as it does from welfare and social policy, saving lives and humanitarian assistance, through to providing equity subsidies to major global companies and enforcing the types of markets they wish to work in through conditionalities. In general, the political economy of development reflects, reproduces and supports the general policy stance and associated government activities which uphold neoliberal markets worldwide. While neoliberalism is a complex concept, it centrally involves a freedom of capital holders to move their money and profits around the globe relatively unhindered by governments (for more comprehensive accounts see Harrison 2005; Saad-Filho and Johnston 2004). In development, these macroeconomic policies of 'liberalisation' (unhindered trade, finance and exchange) are seen to be in contradiction with the former social welfare policies. Pieterse summarised the current political economy of aid and poverty reduction adeptly when he pointed to this 'incoherence' of policy:

> Neoliberal policies widen the global inequality that poverty reduction strategies seek to mitigate. International financial institutions count on 'conditional convergence' while inhibiting the required conditions from materialising. International institutions urge state action while trapping states in structural reform.
>
> (2002: 1042)

He continues that neoliberal policies are probably the 'central dynamic' in widening domestic and global inequality since the 1980s, since they 'bet on the strong, privilege the privileged, help the winners, expose the losers and prompt a "race to the bottom"' (Pieterse 2002: 1032), a view shared by the robust analysis of Milanovic (2003). Meanwhile, for the general public, it is undoubtedly the former social welfare functions of aid that are understood to constitute the aid relationship as a whole: few, in any case, think aid budgets are given to multinational companies in order to build the infrastructure they themselves use. However, it is not the purpose here to support the conservative case for less aid (based in racialised ideas of corruption and waste) by critiquing the private uses of aid budgets, rather to question the pattern of 'beneficiaries' we can expect, and to suggest that aid should be spent in a different pattern.

It is also not the purpose here to reiterate the debate about the inefficacy of neoliberalism to development, particularly in its crude cost/benefit mode, suffice to say that we are returned to the Marxist conundrum about the nature of exploitation mentioned in chapter 1: an absence of capitalism can be normatively as bad, if not worse, than an overdose of it in the neoliberal mode. Many radical accounts are proselytising in their rebukes for a 'neoliberalism' concept which is ludicrously expanded to depict a catch-all of everything that is wrong with contemporary economics in respect of social welfare. At this generic level the argument risks descending into caricature, and we lose the strategic agenda of how social and worker movements can shift the balance of global power in favour of the poor, by democratizing the management of markets in their favour. That current development policy is detrimental to social justice is evidenced by the gratuitously negative statistics on social wellbeing in Africa (see chapter 6) and some parts of South-East Asia and Latin America, and the collective myopia of those involved in high institutions to see their contributions relatively, as the small change that they really are, in comparison to structural relationships that are singularly skewed in favour of the already rich. Cynically, but not inaccurately, the global development 'budget' is no more than a small palliative, a sophisticated public relations machine to undermine the critique of global power to which the international worker and social movement is inclined. It is the 'gift from the American people' stamped on the bag of corn in the television picture. The public relations exercise contradicts popular knowledge, the 'consciousness arising from being', the lived experience of the minute reach of developmental welfare, relative to wider economic exploitation: this consciousness asks 'what global assistance is this, that is so little and so late?'

Pieterse reminds his readers of Thomas Pogge's (2002) 'international borrowing privilege' that 'regardless of how a government has come to power ... can put a country into debt', and the 'international resource privilege' that 'regardless of how a country has come into power ... can confer globally valid ownership rights in a country's resources to foreign companies' (Pieterse 2002: 1035; see also Pieterse 2004: 75). Pieterse goes on to say:

> In view of these practices, corporations and governments in the North are accomplices in official corruption; thus, placing the burden of reform solely on poor countries only reinforces the existing imbalance.
>
> (2002: 1035)

His argument can, however, be extended to development in general, since development policy unquestionably recognises Pogge's 'privileges': it colludes and reproduces political and economic elites who have the power to throw their own populations into poverty and abjection. We do not see, for example, the World Bank turning to rapacious elites and saying, 'No, you can't borrow in the name of your poor people, your personal income is too high already'! Instead structures of inequality are reinforced. The current anti-democratic approach has been summarised by Joseph Ki-Zerbo (with reference to donor policy at the time of the Moi Government in Kenya during the 1990s) as 'Silence, Development in Progress' (cited in Murunga 2007: 288). Development policy and development finance can do this because they critically tip the balance of power in elites' favour relative to the majority population, allowing them to collect rents from the strategic use of the sovereignty they control (see also Harrison 1999: 537–40 on 'boundary politics'; Bracking 2009; and chapter 11). From the perspective of the political economist, it is to the construction of markets that we should now turn in the next chapter to see how these antimonies of power are reproduced.

Conclusion

This chapter has provided a brief overview of the availability of liquidity from the private sector and the public sector in the form of development finance, and has examined the intimate relationship conceptually and practically between flows of money called 'investment', 'debt and debt relief' and those categorised as 'aid'. These carry social and economic relations, what Marxists would call the 'capital relation' to other societies through institutional channels, principally within the frontier of the state, as described in chapter 1. Before returning for a closer look at these institutions, the next two chapters review, first, how markets are made and the principal use of risk as a form of liquidity management; and then, second, how the Great Predators are structured. For those readers who are not economists, this is not as dry as it sounds, and is illuminating of broader concerns than just money itself! Technical language in the area of finance serves to hide and mystify more general relationships of social power, privilege, and status and critically obscures how the divide between the global haves and have-nots is maintained; the technical slights of hand are the implementing policy machine of the political economy of development. It is worth looking beyond the jargon. Similarly, we saw in this chapter how 'big' numbers can hide systemic relationships of power and inequality, such that the apparent generosity of debt relief and aid is variegated and significant only 'at the edges' of the wider capitalism in which it is embedded, and by which it is overshadowed. As Keynes famously noted 'interesting things happen at the edges', so we must now look at these markets for finance further.

Notes

1. 'Right to Food' is contained in the International Covenant on Economic, Social and Cultural Rights (ICESCR), General Comment 12. 'Responsibility to Protect' is contained in the United Nations Security Council Resolution 1674 of April 2006, which endorses the 2005 World Summit statement of the same.
2. In some countries, such as Nigeria, these claims ran into billions of pounds.

3. All $ in this book refer to United States of America (US) dollars.
4. According to Lafay and Lecaillon (1993: 68), two-thirds of Latin American debt was at a variable rate, compared with only one-third for Asia, which was thus 'less hard hit'.
5. As a student at the University of Leeds once memorably put it in an essay.
6. Whether this is astute 'market entry' behaviour aimed at undercutting the prior market leaders or whether Chinese and Indian finance will continue to be relatively condition free, if indeed it is now, remains a difficult question. The special issue of *Review of African Political Economy* (2008), 115, 'The "New" Face of China–African Co-operation', makes some interesting observations in this regard (Power et al. 2008).

3 Making markets

We saw in the last chapter that access to private funds for development for the majority of the poorest countries has been sporadic and difficult since 1982. In Africa, from the onset of the debt crisis, what are termed 'externalised' forms of multinational corporation (MNC) involvement became increasingly common, such as subcontracting and production under license; forms of involvement which involve a thin equity base and which are less risky, often incorporating arrangements for assured payment in foreign exchange for services, brand use and royalties for patented processes (Bennell 1994: 14; United Nations Centre for Transnational Corporations (UNCTC) 1989; United Nations Commission for Trade and Development (UNCTAD) 1994). Thus, as Bond clearly shows in his book (2006), smaller investment volumes do not imply the absence of profitable extractive processes, rather that these are done on a thin equity base, in privatised and sometimes criminalised extractive enclaves. This pattern has contradicted the 1990s proposition that there was a powerful association between 'good' macroeconomic policies and inward investment, since the wider context has not been particularly significant in determining investment patterns (see Ferguson 2006: 194–8). In turn, markets have grown unevenly and irregularly around these uneven investments, confounding economists' predictions in varied and often personalised contexts, with social and political factors more important than a general model would allow for. In this chapter we look further at how markets are structured and the role, in particular, of public 'market makers'; a theme which is developed in the next chapter by a further examination of the relationship between international financial institutions (IFIs) and creditor states. In chapter 5, a case study of the British frontier institutions for capital export is presented. Together, we are exploring how the public sector critically socialises and underwrites risk in favour of the profitability of the private sector. Where investments haven't been concentrated around mineral extraction, informalised or globally integrated through an MNC supply chain, they have been forged under the guardianship of public development finance institutions (DFIs). So, how are markets made?

Markets

It is not sufficient to look only at aggregate data when explaining the political economy of development, since such data measure the outcomes of social process. At a meso-level there are also attendant structural relationships formed and reformed during the processes of investment, trade and exchange which author economic possibilities and denials. In other words, in the promotion of 'The Market' of the structural adjustment programme (SAP) period, a deepening of the management of markets by the IFIs took place: markets were constructed and access to them managed to re-configure the colonial pattern of dependent development. This project involved a lot of work and a lot of change, even where the results were only marginally reflected in the data for growth or capital formation. One of the global market makers, such as typically the International Finance Corporation (IFC), would raise a large umbrella and under it would crowd in a flotilla of lesser investors happy to have some assurance that the privilege of the IFC's position relative to the country's government, and the investment guarantees they would insist on, would shelter them from all sorts of risks and threats to their profits. In this section we need to examine what it is about a market which allows differential outcomes to participants, which serves the function of reconfiguring power, and then see how the particular notion of risk in markets makes unpredictability calculable, such that it serves the interests of the privileged. By means of this exploration, we can then identify ways in which development finance makes and expands markets.

Market structures are not expressions of abstract principles of rationality and efficiency, but instead:

> represent concrete configurations of power; markets are deter-
> minations of power relations, expressions of lines of force
> (domination and subordination) within the global order.
> (Bush and Szeftel 1994: 155)

Markets can free humans from the bounds of certain types of oppression, such as extra-economic slavery, violence, serfdom and debt peonage. They can also shake up patrimonial societies and ensure that people not related to the political class can create independent livelihoods. There are also contexts in which competition within markets can encourage innovation, invention and a better price to consumers. However:

> It is one thing to argue that markets can be mechanisms to
> improve efficiency and democracy, serving to check bureaucratic
> and petty bourgeois accumulation, job patronage and the politics
> of graft, increasing industrial flexibility and removing ethnic and
> racial prejudice from some processes of resource allocation. It is
> quite another to argue that development and democracy require
> that society should be regulated by the market.
> (Bush and Szeftel 1994: 153)

But this latter assertion became dominant from the early 1980s onward, as the specific contexts in which people could enjoy these benefits were obscured in favour of an all encompassing market, eulogising which generalised these to apparently apply everywhere at any time. This was highly unfortunate, because some markets can also protect privileged companies, exclude new producers, keep prices to consumers artificially high and be destroyed in the short term by products from other markets, such as when local manufacturing industry in structurally adjusting African economies was destroyed by import liberalisation allowing cheaper incoming products (see Mwanza 1992; various essays in Onimode 1989; and, on Zimbabwe, Chipika et al. 2000; Beckman and Sachikonye 2001).

Mackintosh provided an early critique which isolated the concept of 'markets' in three different contexts: in its broadest abstraction, in a range of models of different types of market and in actual working markets (Mackintosh 1990). In the broadest abstraction, 'the market' became a token of ideological debate, implying private ownership, 'freedom', entrepreneurial effort and a neutral mechanism with which to organise society equitably by materially rewarding the deserving 'successes'. It is an iconic concept which signifies freedom and has a widespread association with liberal democracy. Because of this, as Murunga has recently pointed out, opponents of structural adjustment were successfully depicted by its proponents as rent-seekers, protectors of anti-democratic privilege and patrimonialism (Murunga 2007: 277). The iconic market implies that market relations exist abstracted from the social relations which provide the market's framework, while market growth or extension can be only a quantitative issue. This is the market of the triumphalist Right; necessary, benevolent and permanent. It is also 'The Market' which worked at an ideological level to drive the class project, which was market restructuring under structural adjustment, back in favour of international capital and a smaller comprador class, and away from the wider, popular nationalist constituency.

However, ideological project aside, in actual working markets, including those for international finance, varying institutional forms take place, there is limited information, and arbitrary and qualitative decisions are taken over risk, often according to the cultural and social background of participants. Social classes are shored up and reconfigured. We can summarise that markets:

> concentrate information, and hence power, in the hands of few: that some participants are "market makers" while others enter in a position of weakness; that markets absorb huge quantities of resources in their functioning; that profits of a

few, and growth for some, thrive in conditions of uncertainty, inequality and vulnerability of those who sell their labour power and of most consumers; and that atomised decision-making within a market can produce long-term destructive consequences – for example on the environment – which may have been intended by none of the participants.

(Mackintosh 1990: 50)

All markets are structured by social relations, by classes and institutions, and more generally by state action. There is no such thing as a free market, only variation in how the terms of their operation are set.

This is particularly the case in very weak and incomplete markets, where those who set operations have a large arbitrary set of powers. The Great Predators enter here as market makers with 'an ambiguous character', to both make profitable capitalist investments and to maintain notions of benevolent development assistance, existing 'between the two' positions of 'donor agency' and 'profit-seeking financial intermediary'.[1] But the complementarity between the two is possible only because the profitability is material and measurable, while the 'development' is asserted normatively. Just as importantly, because the profitability in weak markets is purposively constructed: while the Great Predators often lend at 'market interest rates', and profitability derives from repayments at these rates, it is important to note that these 'market rates' are constructed artificially, in the case of the very poorest countries, by the Predators themselves. Because there is an incomplete or non-existent market for similar products – long-term finance and equity – since no private firms are exchanging, the price of the money is set by the supplier or suppliers, acting like a cartel: it is in this sense of incomplete markets that the Predators manage development.

Moreover, while markets are embedded in, and have multiple effects on society – and the market for international liquidity shapes whether a country can buy productive or industrial resources, can adequately feed and house its people and fund an equitable polity – they are made by a surprisingly small number of people. Those who 'set the terms' of operation, the 'market makers', and who control the allocation of international liquidity, are concentrated in the IFIs and large banks. They exist at the 'commanding heights' (Arrighi 1994: xii), in the boardroom of the global economy, and their relatively small number explains in part both the herd behaviour of investors when markets are in trouble, and the incredible booms and slumps of fortune as the system swings around its own measures of 'confidence'. In turn, the global markets for goods and services are constructed indirectly by this overriding market for finance, since it is the commodity essential to join in any of them.

One of these 'market makers', the IFC, explained the problematic, even at the height of the 'free market' craze, thus:

> It has been argued that the principle of a market economy implies that government and government-financed efforts to assist the private sector should be confined strictly to ensuring that the right macroeconomic policies and legal and accounting systems have been set up. Within this framework, this argument continues, markets should be left to work, and the private sector should be left to look after itself. The view may be characterised as extreme, not to say ideological. Even when government policies are optimal (and, of course, they are not always so), markets do not always work perfectly, and various barriers and perceptions of risk discourage the private sector. It is appropriate, therefore, for institutions such as IFC, although publicly financed, to play a role that will enable markets to overcome these barriers and perceptions.
>
> (IFC 1992: 1)

The IFC report continues: 'Private business has definite needs; if these needs go unmet, growth will occur only slowly, if at all' (IFC 1992: 18). The central signifier of the quality of a market is 'risk', which represents a host of other criteria, such that 'risk' acts to control entry, exit and participation in markets as a governing technology.

Risk as governing technology

Risk per se is not inherently detrimental to growth, development or economic activity: risk is a potential source of profit and the capitalist entrepreneur expects above average returns for investment in risky ventures. To do so, however, the risk must be managed, such that uncertainty, pure and simple, becomes calculable, such that markets can expand. For North and Haufler, economic development is ensured by the institutionalisation of risk, with good business deals judged as those where there is a high degree of certainty about future returns, as the lengthy history of cartelisation illustrates (North 1990: 126; Haufler 1997). This pattern forms the antithesis of a global risk-taking strategy so avowed by capitalist propaganda (see Haufler 1997). Since certainty of outcomes to investment and trade is less in a foreign territory, if this risk is left unmitigated, investment, trade and technological development will be arrested.

Two primary issues emerge: the problem of risk assessment in economic exchange and the distribution of costs and profits in the risk regime as a whole. The problem of assessment prompts the question why some countries are deemed 'risky', indeed why some are 'too risky' to attract private flows of FDI or credit, and others not, particularly when the label also contributes to the denial of some countries' access to international credit completely, while others experience a heightened cost of industrialisation and a higher rate of extracted profits where credit has been granted. However, the assessment of risk is always qualitative, however sophisticated the quantitative modelling undertaken, while the accuracy of risk assessment also relates to the demands of the purchaser of the insurance contract. The argument can be made that these demands are excessive in relation to poor countries: high profits and risky environments are related and can be incorporated into business planning. With the development paradigm, however, it is arguable that something more political has emerged: a synergistic agreement that 'too risky' means 'we can get public subsidy'; if the costs of risk can be socialised and borne by public institutions the result is even higher profits. The development finance system here arguably contributes to rent-taking activity, since historically markets declared too risky have systematically been subject to public subsidy. Sometimes this effect is secured by accounts of risk that are quite clearly racialised and arbitrary, a point which has been substantiated by research.

Thus, the dearth of private investment in Africa is explained by the private sector in terms of Africa being 'too risky'. However, the homogenising and racialised view of Africa in the money capitals of the world does nothing to assist productive investment, even when opportunities arise. Mkandawire carried out research on FDI and found that:

> rates of return of direct investments have generally been much higher in African than in other developing regions. This, however, has not made Africa a favourite among investors, largely because of consideration of the intangible 'risk factor', nurtured by the tendency to treat the continent as homogenous and a large dose of ignorance about individual African countries. There is considerable evidence that shows that Africa is systematically rated as more risky than is warranted by the underlying economic characteristics.
>
> (2005: 7)

Additionally, Mkandawire found that little of even these small flows had reached the all-important manufacturing sector, and as much as 14 per cent was 'driven by acquisitions facilitated by the increased pace of privatisation to buy up existing plants that are being sold, usually under "fire sale" conditions' (2005: 6). These conclusions are supported by another study, in which 'negative perceptions of Africa are a major cause of under-investment' (Bhinda et al. 1999: 72). Here, even successful African countries were unable to attract FDI as 'potential investors lump them together with other countries, as part of a continent that is considered not to be attractive', with investors additionally 'unable to distinguish among countries' and tending 'to attribute negative performance to the whole region' (Bhinda et al. 1999: 55, cited in Ferguson 2006: 7). Bhinda et al. note that 'investor perceptions rather than objective data' are guiding investment decisions (Bhinda et al. 1999: 15), while Ferguson adds that 'such perceptions don't just misunderstand social reality; they also shape it', and concludes that 'it is clear that the spectral category "Africa" looms large in these perceptions, with powerful consequential results' (2006: 7).

To compound the problem of risk assessment there exists the further issue of who bears the risk, since it exists in exchanges between individuals and at all levels and relations between institutions: firms, banks, local, national and international, with negotiation to pay for and underwrite risk, a feature of the relations of institutions including governments and banks. The relationships between these institutions provide safeguards which reduce risk on some international loans, including guarantees by export credit insurance agencies in the lender's own country, internal firms' guarantees by a parent on loans to its affiliates, and guarantees by host government agencies on loans to private firms within their country (Eiteman et al. 1992: 297).[2] A large proportion of money lent to the private sector in developing countries has been guaranteed by sovereign governments, in order that the Northern firms involved in these economic activities, either as contractors or in trading relations with local firms, can deem the risk 'acceptable'. Public lenders in the North to private sector companies in the South have also often sought government guarantees, although the IFC tends to avoid this practice, ostensibly because it can distort calculations of business feasibility.

The public risks regime has also developed 'since credit has become an increasingly competitive component of the terms of export selling' (Eiteman et al. 1992: 538). By 1992, the governments of at least 35 countries have established entities that insure credit risks for exports.[3] Since competition between states to increase exports by lengthening the period for which credit transactions are insured could lead to a credit war, as early as 1934 the Berne Union, officially the Union d'Assureurs des Crédits Internationaux, was established to regulate voluntary understandings governing credit terms. The UK institution for insuring exports, the Export Credit Guarantee Department (ECGD) and fellow European institutions are all members. As members of the Union they are subject to the rules in markets for export insurance, although that does not prevent differentials in price affecting market outcomes.

Governments' involvement in export credit as a form of risk management has also grown because the set of economic transactions that the private market for insurance is prepared to cover is invariably less than the potential market size desired by firms and states. Where the private banking sector refuses to lend, international development institutions meet demand, such that the larger the number of countries deemed uncreditworthy, the greater the burden placed on public institutions, with the risk that 'Their limited funds will inevitably be diverted away from the poorest developing nations, which have no hope of qualifying for loans from private banks' (Eiteman et al. 1992). There are also problems here for DFIs, reviewed in Storey and Williams (2006), that the public institutions will only garner business that is ultimately inefficient and unproductive, in so far as it has already been rejected by private markets as unethical and 'dirty', a charge that has been increasingly levelled at the ECGD in the UK because of its disproportionate coverage of arms exports and environmentally damaging dam projects (see chapter 5). Extending markets for the benefit of poor people is only one potential modality of a risk-taking public sector institution, although it is potentially an important one, while promoting dirty industries could be another.

In fact, states and firms share the same capital markets in order to fund economic activity through the issuance of government bonds and shares respectively, such that reinsurance companies know that a high price or exclusion of a country in terms of their private sector clients will be picked up by the public sector, just as dirty industry work, which can fatally damage a private firm's reputation, can be better borne by a government, whose electorate is weighing a number of more pertinent issues in its choice of leaders. Public accountability through the vote is thus less acute than private accountability through the market in some instances. In short, a firm can go bankrupt and a government can't, while an election has, to our knowledge, never been won or lost because of export credit policy. But the importance of government involvement is also underscored at a more fundamental level. This interdependence of both sectors on the same capital markets is analysed, with respect to the capitalist state, by authors who stress that the state is guarantor and enforcer of the capital relation and is itself funded by surplus value created in private accumulation (see for example Offe 1975 and 1984; see also various authors in Clarke 1991). Also, without the state as guarantor and arbiter of class power in society, the value and function of money could not exist in the first place (see Bonefeld and Holloway 1995). More particularly, Offe defines the capitalist state:

a) by its exclusion from accumulation, b) by its necessary function for accumulation, c) by its dependence on accumulation, and d) by its function to conceal and deny a), b) and c).

(Offe 1975, cited in Held and Krieger 1983: 488)

This quote underscores that interdependence is also political and social. For example, recent events in the 'credit crunch' illustrate the pressure on creditor governments to bail out banks facing bankruptcy (Northern Rock in the UK), and privilege large employers with industrial policy subsidies in order to keep powerful private interests happy. This is necessary because when they withdraw their money, the political fallout of recessionary economics and unemployment can unseat governments.

From this perspective the relationship between the two sources of revenue for export credit and insurance (government or firms) is more intimate, with the vulnerability of risks insurance compounded, given that both systems are likely to be under-resourced at the same time. In this event, liquidity can be restored by increased government borrowing pending readjustment to profitability in the private regime: a readjustment supervised by creditor states since it involves them promoting structural adjustment in the borrower countries. Structural adjustment, Poverty Reduction Strategy Papers (PRSPs) and neoliberal conditionalities more generally can be seen as serving this purpose of restoring profitability through adjustment (and workers' subsidy to the private sector through the tax systems of both creditor and debtor countries), in order to reduce risk by monitoring and supervising the borrower country's side of the economic contract with firms. States are then acting to adjust the risk regime on behalf of private firms, while also meeting a proportion of the 'excess demand' for underwriting capitalist activity through a lattice of state bilateral guarantee. Meanwhile, workers and taxpayers foot the bill.

For firms wanting to go to poor areas falling outside the insurable geography dictated by the private market, recourse to guaranteed credit from quasi-public financial institutions and to bilateral finance is necessary. From an economic perspective, this can be viewed as rent-seeking (following Krueger 1974; Tollison 1982), where private groups use the political system to guarantee them a portion of a market, reducing their risks to near zero. Alternatively, state bilateral guarantees can be viewed as a form of public subsidy, a kind of Keynesian injection to catalyse development in poorer areas. It is in this later sense that the DFIs and export credit agencies (ECAs) represent their activities to the public. Thus, a firm or group of firms may lobby government to take actions to prevent a loss or to take a share of that loss. Haufler summarises that from a public goods standpoint, government intervention would be justified as a correction of market failure (citing Mendez 1992), but that the redistribution of loss could also be viewed as using public agencies for private gain (Haufler 1997). From the perspective of the insurance firm, recourse to the state is justified since insurance itself can be seen as a quasi-public good, supporting the market system and facilitating investment and exchange (Snidal 1979).

Political risk: uncertainty or calculable risk?

Thus, risk acts to regulate market participation and the prices accrued to that participation in the form of profits. These risk calculations are derived from investor perceptions and subsequently fix market activities, which in turn condition people's livelihoods and income. The public institutions work in a similar way and also use risk calculation in the process of investment decision-making. However, in this the mathematical basis is even more fluid, if not arbitrary: the market for development finance is culturally, politically and racially embedded, as we will see in the coming chapters. However, despite this, two outcomes are fairly constant. First, that a favourable rate of return is generally produced. For example, the Commonwealth Development Corporation (CDC) rate of return on its portfolio in 2004 was 22 per cent, matching the Morgan Stanley Capital International (MSCI) Emerging Markets Index, while in 2007 it outperformed the index by 20 per cent with a portfolio performance of 57 per cent, up from 14 per cent in 2006 (CDC 2008). Second, that development finance has the effect of under-girding class structures and maintaining inequality by supporting elites; although there are exceptions to this, as in the high-profile CDC support for indigenous ownership in the South African hotel industry.

That risk assessment is fluid is confirmed by qualitative interviewing, and evidence from various sources which suggests that the empirical or scientific basis of such methods is less than absolute. Banks and firms also still get it wrong – sometimes incredibly so, as illustrated by the UK's Financial Services Authority's (FSA) errors in regulation in regard to Northern Rock and that bank's own lax risk assessment procedures – and change their means of assessing risk frequently. By the early 1990s, sensitivity testing and projected rates of return were commonly used by international firms in in-house calculations of political risk. The continued complex application of 'scientific method' is aimed at accounting risk, but as is demonstrated resoundingly by the 'credit crunch', large-scale failure to properly account liabilities and income can still occur, arguably because a monetised value is being applied in the futures and derivatives markets to expectations of income streams which may or may not occur. In the credit crunch fiasco it transpires that the companies owning the expectation of an income were not even the same companies which owned the actual asset which would generate it, but holding companies in tax havens (see Hildyard 2008). For example, the expected income stream from credit card debts and mortgages sold to poor people had been circulated around the global system to distribute and resell 'risk', which proved highly contagious, spreading what has been termed 'toxic debt' because of the very low likelihood of it ever being repaid.

Sovereign political risk and market makers

Historically, the problem of political risk was solved by colonialism in Africa from the 1880s, such that trading companies' risk was increasingly managed by administrators and political authorities grafted on to African territories, who later claimed territorial control and enforced their rules by violence and oppression. This process extended and assisted a long history of state-sponsored capital export by the European states, a process neatly summarised in a contemporary study by Hobson in 1902 for the British case:

> It is not too much to say that the modern foreign policy of Great Britain has been primarily a struggle for profitable markets of investment. To a larger extent every year Great Britain has been becoming a nation living upon tribute from abroad, and the classes who enjoy this tribute have had an ever-increasing incentive to employ the public policy, the public purse, and the public force to extend the field of their private investments, and to safeguard and improve their existing investments. This is, perhaps, the most important fact in modern politics, and the obscurity in which it is wrapped has constituted the gravest danger to our State.
>
> (1938 [1902]: 53–4)

These tributes, combined with the modern equivalents relating to patents, licensing and royalties, still produce a healthy income as the legacy of colonial conquest lives on in the stock of metropolitan-owned income-earning assets associated with past economic process. These include long-running patents and intellectual property. This legacy gives moral weight to the increasing demands for reparations heard in global and regional forums, often voiced by activists from the World Social Forum movement (see Bond 2006: 141–51), since the North's head start, which still earns them money, was only won by conquest, plunder and slavery.

Within the colonial period, the imperial power and the local territorial administration made markets work in favour of the occupier, under the conditions of the 'Colonial Diktat' or contract, which specified controls on trade and investment which might compete favourably with the metropole's manufacture. Milanovic summarises these terms, showing that autochthonous industrial development was effectively precluded, since:

(a) colonies could import only products from the metropolis and tariff rates must be low, normally 0%, (b) colonial export could be made to the metropolis only from which they could [be] reexported, (c) production of manufactured goods that could compete with products of the metropolis was banned, and (d) transport between colony and metropolis is conducted only on metropolis' ships.

(2003: 671–2, citing Bairoch 1997, vol. 2: 665–9)

The aim was to prevent industrial competition in the occupied territories and make the market conform to metropolitan interests.

The issue of the construction and pricing of markets was already a feature of the early teething problems of the CDC, who drew attention to:

the lack of uniformity in Colonial Taxation systems, to Land Tenure policies which in some cases discourage high capital investment, and to the high cost, often unavoidable, of public utility services, roads, and other engineering works in the Colonies.

(CDC 1949: 7)

The CDC was already aware of the more particular interests of the primary producers who they would employ when they term the policy of His Majesty's Government as 'somewhat obscure' despite 'the fundamental importance of markets and prices for Colonial products'. They suggest, 'however complex the factors involved', that the government be required to pay 'closer consideration' to the 'relative place in the UK markets of the primary producers of the United Kingdom, Dominions, Colonial territories, and foreign countries' (CDC 1949: 7). In the post-war colonial period, risk was managed in the colonies by trading patterns which concentrated economic activities within firm structures which privileged British parties, either subsidiaries of British-based companies, associates or within economic spaces authorised and populated by settler populations.

After independence in the majority world, private bank lending predominated in the 1960s and 1970s, but following the mid-1980s debt crisis in the middle-income developing countries, central banks in core creditor states began increasing supervision and imposition of provisioning against country risk in commercial banks. This was as a consequence, in large part, of the role central banks assumed in mopping up bad debt in the 1980s. In the UK in August 1987 the Bank of England circulated guidelines on country debt provisioning with the 'matrix', an objective empirical framework for analysis of risk, to all UK incorporated institutions authorised under the Banking Act (HC 1990: 132–6).[4] The matrix was designed to identify countries with potential repayments difficulties, a task which made the matrix ever more complex (HC 1990: 132). Nonetheless, singularly for Africa, factors were tightened over time to trigger provisioning at earlier stages of risk (HC 1990: 132). In 1990, one factor which could trigger a provisioning requirement was:

> 'not meeting IMF targets/unwilling to go to IMF', with a country scoring here (amount unspecified) 'if it is in breach of IMF targets (ie performance criteria for any programme) or is unable or unwilling to go to the IMF'.
>
> (HC 1990: 136)

Thus, the increasing conditionality of lending which occurred in the 1980s was written into country-risk management, such that commercial banks were expected to have higher provisioning (resources in case of default) for those countries not strictly following IMF programmes. The Bank of England was asked by the Treasury and Civil Service Select Committee in 1990 to comment on the 'likely result that virtually all lending outside the fully developed world will need to be provisioned for', to which the bank replied that the matrix was not a 'mechanistic tool' where the central bank would impose provisions but was for 'guidance', with a 'forward-looking element', to encourage banks to 'take proper account of a country's economic position when pricing a facility to be provided to it' (HC 1990: 137). These comments indicate that the actual supervision by the Bank of England at this stage remained predominantly discretionary, although further international codes on provisioning levels were agreed during the 1990s. The Basle Accord of 1988 set a precedent of regulation, setting a framework for measuring bank capital and setting minimum capital adequacy standards following the debt crisis (Eiteman et al. 1992: 307), but the increased codification of bank behaviour picked up apace, not least as a consequence of the security and anti-terrorist agendas with, in particular, the Financial Action Task Force (FATF) from 1989 catalysing the deepening of banking regulation on many fronts.[5]

The International Finance Corporation
and sovereign economies

Large companies in the core states have currency and interest rate swaps made available to them by international investment banks which bring benefit to their financial positions. However, 'country risk' considerations preclude international banks from making these services available in poorer countries, such that the International Finance Corporation (IFC) has assumed a role of mediation, organising swaps between companies in poorer countries and the international banks. For example, the IFC describes how a loan by it to a Turkish bank in the early 1990s allowed the bank to access other funds from Japanese, European, Scandinavian and US banks, who otherwise would have deemed 'Turkey' too risky. The IFC basically underwrote the bank, providing an insurance for convertibility in an 'IFC-led and -syndicated "liquidity backstop" feature', and by so doing contributed to greater integration and cross-provisioning in the international financial system, allowing the whole geography of 'Turkey' to effectively 'join in', and move closer over the subsequent period to the European Union. The IFC explains that 'these banks were [then] willing to lend to the Turkish bank because of cross-default provisions in IFC's loan and the comfort provided by IFC's reputation' (1992: 12). This 'reputation' is of course a reflection of the power of the IFC itself and of those core states which underwrite its activities and help in the reduction of investment risk through political intervention.

Apart from direct liquidity provided to banks for on-lending, the IFC also intervenes to enlarge equity markets, partly by the direct involvement, particularly in Eastern Europe, of the IFC's Corporate Finance Services Department (established in 1990), which manages privatisations and often invests in enterprises being privatised. The IFC also promotes country funds, mutual funds and securities. These functions are most commonly practiced as countries become more creditworthy and IFC-sponsored companies within them become more sophisticated, such that the IFC focus can shift to helping firms access global credit markets, including European and North American pension funds. The IFC organises and promotes developing country funds, pooling securities from a number of companies, in order to reduce the otherwise excessive risk associated with investing in one singularly, and then offering shares of the pool on the world market. From 1956, when the IFC was founded, to 2005, the IFC committed more than $49 billion of its funds and arranged another $24 billion in syndications 'for 3,319 companies in 140 developing countries', such that its portfolio at year end of 2005 was $19.3 billion in its own account, and $5.3 billion 'held for participants in loan syndications' (IFC 2006: ii).

These relatively large sounding numbers notwithstanding, the IFC actually has a number of rather different and potentially contradictory jobs. Ostensibly, there is a progression in the model of IFC assistance whereby economic growth eases countries' capital constraints and the IFC becomes displaced in company financing, a desirable progression born of 'good' government policy and effective assistance. Once displaced in direct company financing, however, the IFC would still expect a role in capital market operations which are not so much the subject of displacement, significantly for this analysis of the political development of the poorest, because state power (collective and institutionalised) is required to make those markets happen. These different priorities reflect differing roles for the IFC, depending on the relative size and profitabilities of the different circuits of capital in the countries concerned. Once profitability is assured in productive units of capital through direct participation, and programme funding with conditionality assures the greater profitability of merchant capital through 'opening' markets and the promotion of 'free' trade (and the associated reduction of the ability of governments to tax moving goods), the role of assuring profitability in the circuit of finance capital, particularly at the international level, falls to such organisations as the IFC. In a sense, countries are adjusted 'up' to boardroom-level interventions.

We examine in chapter 5 the bilateral history of the CDC in managing liquidity in the Anglophone colonies and subsequent independence era, but can just observe here that the CDC advocates a similar 'progression', whereby the weight of its earlier interventions were directly at the company level (parastatal and then private), but it progressed, particularly from the late 1980s, into a heavier workload in the finance sector, mounting increasing numbers of country funds, until the ultimate logic of this made it see itself as a fund manager. Other European bilateral DFIs behaved similarly, as we explore in chapter 8, with the effect that the volume and boundaries of the constructed 'market' for finance are moulded by the IFIs – both multi- and bi-lateral – the dominant instrument of this being their deepened institutional control; the explanatory mechanism being the allowable or prohibitive measurement of perceived 'country risk', which translates into various pools of money organised by cultural and political proximity to the Northern financial core. For example, the Turkish syndication referred to above is part of a wider and contested social process of incorporation of Turkey into the global economy, with 'Western' states as its sponsor, a process which remains incomplete and problematic as the issue of European membership illustrates.

Bilateral DFIs still rely on post-colonial histories and shared business cultures in their management of risk, in addition to financial instruments and sensitivity testing, and other modes of quantification and provisioning. In this there is also a modern realm of discretion, arbitrary decision-making and political manoeuvring more generally. The Monopolies and Mergers Commission (MMC) in 1992 concluded that political risk was:

> not normally addressed specifically in CDC's project appraisals. CDC told us that political factors were primarily a matter for its Board to consider and did not need to be covered in every appraisal report.
>
> (MMC 1992: 70)

However, after examining four CDC projects in difficulty, the MMC noted that the 'common feature' was:

> the high degree of government involvement either as a share-holder, loan guarantor or granter of derogations from existing legislation, without which projects would not be feasible at all.
>
> (ibid.)

Noting that a change of government could cause further difficulties and that solving the difficulties would require resolution at a govern-mental level, 'or by a number of DFIs acting together, and not by CDC alone' (MMC 1992: 70), the MMC helped to underline the reliance of the CDC both on the actions, legislation or derogations from legislation given by host governments, as well as on a sphere of collectivised power which expresses itself in the institutionalisation of DFIs as a group.

The view 'from the top' illustrates the surprisingly personalised basis in which key financial regulations are embedded. It also helps explain why DFIs often end up in a cul-de-sac, bound by their own histories to continue lending even when the likelihood of the loan being used productively is slight, and the chance of eventual repay-ment even more remote. For example, a senior official in the CDC in 1993, referring to the case of Kenya, noted that the CDC would take investment decisions:

> by understanding the human nature of these people, how they are moving and the politicians, rather than looking at computer figures. So I think there is a lot of, in this business of investing in developing countries, there is an awful lot of experience, that comes in.
>
> (Interview, London, 1993)

In fact, as a whole, the donors continued to lend to Moi for two decades, despite any real effort on that government's part to meet conditionalities at a country level (see Murunga 2007). In general, when governments faced debt-servicing problems (sometimes because of political reasons which 'blocked' the export of capital, but sometimes also merely because of foreign exchange shortages) the logic of the 1980s and 1990s at the CDC was to reinvest, as an incentive to encourage debt servicing or simply to stop blocked funds lying fallow (see for example National Audit Office (NAO) 1989: 22). Thus, the obduracy of dictators could merely prompt further political engagement and new money offered for debt rescheduling or increased equity stakes, preferably in a, or indeed another, foreign exchange generating project (see MMC 1992: 86). A cycle of country dependence on foreign exchange and CDC commitment to export-oriented enclaves was produced. Incentives for local elite financial delinquency sat alongside the surreptitious removal of some profits in the short to medium term for the CDC. However, it would be difficult to view the product of such a Faustian deal as developmental.

Conclusion

In this chapter we have examined how the apparent spontaneity of markets is in fact engineered by human agency: on a theoretical level when the practicalities and logistics of real markets are explored; on an everyday level through calculations of risk at many levels, such as the firm, the country and within banks; and then at an international level by looking at the example of the 'kingmaker' of sovereign markets: the IFC. Within this study it should be apparent that the political economy approach is heterodox, and post-structural. In other words, issues of race, place and identity are not residual factors in our analysis but key to how the hierarchy of global space is ordered. We saw this illustrated in this chapter in relation to the management of money and the construction of markets. In the next chapter the specific relationships between rich states and governing institutions is examined, before the sum of these systemic relationships is modelled.

Notes

1. Phrases used by the National Audit Office (NAO) about the CDC (NAO 1989: 3).
2. Eiteman et al. note that while the latter two do not apply to reducing risks on sovereign loans, they do serve to reduce overall country risk (1992: 297).
3. Details are in annual editions of the International Export Credit Institute's *The World's Principal Export Credit Insurance Systems* (New York).

4. Appendix 10 (HC 1990: 132–6) with Annex: Bank of England Guidelines on Country Debt Provisioning (Matrix) sent to UK Incorporated Authorised Institutions with Exposures to Countries Experiencing Debt Servicing and Repayment Difficulties, Banking Supervision Division, Bank of England, January 1990.

5. 'The Financial Action Task Force (FATF) is an inter-governmental body whose purpose is the development and promotion of national and international policies to combat money laundering and terrorist financing' (FATF 2008) from their website at: www.fatf-gafi.org/pages/0,2987,en_32250379_32235720_1_1_1_1_1,00.html

4 International development banks and creditor states

The Bretton Woods banks and regional development banks (RDBs) (collectively referred to here as international financial institutions (IFIs) or, when the bilateral development finance institutions (DFIs) are included as well, as the 'Great Predators') can only generate and regulate markets because they themselves are underwritten and their risk is managed by their joint owners: the rich economies of the global system, principally those who were the 'winners' of the Second World War. Since 1948, these have pooled their resources in a global system of public credit. Politically, this system collectivised the management of empire, as the economies of the bilateral colonies came under collective management. When most colonies were territorially 'lost' to the creditor states at independence, they joined with the looser spheres of economic influence of the United States and Japan into a new monetised zone for capital export, which became known as the Third World. Other European countries and newcomers such as Saudi Arabia have joined in at the board level. Membership of the global credit club is essentially simple: if the other members allow, a country can put in capital and then it is allocated votes in direct proportion to the country's stake in the bank, in this case, the World Bank and IMF. In regional development banks the voting is slightly more complicated, with older members not so keen to give over voting stakes in exchange for capital: new members are often just allowed to put their money into rolling funds which attract lesser rights to power. When the Bretton Woods institutions (BWIs) periodically enlarge their core stakes, denominated in special drawing rights or SDRs, it is a political and sometimes highly charged exercise for that reason: power is also being reallocated and redistributed.

In turn, these SDR contributions are duly underwritten through a liability in the creditor countries' central accounts. The payments to the multilaterals then increase the scope, reach and volume of money flows in the world system, in accordance with the role of money in regulating the pace and output of production (Harvey 1982: 284–8). These monies are recycled through the poorer countries, representing the barometer of their allowable liquidity; their allowable net present consumption of finance and working capital. In the case of the poorest, there has even developed a tendency to highlight the relevance of such flows by the use of the annual 'net receipts' concept to describe their liquidity position. These funds may form only a small part of the total capital mobilised for export by the creditor states (the substantial volume of which is either private, or institutionally channelled through bilateral financial institutions (see chapter 8)), but they are the pin on which the upside down pyramid of investment is crowded in from the rest of the private sector and bilaterals, who are reassured that their risk is controllable because of the presence of IFI capital in a country, sector, project, company or bank. It is the underwriting function of the multilateral DFIs which helps to maintain the lattice of the bilateral institutions, and attached to them, those companies who will do business at the periphery of the Westphalian capitalist system.

The direct payment of funds to multilaterals provides provisioning for them, such that the core creditor states become the underwriters of the multilateral finance organisations, who then disburse monies and produce a profit. It is interesting to note then that in aggregate, provisions provided for the International Monetary Fund (IMF) most often stay in the country of the creditor and actually generate a flow of funds from the IMF to the treasury of the core state. For example, the UK quota at the IMF changes as debtor countries demand sterling, which the IMF then either takes from its reserves or draws from the UK National Loans Fund, with the effect that the UK's reserve tranche position, which is a claim on the IMF and forms part of the UK's official reserves, itself increases. The UK Treasury explains that 'interest (technically called "remuneration") is received on that part of the reserve tranche which is "remunerated" and this is credited to the official reserves' (HC 1990: 140). The IMF holds securities, which form part of the UK quota, which it presents to the Treasury when sterling is required, such that, to summarise, 'The drawing of sterling by the IMF increases the UK's reserve tranche position, and hence the amount of remuneration (interest) it receives' (ibid.). Additionally, when debtor states fall into arrears on interest a mechanism of 'burden sharing' takes effect, whereby 'charges to all debtors and remuneration to all creditors are adjusted to offset the unpaid charges', which again generates an increase to the UK tranche position (ibid.).

In the case of the World Bank, the creditor states supply contributions to the Bank's capital as shareholders. However, only a small proportion of the Bank's capital available to borrowers is provided in this way. For example, in 1988, following a General Capital Increase process by the Bank involving a UK contribution of $110 million, which grew the overall callable capital sum (contingent liability) of the UK to £4.6 billion, only 3 per cent of the Bank's capital had actually been paid in by members, with the rest borrowed in the international capital markets (HC 1990: 140). Thus, the relationship between the Bank and the core states has them as shareholders and underwriters. In the former role they have rights to profits against their contributions, reflected in an increasing value of their shares. These increases could be substantial since the World Bank has never made a loss and has substantial reserves of its own. The contributions can thus be viewed as a form of underwriting or provisioning, which enables the Bank to have Triple-A ratings when it borrows from capital markets, which in turn allows it to borrow at the lowest rates available against the collective guarantee of the creditor states and their governments. The UK Treasury noted in 1990 that while the members contributions are 'on call, if necessary, to meet the Bank's obligations', 'no calls on this portion of the capital have ever been made' (ibid.). The members' contributions are termed the 'callable' or 'unpaid proportion' of the Bank's capital. Should the Bank make a loss not coverable by its substantial reserves, the Bank would call on the 'unpaid proportion' of its capital, which comprises the contributions of the creditor states, which are in practice accounted liabilities in national accounts.

Similarly, the International Finance Corporation (IFC) has a low gearing ratio of actual contributions, or share capital from members relative to borrowings, with the members having voting rights in proportion to the number of shares held. It is the largest source of direct project financing for private investment in developing countries, and is also confined to invest only in the private sector. In the early 1990s, 80 per cent of lending requirements were borrowed in international financial markets, with public Triple-A bond issues (from Moody's and Standard & Poor's) or private placements, while the remaining 20 per cent was borrowed from the International Bank for Reconstruction and Development (IFC 1992a). In a trend also seen in the rapid portfolio growth of the Commonwealth Development Corporation (CDC) from the mid-1980s, the IFC demonstrated that funds extended in this way, borrowed from capital markets and then on-lent to private sector projects, attracted other investors to join in syndications and joint ventures.

In 2008, the African Development Bank summarised that all bonds from the regional development banks – from the African Development Bank (AfDB), Asian Development Bank (ADB), European Bank for Reconstruction and Development (EBRD), International Bank for Reconstruction and Development (IBRD), Inter-American Development ment Bank (IADB) and Nordic Investment Bank (NIB) – were all Triple-A rated (Standard & Poor's 2007: 23). The AfDB in 2007 boasted a paid-in capital of nearly 2.2 billion 'units of account' or UA (equivalent to $3.4 billion) and 'AAA callable capital' of $8.6 billion (capital held in countries which were Triple A, which the AfDB could ask for if it needed it), and then 'other callable capital' of $21.9 billion (from countries who were not so creditworthy). The AfDB was leveraging its usable capital in international money markets in a way that nearly doubled it (AfDB 2008: 19). The bank defined usable capital as paid-in capital and reserves ($3.4 billion and $4.0 billion respectively in 2007), plus callable capital of countries with Double-A rating and above (AfDB 2008: 21). They were projecting in December 2007 a borrowing programme in capital markets planned for 2008 worth $1.9 billion (AfDB 2008: 25).[1]

Good banks or powerful owners?

The multilaterals often claim that default on loans extended by them is rare, such that their status as prudent institutions is respected, which in turn guarantees their continued ability to borrow money cheaply, in order to pass it on as development finance to poor countries, helping 'aid development'. The ongoing debt crisis illustrates, however, that while creditor states may co-operate to create such institutions for the public good dividend, this is not without reward to them, while the price of the development on offer is not as cheap as advertised. In terms of the creditor states, they get back from their investments derivative procurement benefits (explored in chapter 7) and increases to the value of their shareholdings. Meanwhile, the conflict between their various bilateral interests is not resolved so much as displaced to this other forum, while the activities of their various bilateral finance institutions remain paramount and lucrative, particularly in so far as they represent commercial constituencies and imperatives. Indeed, bilateral Official Development Assistance remains the channel of choice for pursuing commercial and geostrategic interests, as discussed in chapter 8. The multilateral contributions help guarantee a marketplace in which the real business of bilateral competition can continue. In this latter sense, the public good produced is not 'development' as such, but the institutional infrastructure of an international market in the export of capital business.

The success of co-operation is that default risk can be reduced both by the extension of conditionality – through programmes such as structural adjustment programmes (SAPs), the Highly Indebted Poor Country Initiative (HIPC) and the poverty reduction strategy (PRS) process – and by the Paris Club and London Club mechanisms, if a debt negotiation becomes necessary. It also means that the collective populations of Europe and North America are on standby to pay up if the system crashes, through generalised wage labour and taxation relationships. Ultimately, for a poor country which has outstanding debts to both bilateral and multilateral institutions, it is the multilaterals which head adjustment negotiations, using indebtedness to oversee and regulate access to usable liquidity or 'receipts net', through an increasing volume of rules governing liquidity tranches granted. Repayments to multilaterals are accepted as predominant as compared to other credits owed bilaterally or commercially, while multilateral debt is becoming more prominent as a proportion of the debt profiles of the 'severely indebted low income countries' (SILICs). Between 1980 and 1997, as a consequence of the 'debt crisis', debt owed to multilateral creditors rose from 22 to 28 per cent of debt stock, and from 20 to over 50 per cent of debt service payments, representing a transfer of between $3 billion and $4 billion annually to multilateral institutions (HC 1997: 72).

Indeed, when there is a 'credit crunch' in the development finance system, the multilateral institutions are historically adept at ensuring that they are at the front of the queue, relative to other creditors, when poorer countries face a squeeze on their financial resources. For example, the 1996 Halifax Summit of G7 countries was supposed to have set in train a coordinated framework for debt sustainability, involving 'an "exit" strategy in which the target is overall debt sustainability, rather than the competitive pursuit of creditor claims' (HC 1997: 71).[2] However, different core states had different interests: the UK was pushing for reform, while Germany and Japan remained 'opposed in principle to multilateral debt relief' (ibid.). At this time, the problems of illiquidity and bankruptcy suffered by the SILIC countries, many of which were located in sub-Saharan Africa, were impacting on the institutions and companies of the British state predominantly, creating a claim on their underwriting resources, which they in turn were seeking to share with other, less financially compromised core creditors.

However, the IMF was also pursuing its own institutional and particular interest. First, according to Oxfam, it 'systematically understated the extent of the multilateral debt problem, notably that part which pertain(ed) to its own operations' (HC 1997: 71–2). Then the Fund's managing director 'signalled that he would not countenance involvement in such an initiative without prior action by the Paris Club of official creditors to provide 90 per cent debt stock reduction',[3] effectively a precondition for IMF participation, and that it would only participate through its Enhanced Structural Adjustment Facility (ESAF), which was only marginally concessional and which had rigorous and deflationary conditionalities attached (ibid.). Oxfam summarised that the IMF approach violated the framework paper of the IMF and World Bank boards:

> namely, that multilateral institutions should contribute to debt relief on a broadly equitable basis, according to their exposure in the country concerned. The dominant view in the Fund appears to be that debt reduction should be regarded as a priority for all creditors other than itself.
>
> (HC 1997: 71)

From the mid-1980s to the mid-1990s this institutional interest seems to have been well served, given figures relating to the IMF's exposure and share of debt service repayments. Thus, for example, the IMF accounted in 1997 for about 12 per cent of the total SILIC debt stock owed to multilaterals and yet received about 20 per cent of service payments made, amounting to some $600 million annually, while repayments for the years 1987–97 had constituted a net transfer of $4 billion more in repayments from the SILICs than the IMF has transferred in new loans (HC 1997: 72). Oxfam explained this higher IMF share of debt servicing relative to debt stock by the meaner concessionality terms of the ESAF facility relative to others, such as the World Bank's International Development Association (IDA) loans. The logic in the IMF position was that if other creditors refinanced their loans first, this would create the liquidity to ensure repayment to itself through transfer and displacement processes in the poorer countries, since finance is fungible. In this way, bilateral donors meet the costs of multilateral creditors by allowing accumulation of arrears on their own claims, with the SILICs not untypically meeting less than half of payments due in 1996, such that by 1997 capitalised interest payments accounted for about 50 per cent of total debt servicing and arrears had quadrupled to $56 billion since 1989 (ibid.).

In short, debt relief in the 1990s was largely a zero-sum game, because of these transfers of liabilities between institutions, which made little difference to countries' overall liabilities. Resources were merely transferred from other aid budgets, with Oxfam conservatively estimating that around $2 billion annually was transferred from national aid budgets to repay multilateral creditors, while an increasing share of the IDA's budget was merely recycled to meet the costs of repayments on past loans from the IBRD (HC 1997: 73). The World Bank covered the gap between repayments to the IMF and new disbursements by using financing through the IDA to pay the IMF! Indeed, Oxfam cite the shocking statistic that, in the case of Zambia during the late 1990s, 'well over half of the finance provided by external donors represents payments to, or between, themselves', and add that:

> viewed through anything other than the distorting prism of financial accountancy, there is something curious about the concepts of cheques crossing 19th Street in Washington from the World Bank to the IMF, and about donors repaying themselves, ostensibly in the name of development.
>
> (HC 1997: 73)

Given Oxfam's evidence here, even the House of Commons Select Committee summarised that there was a 'danger' of a growing share of a (then diminishing) Overseas Development Administration (ODA) budget being spent on refinancing multilateral debt with countries remaining on the 'debt treadmill, on which they use aid to repay money due on earlier loans' (HC 1997: 74).

Not much has changed in the 2000s, principally because the system itself is still privatised, although publicly underwritten. From the perspective of 'receipts net' it makes little difference if a country owes x amount or 100 times more, if actual liquidity received is constant: what is being adjusted is instead the valuable exchange of political claims, historical guilt and obligation, and what is being traded are relative moral claims and the possibilities of a better quality of life, or not, for countless people. But these negotiations, counterclaims and representations are negotiated and contested by a small privatised cabal of bankers, working ostensibly with the 'public good' in mind. And as we saw in the last chapter, in the boardroom of the system it is the perception of borrowing elites' attitudes and behaviours which ultimately matter to calculations of country risk and profitability, so 'being good' is 'rewarded' with debt stock reduction in expectation of future political compliance and pro-capitalist cultural responses. Meanwhile, the 'institution first' approach in the actual negotiations has meant that the reputation standing of IFIs in the credit markets is still high, despite any problems that they have, and many IFIs and RDBs enjoy Triple-A rating. They are first in the queue for international money, because they are the best at bullying other people to pay up.

This private rating, for example by Standard & Poor's, is a judgment of the relationship between capital owners (represented by states) and sovereign borrowers over time, and the ability of creditor countries to write-down or write-off any bad debt that surface. But it would be misleading to take the Triple-A rating as evidence that DFIs 'always win' in a singular instant or with a singular country: it is only the system which is being endorsed. Ultimately, getting paid can rely on 'what our standing in the particular country is, and how well our representatives, how close they are to the government' (CDC official, interview, 1993). DFIs can also carry more loss over time because of reputational and institutional features and associations with core states: funders can wait until the borrowing government changes its policy. In any commercial joint venture, losses are shared between the various shareholders, and sometimes firms or banks go into receivership or bankruptcy. In a recent anachronistic twist in Britain, Northern Rock was nationalised. However, the peculiar nature of multilateral financial institutions is that any 'bankruptcy' or loss of payments due to the position of debtors may affect this year's net receipts, but can be absorbed quite quickly, such that it doesn't even affect the value of assets or future claims.

Thus, the IMF has been historically opposed to debt relief because it fears reputational damage, which would create a moral hazard where borrowers would take funds expecting that a proportion would be written-off at a future later date. However, this argument is weak, since the critical difference between the IMF and a truly private bank tempers this damage: even when things go seriously wrong, such as in Argentina in 2003, the bank seems to walk away unscathed, principally because the markets think that the core creditor states are a secure bulwark to their investments in bank bonds. Thus the financial collapse in Mexico in 1995–96, which accounted for around 10 per cent of the IBRD's portfolio, did not register on bond markets, 'confirming the view of most analysts that it is the guarantee of its OECD shareholders which determines market perceptions' (HC 1997: 74). In fact, there is little relationship between the debtor's economic situation and the asset value of the IMF's portfolio since the value of the latter is more fundamentally related to bankers' and investors' belief in the power of the creditor states to control risk on their behalf, ominously, by more crude political means if necessary. The banks endorse the political management of the system itself.

In terms of the debtor country, the scenario here is one in which, since sovereign entities cannot, by definition, go bankrupt, their failure to pay merely causes the claim on their resources to be elongated, transferred from a forex to a soft currency, equity or merely resource claim (for example, the money for oil deals with Angola). It is politics which is adjusted and power relations between creditors and debtors which are reorganised, using the mechanism of supplying or depriving a country of liquidity, in the context of 'virtual' bankruptcy. Liquidity in this context is what debtors are negotiating for. However, when liquidity is granted, the subsequent arrangements for its use can also reflect the weakness of the borrowers' position: in chapter 8 we see further how even the liquidity provided to a country is often 'walled in' within an institutional context – such as within a Northern firm – which can be controlled vertically from the creditor state. Also, those economic sectors and companies of particular benefit to donors seem to receive the most money, as we explore further in chapters 7, 8 and 9. In other words, the problem referred to above about the recalcitrance of the Nigerian Government would also be addressed at a meso-level, once country negotiations were concluded, to protect future investments at firm level. Since the mid-1990s such deepened intervention has become more common, as the proposed, but thwarted, revenue structure for the Chad–Cameroon pipeline project illustrates.

The process of capital export is implemented with these deep institutional guarantees in mind, through the lattice of bilateral finance institutions headed by multilaterals, which gives any particular project a particular coalition of interested parties, other than, of course, the domestic borrower state and people. Bilateral and multilateral DFIs often have intermeshed equity and ownership, quite apart from their shared management cultures, with, for example, the British Government owning a large part of the IFC and then encouraging it to work with the CDC as the latter's 'closest multilateral analogy' (HC 1994a: 5). This intermeshing of equity, and the institutionalisation of risk which underwrites it, forms the skeleton of the political economy of development in the poorest and most indebted countries. It secures and returns for posterity the profits of extractive industries, environmental resources, and the labour of millions of underpaid workers in the global South to the traditional power centres of their historic colonial occupiers and their modern-day clubs and banks. Meanwhile, newly industrial countries have bought into the clubs.

The global Keynesian multiplier

We can model this system of risk management and institutional underwriting of the political economy of development by the rich creditor states of the OECD, as the 'global Keynesian multiplier' (see Figure 4.1). In this system, value (which is a Marxist term that is more accurate than money as such, since some of the resources transferred might be in derivative instruments or promises, such as export insurance credits, liabilities or even non-pecuniary assets) flows around the diagram clockwise, starting in Box 1 where it is underwritten by the governments of the rich states. It flows first to the development finance institutions or DFIs – bilateral, regional and global – the regional counterparts of which are sometimes referred to as the regional development banks (RDBs), the global as international financial institutions (IFIs), which means the World Bank, IMF, IFC and MIGA (Multinational Investment Guarantee Authority), in Box 2. Export credit agencies (ECAs) also receive value. All of these then on-lend the money to borrowing governments, in Box 3, who accept a liability in the form of sovereign debt to be paid back by their citizens, although some might be the subject of a future debt-forgiveness deal, in which case citizens of creditor countries pay some back. The political elite in the 'soft currency' state (called this because it will generally not possess an internationally exchangeable currency) then use the foreign exchange denominated loan to, variously, purchase development goods such as infrastructure, social services, plant and equipment, or use it to plug fiscal deficits, pay public sector wages or merely pay themselves. At best, the investment will act in the way Keynes would have predicted, thus justifying the title given this system here, of generating multiplier effects, galvanising and catalysing more investment around itself, which then kick-starts a growth spurt in the receiving economy. However, a majority of contracts which derive from these purchases, when they are made, have been historically met by the large companies domiciled in the creditor countries, Box 4 – such as the large construction firms, Balfour Beatty, Halcrow, Acres and so forth, who build hydroelectric dams – whose profits are then stored in global banks, also often domiciled in creditor states and taxed by creditor governments. In other words, the profits from the market in development, which is managed from the core states, mostly returns to these same jurisdictions. There is also a short-cut route, where money goes straight from Box 2 to Box 4, sometimes without a government guarantee, but the effect on the national economy and pattern of profits is similar. The profits and returns are explored in chapters 7 and 8.

A key objection to this model will be that there is no singular incarnation but many such circuits, and that Asian sovereign wealth funds, in particular, are at least as significant in scale and volume but are not covered here. Another will be that not all development finance is used in this way, and that much now bypasses state structures entirely, being used to fund NGOs and the private voluntary sector (see Riddell 2007). Another objection will be that when it fails, the multiplier's debts have been written off, as in the current period, so the cost of reproducing capital is not in fact borne by the poorest. The point about newcomers to the business is correct in part, but as yet this is the only system in place which pretends and largely actualises a global set of economic behaviours, although that might not be the case in 20 or so years time. The second point about pecuniary and non-pecuniary gifts and the private voluntary sector is also correct in that this might provide development goods, but again it is not an institutional system as such with the power to underwrite an accumulation process; it also does not compensate for the failures of the intergovernmental equivalent. The third objection actually underscores the importance of democratising capital allocation globally: debt may have been written off, but there is no other future available unless this systemic multiplier changes, since countries will just go around again. Unless poorer people can earn a living by other means they will need to be funnelled through this system, and indebtedness will result, just as it did last time; a point that the new advocates of increased spending on the private sector would do well to bear in mind. In short, if a country has nothing to spend today, however the historical liabilities are calculated, it will also have nothing again tomorrow, if nothing changes in terms of relative power in the political economy of development.

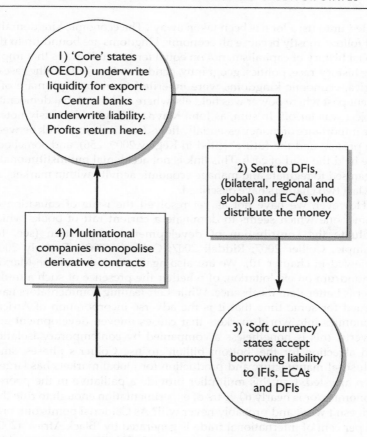

Figure 4.1 Recycling value: the global Keynesian multiplier
Source: An earlier version appeared in Bracking (2003).

Conclusion

From the perspective of Africa, this system is not delivering prosperity, which we explore further in chapter 6, and additionally it looks like the bearer of an equally bleak future. The post-independence period has not met expectations, and alongside nationally based processes, part of this failing must be assigned to the experience internationally of the political economy of development. Thirty years after Kwame Nkrumah's exhortation following the independence of Ghana: 'Seek ye first the political kingdom, and all else shall be added unto you', Chinua Achebe remarked: 'We sought the "political kingdom" and nothing has been added unto us; a lot has been taken away'. The economic kingdom did not follow, mostly because all economic kingdoms are bound up in the global history of capitalism, not on equal terms but in ways that implicate history, race, politics, geography, gender and so forth. In the case of Africa, economic kingdoms were inherited from the nightmare of a recent past where power was held elsewhere and the global democratic project was far off. In sum, as John Maynard Keynes famously noted, 'the importance of money essentially flows from its being a link between the present and the future' (cited in Kegley 2009: 256), and somebody else held the wad of cash. This link is not accidental but institutionally organised to regulate and manage economic activity within markets, as the last two chapters have described.

However, we have not as yet resolved the issue of causation or blame, one which seems to dominate a current raft of books which evaluate the contribution of development co-operation (see, for example, Collier 2007; Riddell 2007; Calderisi 2006; Easterly 2006; reviewed in chapter 10). We are also again reminded of the Marxist conundrum on exploitation, of whether the presence of such a multiplier is better than its absence. While Left-leaning commentators have argued for some time that it is the adverse incorporation of African economies into world markets that causes uneven development and poverty, this is nonetheless accompanied by contemporary isolation and abjection for the 'bottom billion' to use Collier's phases, since industrial manufacture and production for global markets has largely been arrested. Can this multiplier provide a palliative in the poorest economies, or is nearly 60 years of experimentation enough to rule that is doesn't work and probably never will? As Calderisi points out, only 1.5 per cent of international trade is generated by 'Black Africa' (2006: 144), while Africa has lost the equivalent of $70 billion per year (in 1990 dollars) in market share every year since the 1970s, or $700 per family per year (2006: 141), a haemorrhage which, according to Calderisi, has been accompanied by widespread dictatorship and 'obscured by decades of Western generosity' (2006: 153). While we can resist the description of 'generosity', this system of capital injection, called aid, which Calderisi values at $40 per person (2006: 142), has undoubtedly assisted some areas and peoples to integrate into internationalised accumulation (an aspect we explore further in chapter 10), while shoring up some relatively undeserving political elites, such as the Cameroonian Government who were given debt relief of more than $100 million in October 2000 but who, 15 months later, had failed to spend a cent of it on social and economic services for the poor (Calderisi 2006: 132). In short, is this economic decline despite of, not related to, or because of the political economy of development? This book argues that it is partly to blame.

Notes

1. 1 UA = 1 SDR =1.35952 US$ (2002) = 1.58025 USS (2007) (AfDB 2008: 36). The figures in this paragraph have been converted from their original UA amounts into US$ at the 2007 exchange rate quoted by the AfDB in the same source, and then changed from millions into billions and rounded up to one decimal place. The same conversions are used for data in chapter 7.
2. HC (1997), Treasury Committee, International Monetary Fund, Minutes of Evidence, Wednesday 29 January (London: TSO). Substantive information is provided by the Memorandum submitted by Oxfam (UKI), pp.71–80. Pages within this range thus refer to the Oxfam submission.
3. Michel Camdessus, at the spring 1996 meeting of the World Bank and IMF.

5 The British market makers

In order to illustrate the historical development of the global multiplier which occupies the centre of the political economy of development (but which is actually a many-to-many system or set of similar bilateral multipliers), this chapter uses a case study of the British state, which has been a key author of power in the international system. The Commonwealth Development Corporation (CDC), Export Credit Guarantee Department (ECGD) and Crown Agents primarily express British economic power in the frontier zone and help regulate and police those economic spaces in favour of British concerns. They are all ultimately underwritten by the Treasury, although they were all partly privatised in the 1990s (see below). These organisations all have their roots in the British Empire. Thus, while the Department for International Development (DFID) is the lead department for development issues in practice this is only a small component of the far larger enterprise of UK plc. Indeed, a cynic might attribute its social welfare focus to a public relations exercise on behalf of the other more profitable sectors of British outreach. It could equally be compared to that part of the iceberg visible above the waterline, heading a much larger rump of institutions dedicated to capital export.[1] The CDC and ECGD are the bilateral institutions of economic intervention, the former by means of investments, the latter by means of trade and investment insurance, while the Crown Agents manage international logistics and supply for the UK, World Bank and Japanese bilateral aid budgets. Together, they are the submerged part of the larger iceberg. Both the CDC and ECGD have historically disbursed development finance and export credits that are larger than the sums managed by DFID. These organisations are located metaphorically in the frontier state, that part which is internationalised or 'extraverted' to use Bayart's term (Bayart 1993) and focused on the globalised economy as a whole. We will first examine each in turn, then review their collective contribution to promoting a neoliberal global economy.

The Commonwealth Development Corporation

The CDC was established as the Colonial Development Corporation in 1948 by Act of Parliament, at the end of a war in which, as George Orwell noted in 1939, 'six hundred million disenfranchised human beings' would fight for the Franco-British alliance against Nazi Germany as members of their combined empires, hardly a 'coalition of democracies' (Orwell 1939, cited in Crick 1980: 367–77). Even the British Ministry of Information, during the Second World War, had noted that:

> We cannot afford to ride rough-shod over the peoples of the Colonies whilst maintaining to the World at large we are fighting for the freedom of mankind.
>
> (Cited in Smyth 1985: 76)

This problem of a democratic deficit was partly offset by the establishment of the developmental discourse and its institutions, including the CDC. Even in 1937 and 1938 there had been widespread riots in the West Indies against colonial rule, which had woken the Colonial Office to the prospect of resistance; India had been mounting pressure for independence; and Lord Hailey's highly critical 'African survey' had been published in 1938. The Government had produced a Colonial Development and Welfare Act in 1940, which promised £55 million over 10 years, and then another of the same in 1945, this time promising £120 million over 10 years. Moreover, in 1941, Roosevelt and Churchill had felt obliged to endorse the Atlantic Charter, a joint wish to see 'sovereign rights and self-government restored to those who have been forcibly deprived of them' (see Smyth 1985). Thus, with widespread war service taken from the people of the colonies, combined with pre-existing resistance and the ebullient promises made during the war in order to secure supplies, the British Empire was suffering a legitimacy crisis in the colonies. It was in this context that in 1943 the Financial Adviser to the Secretary of State for the Colonies, Sydney Caine, advised that it was:

> necessary to set up a body independent of existing authorities … to conceive and carry out major projects, preferably as a company clothed in commercial form but in fact working as the agent of government.
>
> (Cited by CDC 1997)

In 1948 such an organisation was born, just before US president Harry S. Truman 'invents' poverty and underdevelopment in his 'Four Point Program' of 1949. A new focus on the material needs of the peoples in the South was required and globalised in the Truman speech, in part to avoid revolt as the expectations of liberation raised during the war were quashed and postponed. A timeline of other key events in the history of the CDC is reproduced in Figure 5.1.

1949	CDC acquires Borneo Abaca Ltd (BAL) to produce hemp fibre. In 1957 BAL pioneered palm oil in the area, which produced 7% of world output in 1996.
1950	Lord Reith is appointed CEO of the CDC by UK Prime Minister Clement Atlee to create a firm basis for growth. First question asked is whether CDC is withdrawing from 'real' development and becoming a finance house.
1954	CDC moves into profit.
1963	As Britain's former colonies become independent, the organisation is renamed the Commonwealth Development Corporation.
1969	In a desire to have a wider impact in poorer countries, CDC is given authority to invest outside the Commonwealth.
1981	CDC's loan portfolio reaches £385 mill. and an investment in Bangladesh is the first in the Indian subcontinent.
1997	UK Prime Minister Tony Blair announces that CDC is to become a public–private partnership in order for it to benefit from association with the Government and participation from the private sector.
1999	CDC Act 1999: CDC becomes a public limited company (plc).
2001	Aureos Capital joint venture launched.
2002	No private partner found, 'CDC Capital Partners' concept abandoned, CDC 'unbundled'.
2004	Management function privatised as Actis, a fund management company.

Figure 5.1 A short history of the CDC
Source: www.cdc.group.com, accessed November 1996; see also Tyler 2008.

The 1948 Act charged the Corporation with:

> the duty of securing the investigation, formulation and carrying out of projects for developing resources of colonial territories with a view to the production therein of foodstuffs and raw materials, or for other agricultural, industrial and trade development, Clause 1(1).
>
> (Rendell 1976: 276)

It 'should have particular regard to the interests of the inhabitants' (ibid.), Clause 7(1), and had to balance revenue and expenses year-on-year, Clause 15(1), which 'meant that the Corporation was expected to budget on a commercial basis for a modest profit' (ibid.). Lord Howick, CDC chairman from 1960 to 1972, later called this Act 'admirably flexible', excepting the 'rigid terms' of financing solely in loans (with no equity). Indeed, this exception was a position later condemned by the Sinclair Committee in 1959, although the Government still rejected its recommendation to provide equity (CDC 1971: 9). Thus, the CDC was to 'maximise development, not profit, but ... operate in a commercial manner' (NAO 1989: 3). In this, it was an experiment and precursor of the application of ethical corporate governance, maintaining a triple bottom line, if not with environmental at least in accordance with economic, social and developmental prerogatives; although, at actual sites of investment this was not without problems.[2] The CDC saw its mission as to prove that viable projects could be found in developing countries, and by so doing, to reduce the real and perceived risk to other investors. It would, and did, 'augment' capital flows, with the 'original idea ... that it should fill a gap between direct government aid and private enterprise commercial operations' (Rendell 1976: 182).[3] The UK Government, through most of the Corporation's history, has seen no obvious conflict between its developmental and commercial objectives, and in 1994, when it was the subject of review, stated that the role of the CDC as a provider of direct private investment was, de facto, of developmental benefit (HC 1994: 5).

From its earliest days the Corporation's policies were liberal and participatory as compared with the more conservative views of first the Colonial Office and then the Overseas Development Ministry. The Corporation saw its role from 1948:

> as being primarily to raise the living standards of the rural population, and considered that this could be affected most directly by the promotion of increased agricultural production.
> (Rendell 1976: 223)

Already by 1949 it was negotiating between two different interests: those of the British state which sponsored it and the particular interests of the people it would employ overseas given the structural position of the colonies in the world economy and sterling area. Thus, in 1949 they urged the British Government to pay 'closer consideration' to pricing policies and the 'relative place in the UK markets of the primary producers' (CDC 1949: 7). Its early interest in agricultural production also remained central to its portfolio, although from 1964 to 1974, it reclassified its agricultural processing plant as industry:

> [a] gesture towards the new independent governments among whom there was a tendency ... to claim that their countries had

been exploited by the former colonial powers as merely producers of primary products, and (abetted by some academic economists) to look to rapid industrialisation as the key to economic progress.

(Rendell 1976: 223)

It was a pioneer of the core-satellite estate model of contract farming, as in the Kenya Tea Development Authority model, and also successfully ran very large plantation systems.

The Corporation in its earliest years made substantial losses[4] as the immediate needs of the British Empire and the general shortage of dollars in the sterling area caused the Colonial Office to press the Corporation into large-scale food production and uncommercial ventures, without, according to Rendell, sufficient attention to land titles and contractual arrangements (Rendell 1976: 36–8, 273). In 1950 CDC wrote that 'it is desirable that colonial peoples should be able to understand, approve of and co-operate in the Corporation's schemes and objectives' (CDC 1950: 2). By 1955, a 'rationale for future operations, which would start from the needs of the overseas territories themselves, was being worked out', although financial stringency, staff shortages and the 1956–63 British Government ban on investments in the ex-colonies mitigated against the policy, with this latter putting the CDC's future at risk from 'slow strangulation' as its area of operations shrank (Rendell 1976: 276). The CDC strategy involved raising living standards 'on a basis which might continue permanently after expatriate aid had been withdrawn'. To which end smallholder agricultural schemes, development companies in support of indigenous entrepreneurs and house building were given priority since they were judged to directly help the individual (Rendell 1976: 277). These types of project were unique, and so CDC management responsibilities became unavoidable, 'despite continued official disfavour' expressed in an official policy of 'no solo projects' which was only 'grudgingly' withdrawn in 1961 (Rendell 1976: 279). By 1973, with oil prices rising rapidly, the Corporation urged the donor countries to have 'a greater awareness that the prosperities of the industrialised and developing countries are inextricably linked', and to augment, rather than reduce, their finance (CDC 1973: 11).

The Corporation was placed in a contradictory position by demands for independence which placed its own future at risk but also ultimately remade it. The Far East Regional Controller was murdered in 1954 during the Malayan Emergency, and 'colonial governments under notice of termination became reluctant to take the initiatives that major development projects often required' (Rendell 1976: 37, 72). Land tenure was problematic, while the Mau Mau insurrection and post-colonial nationalisations of estates belonging to CDC's business partners limited operations in Kenya and Tanzania respectively (Rendell 1976: 72, 74). The problems were exacerbated by the British Government ban on all new investments after a country became independent, thus militating against investigations when the project could be declared 'out of time' (Rendell 1976: 72). When the Ghana Independence Bill was going through Parliament, Reith, the CDC chairman, mobilised support against the permanent exclusion of the CDC from the newly independent countries, which he believed would:

> spell the end of the Corporation as a separate viable concern, exert(ing) every effort, when the government's decision could not be changed, to get the machinery of exclusion modified.
>
> (Rendell 1976: 275)

This 'provided the essential foundation for Lord Howick's sustained and successful campaign for reinstatement in 1962 to 1963' (Rendell 1976: 275).

The limited autonomy of the CDC from the British Government eventually worked in its favour. As Rendell notes of this time:

> any hint of direct British Government intervention in Corporation operational decisions would have gravely prejudiced the Corporation's acceptability by most overseas governments both before and after independence. Indeed the Corporation had actual experience on several occasions of how difficulties tended to dissolve when local suspicions about CDC's actions being influenced from Whitehall were dispelled.
>
> (Rendell 1976: 275)

Corporation operations in newly independent countries maintained:

> the British connexion ... on terms which nationalistic sensitivity would have regarded as unacceptable if exercised by an agency under the direct operational control of the British ... government.
>
> (Rendell 1976: 170)

Thus, arguably, the Corporation became the sole acceptable representative of the British state, with promotion of local citizens and the presence of the Regional Controller and office which 'took the edge off the expatriate image' (Rendell 1976: 281) important to continued good relations. These comments illustrate the continued role of the CDC in winning back legitimacy for British commercial and state interests.

In 1961 the CDC won the 1961 Financial Settlement and the primary responsibility for maintaining a proper balance in its own portfolio, and in 1963 restoration in the independent territories (Rendell 1976: 181, 168). In 1962, the CDC began to publish figures of its contributions to British exports and invisible earnings, reflecting an increasing need to win support at home when balance of payments problems loomed, while it supported pleas for more money by stressing its catalytic effect in attracting World Bank and IDA money to the Commonwealth (Rendell 1976: 169). Its future had been assured and the terms on which it borrowed from the Exchequer were gradually eased, which in turn allowed for expansion (Rendell 1976: 184). In 1965, a limited amount of interest-waiver money was conceded, which 'established the principle that the interest rate on Treasury advances to CDC might be subsidized' (Rendell 1976: 174). In 1967–68 – 'a watershed in the CDC story' – the CDC was established as 'an integral part' of the Aid Programme: the 1967 'framework' settlement allowed for four-yearly forward planning and left the Corporation otherwise to 'run its own affairs'; while the 1968 Treasury decision to roll over unused Treasury quota allowed for more financial flexibility (Rendell 1976: 166–7). In 1968 and 1970 the CDC received glowing praise from House of Commons Select Committees, and an Act of 1969 allowed it to operate outside the Commonwealth subject to ministerial approval in each country, while also doubling its borrowing limits and the Treasury's lending ceiling (Rendell 1976: 170, 178). From 1970 it expanded rapidly (Rendell 1976: 174), helped by a new form of concessionary money in 1972–73 when the Treasury was finally prepared to accept an overt, flat rate of subsidisation of 3 per cent for renewable natural resource projects (Rendell 1976: 177–8, 183).

This consolidation of the CDC within the official 'aid' programme of a Labour Government allowed it to develop and reinvest in a lattice of interdependent arrangements with other IFIs that it had been developing since its earliest days. In this sense it was a handmaiden of the globalisation of newly independent African colonies and helped introduce their governments to the more multinational IFIs. This served to collectivise the control over independent African countries' reintegration into the world economy, with the CDC acting as the chair of the 'committee managing the common affairs of the whole bourgeoisie', to misquote Marx. The CDC was in co-operation with the World Bank as early as 1950 in the co-financing of the Kariba Dam project in the then Central African Federation, 'much the largest single CDC investment at the time' (Rendell 1976: 72). The first association with the IFC and Netherlands development agency was the Kilombero Sugar Company in Tanzania in 1960, a project later transferred to the Tanzania Government due to financing problems related to the IFC being debarred by constitution at the time from holding ordinary shares and CDC's reluctance to provide enough equity, 'while an international development agency took prior charge securities only' (Rendell 1976: 264–5). By 1964, the CDC was working with the World Bank and IDA on the Kenya tea development project, and by the early 1970s with the World Bank and EC on oil palm estates in Cameroon (Rendell 1976: 207, 215). Meanwhile, development companies in East Africa acted as 'a forum for the co-operation of European development agencies' (Rendell 1976: 227). By 1969, 'good relations' with the international development agencies in Washington D.C. and the European national agencies led to 'official invitations to CDC representatives to attend at meetings of the Development Aid Committee of OECD in Paris' (Rendell 1976: 270–1).

In 1968, Sir Andrew Cohen, Permanent Secretary at the Ministry of Overseas Development, stated before the Estimates Committee of the House of Commons that:

> The Ministry of Overseas Development regarded the CDC as probably as efficient a form of aid as exists in this country or anywhere in the world, a view which I know the World Bank holds.
>
> (Rendell 1976: 270)

In 1971 the World Bank president, Robert McNamara, affirmed this, and termed the CDC 'a unique organisation which has shown the way to the rest of us' (quoted by CDC 1971: 7), written in the:

> light of a number of agricultural partnerships between the World Bank and CDC and an agreement in accordance with which CDC does agricultural investigations for the World Bank.
>
> (CDC 1971: 7)

The CDC and the other bilateral and multilateral institutions, from this highpoint, then intermeshed operationally and financially in the 40 years from 1968, but how they did that changed periodically.

In fact, CDC subsequently showed remarkable flexibility, experimenting with different ways of working with the private sector in particular, as 'lender, minority shareholder, joint-venture partner, independent project promoter, [and] venture capitalist' (Tyler 2008: 25).[5] In short, following government reviews held roughly every ten years, CDC changed its operating character along with fashions in development practice or, as Tyler summarises, it 'demonstrated a remarkable capacity to move with the times, reinventing itself when necessary to maintain both economic and political relevance' (Tyler 2008: 14). From

1964 to 1983 it acted like a 'Development Bank', focusing on the then in-vogue rural development, especially small-holder agriculture where high returns weren't expected. From the 1975 Ministry and CDC review, which prioritised investments in 'Renewable Natural Resources', the CDC resembled very much the World Bank, with its focus on lending to governments for rural development, in accordance with a political climate which was critical of private sector 'exploitation' and favoured a state-led 'nationalistic model' (Tyler 2008: 15). Loans were made directly to governments and statutory authorities, corporations and state-owned companies, often with a government guarantee, with a view to eventually selling any equity holdings to national governments and to indigenise local management. Many successful projects in this era involved sugar, tea and coffee out-growers, but there were also large 'white elephants' such as the Southern Paper Mills venture in Tanzania (also remarked by Calderisi 2006) and the parastatal Smallholder Sugar and Coffee authorities in Malawi, which despite taking huge rents from growers nevertheless eventually went bust.[6] Some CDC money was loaned for the purpose of nationalising ventures on behalf of governments, such as for the Kilombero Sugar project in Tanzania (Tyler 2008: 15). In sum, in the period 1975–79, there was a predominance of public sector partnerships and little work with the private sector: 46 per cent was co-financed with the World Bank, 93 per cent with a government or state agency, and only 29 per cent with private sector participation. Of 40 new African agribusiness projects supported by CDC from 1964 to 1983, up to 1979 only three were controlled by private sector partners (excluding CDC itself) and one of these, Zambia Sugar, was subsequently nationalised (Tyler 2008: 16).

Tyler summarises this period as one in which it is difficult to establish the viability of separate projects when the loan was made to a government, and that:

> In most cases sustainable agricultural activities were created but often at an unreasonably high financial cost for the government concerned, which in turn contributed to the growing crisis of Third World debt. In practice CDC had been helping to financing [sic] the unsustainable growth of the African public sector bureaucracy.
>
> (Tyler 2008: 17)

Certainly, by the time of the 1986 Overseas Development Administration (ODA precursor of DfID) Review, the investments in agribusiness and plantation agriculture in sub-Saharan Africa had been identified as of high risk and low return, features which accentuated CDC's significant (and now politically unacceptable) exposure (NAO 1989: 21). This ODA Review was followed by a highly critical Overseas Development Institute (ODI) Report on CDC's assessment of risk, which examined 14 projects and concluded that in 'no [CDC] report was risk treated systematically', and that the treatment of risk 'was usually brief and desultory' (MMC 1992: 69). Political fashion had changed, and alongside it so did the CDC. According to Tyler, from 1984 to 1994, the CDC worked as a 'Development Finance Institution', in the model of the IFC, rather than the World Bank, as the perceived failure of state-led development prompted a shift to the Right. The 1985–86 ODA and CDC review mirrored the Thatcherite turn, with a new emphasis on projects with the private sector, while the Renewable Natural Resources target was weakened (Tyler 2008: 17–18). CDC was instructed to meet private sector levels of profitability to avoid 'market distortions'.

However, the 1980s model contained a contradiction: there remained 'an inherent weakness in a public sector body, with "developmental" goals and bureaucratic tendencies, trying to both work with, and compete with, private enterprises' (Tyler 2008: 25). It could afford to fail more often, and it did fail a lot, but:

> Ultimately the view was taken that CDC could only realistically be expected to achieve private sector levels of commercial performance in developing countries, and to compete fairly, if it was itself controlled by private investors.
>
> (ibid.)

This contradiction prompted the next changes in the CDC, as it experimented with ways to privatise first all of itself and then part of itself, through the 1990s to 2004. The mid-1990s review was undertaken at a time where CDC was anticipating privatisation, alongside most other UK parastatal enterprises, such that changes involved making CDC more 'privatisable', more liquid and with healthy market rates of return on loan and equity (Tyler 2008: 20). 'Development' prerogatives were seen as having overridden the good common sense of profitable commercial investment in the creation of internationally competitive businesses. The answer, it was concluded, was to specialise in 'world-class sectors' where CDC had expertise (palm oil, sugar, horticulture, cement, electricity) and the targeting of venture capital investments in profitable new sectors such as telecoms and information technology, while incorporating separate venture capital funds with specific foci for other remaining parts of the portfolio (Tyler 2008: 20), a strategy which was to become dominant after the 1999 privatisation proper. Following the 1997 announcement by New Labour that CDC was indeed to become a public–private partnership, equity investments were prioritised to the point where lending more or less stopped completely (Tyler 2008: 21).

The CDC Act of 1999 transformed it from a statutory body into a limited liability company renamed CDC Group plc. At this point, all shares were owned by the British Government but efforts were made to find a private sector partner to buy a majority holding. To become saleable the portfolio was 'notionally split into two', with CDC Capital Partners the 'new-style' 'private equity investor' and CDC Assets, representing the 'old-style' development corporation. The assets of the latter, which were mostly old loans, were to be realised by loan servicing and the sales of any equity stakes, with the cash generated transferred to support the new fully commercial investments of the newer incarnation. The new senior management brought in to 'spearhead privatisation' saw agribusiness as generally too low profit and CDC's existing portfolio as having a low reputation, such that most of these projects were placed in the 'CDC Assets' umbrella to be sold off (Tyler 2008: 21). The portfolio of agribusiness ventures was written down from '278 million in 1999, to £213 million in 2000, to reflect its new "for sale" rather than "going concern" status' (Tyler 2008: 23). Many assets were sold off, some to managements, some to specialist investors, and the share of agribusiness in CDC's portfolio fell from 20 per cent in 2000 to 5 per cent in 2005. This, however, did not stop a new joint venture, 'Aureos Capital', formed in 2001, from finding new investments in African agribusiness, the food industry and other sectors at commercial rates. Aureos is 'owned by CDC, Norfund, FMO and its management team to run existing and promote new national and regional venture capital funds for Africa and elsewhere' (Tyler 2008: 22).

However, CDC as a whole still hadn't found a private investor by 2002, at terms that the UK Government were prepared to accept, such that the 'CDC Capital Partners' concept was dropped. There were significant concerns about investors asset stripping the portfolio, so instead, the Government decided to privatise just the management function and achieved this in 2004 with the creation of Actis, a fund management company owned by the bulk of the former senior staff of CDC, which works in emerging markets as a private equity fund and which was to become the main source or 'driver' of the super profits recorded in 2007 (Craig 2008).[7] While CDC was thus not technically 'asset stripped' as such, this arrangement has allowed Actis to create a number of separate funds to differentiate between aspects of CDC's historical role which are more profitable than others, with funds for different geographical areas and different sectors, such as 'China', or 'power', or 'mining' (seen as more profitable), or in 2006, the 'Actis

African Agribusiness Fund' (seen as less profitable and initially spon-sored by Actis without interest from others) (Tyler 2008: 24). The rump of CDC is still wholly owned by the British Government, while Actis is 40 per cent owned by the Government, through DfID, while both have independent and separate boards. CDC invests in Actis funds and monitors the performance of Actis as the fund manager. As Tyler summarises:

> Actis is free to invite third parties to invest in its funds and CDC is free ... to invest in emerging market funds promoted by fund managers other than Actis.
>
> (Tyler 2008: 23)

CDC had been 'unbundled', with Aureos managing smaller venture capital funds, and Actis the bulk of CDC's portfolio, without the dampening effect of lower reputation projects.

Thus the longer term history of CDC has it successively withdrawing from direct investment in productive enterprises, and more latterly from direct involvement in financial companies in-country, and becoming instead a private equity emerging markets 'fund of funds', choosing to place its own funds in other fund management companies, principally Actis, which it has continued to prefer since 2004. Thus, taxpayers' money is effectively contracted out into a limited liability partnership between the (old) staff of the CDC and government (DfID with its 40 per cent stake) (Storey and Williams 2006: 5). Its fund managers have done a good job and in 2007, net assets increased by 33 per cent and total post-tax returns were £672 million, meaning that the CDC outperformed the MSCI Emerging Markets Index by 20 per cent in 2007 (CDC 2008a). In perspective, these returns represent a total return after tax which had increased by 79 per cent, compared with £375 million in 2006, while the annualised return on investments was 33 per cent (Craig 2008). At the year end of 2007 the CDC had outstanding commitments of £1.4 billion to 100 funds with 42 managers (ibid.), while its net assets had risen in value from £2 billion in 2006 to £2.7 billion in 2007, prompting fresh talk of privatisation. As a consequence, criticism has been growing of both the heightened, and somewhat unsavoury, profits of Actis, and the ethical quality of its projects.

Actis supports activities which many would only nominally term 'developmental'. The fund represents 62 per cent of CDC's commit-ted funds under management, and recently, as an illustrative exam-ple, it was in charge of running a portfolio of power assets which included Globeleq. In 2007, the Asian and Latin American operations of Globeleq were sold for £621 million, generating gains of £281 million, or more than a third of Actis's total return for 2007 (Craig

2008). Globeleq, formed by Actis since 2000, acquired power assets in Asia, Africa and Latin America in energy generation and distribution, many of which were privatised by close institutional relatives, such as the Crown Agents and (other parts of) the CDC, such as the newly privatised Umeme electricity distribution network in Uganda. These assets have also been increased in value by bilateral development finance and project funds which have gone to large MNCs to upgrade power facilities prior to privatisation. The power assets in sub-Saharan Africa, valued at $167 million, remain with Actis, with a core business development team which includes personnel from the Globeleq company. CDC has recently placed another $750 million 'in cash' for further investments in sub-Saharan power assets through the fund (Craig 2008). However, there is much evidence already that the development credentials of Umeme and Globeleq leave much to be desired. Umeme was taken to court for price hikes by Ugandan consumers (Hall 2007: 10), while a report by War on Want UK has questioned Globeleq's developmental credentials, including in the case of Ugandan privatisation (War on Want 2006).

In effect, coordinated British bilateral aid delivery mechanisms, through both technical assistance contracts and derivative business to power companies, have generated an enlarged British stake in the business of power generation and distribution in Anglophone African countries, particularly in the post-privatisation period. The World Bank procurement database, for example, lists $223,427 million, as the total supplier contract amount won by British businesses in the energy and mining sectors in Africa from 2000 to 2007 (World Bank 2008a). Many of these projects, for which UK consultants and suppliers were involved directly with the World Bank, were also cross funded by UK bilateral agencies. This coordinated effort also generated private wealth for the CDC managers who bought Actis following the part privatisation. Led by senior partner Paul Fletcher, CDC's management function was bought for £373,000, a figure that *Private Eye*, citing one executive close to the deal, deemed 'too cheap'. Government documents valued the remaining stake at between £182 and £535 million (Craig 2008, citing *Private Eye*), while *Private Eye* noted that many of the beneficiaries of the sale of the 60 per cent became multi-millionaires. During 2007, buoyed by excellent profitability, CDC made commitments to 31 new funds, of which 16 were also new fund managers:

> as it sought to diversify its investment reach which includes large buyouts, venture capital, microfinance, mezzanine finance, small to medium-sized enterprise and sector-specific funds.
>
> (Craig 2008)

All good news to those who support a neoliberal approach to poverty reduction, since, as Richard Laing, chief executive of CDC, summarises: 'it is only possible to defeat poverty through the generation of wealth' (cited by Craig 2008), or as Allan Gillespie, head of CDC Capital Partners back in 2002 said in response to Tony Baldry, then chair of the International Development Select Committee, who accused CDC of 'putting profit before poverty relief': 'We don't carry the socially responsible investment label, but to dedicate capital to these countries is, in itself, an act of social responsibility' (cited by the *Financial Times* 2002). This social responsibility has led CDC, through Actis, to place a 19.1 per cent stake in Diamond Bank plc of Nigeria, as an example, the first West African bank to list on the Professional Securities Market of the London Stock Exchange (Touch Base Africa 2008). In other words, lucrative private wealth creation, buoyed by state subsidy, is now promoted as developmental, despite its poor calibre in that regard.

The Export Credit Guarantee Department

ECGD does not make investments directly, but without it the private sector would not be able to either, so it acts as a facilitator of trade and investment, since without insurance cover economic exchange would not be able to take place. It is in this sense that ECGD is also a market maker and gatekeeper of public and private liquidity. It is a department enjoying the sovereign guarantee of the Treasury for its investment portfolio, and supports 'long and large' business and the provision of export credit to the poorest countries where the private market is unwilling to participate because of so-called 'country risk'. They have been intermittently in the news for providing a heavy subsidy for arms exporters and credit for some of the most notorious large dam schemes, for example, the Ilisu in Turkey, which evicted many Kurdish people (Amnesty 2000); the corruption-ridden Lesotho Highlands Water Project; and the Kenyan Turkwell Hydroelectric and Ewaso Ngiro dams (HC 2001: HC39-I, paragraphs 190, 191). Along with other European and global export credit agencies (ECAs), ECGD are the target of a permanent social movement seeking their reform. In the UK, Cornerhouse reviews the performance of ECGD, while FERN is an organisation aimed at European ECA reform and ECA Watch heads the global campaign.

In the first years of New Labour in the late 1990s ECGD also became a conduit for the insurance of large exports of weaponry. Robin Cook when in Opposition was concerned that the Tories had watched the percentage of ECGD cover for military equipment rise from 7 per cent of all capital goods to 'a staggering forty-eight per cent' (Cook 1997). However, in the financial year 1998 to 1999 when Robin Cook had become Foreign Secretary, this rose again to an even higher 52 per cent (ECGD 1999: 5). ECAs are also environmentally notorious:

> ECAs are estimated to support twice the amount of oil, gas and mining projects as do all Multilateral Development Banks such as the World Bank Group. Half of all new greenhouse gas-emitting industrial projects in developing countries have some form of ECA support.
>
> (ECA Watch 2008)

This problem with their development role, combined with a long history of association with bribery and corruption (see Bracking 2007: 237–39), led to the Jakarta Declaration for Reform of Official Export Credit and Investment Insurance Agencies in 2000, which has been endorsed by over 300 NGOs. However, ECAs are good at playing the national economic interest card in order to avoid social regulation. For example, in the British case, a Government review in 1999 led by the International Development Committee, urged the ECGD to adopt best practice in investment, but the ECGD successfully countered ethical regulation in terms of the argument of compromised competitiveness (HC 1999). In other words, they successfully argued against the Government imposing unilateral regulation on the basis of 'best prac- tice', by claiming that their clients would be priced out of the market relative to other national competitors such as French and German firms, although this was considered not such a bad thing by some commentators reflecting on arms to Indonesia and the compulsory eviction of Kurdish people to make way for the Ilisu Dam (HC 2000).

In recognition of the collectivised but competitive interests of the firms of the richer states and the transnational regulatory framework that they adhere to, the International Development Committee (IDC) deferred a decision in this example and recommended that any change should be placed within internationally agreed reform plans with other ECAs in the OECD Consensus Group. Of course other national agencies make similar arguments, such as the government-owned or supported export credit insurance schemes HERMES in Germany, COFACE in France and DUCROIRE in Belgium. While each argues nationally for a competitive edge, and governments indulge them, the collective market and market abuses continue to grow. In international comparative terms, Gianturco summarised that ECA activity levels vary widely due to a number of factors, 'including the strength and risk appetite of other types of financial institution, the age and experi- ence of the ECA, the support it receives from public and private sectors, and its geographic region' (2001: 5). Compared regionally, support for exporting is:

highest among the Asian ECAs (which financed an average of $15 billion of exports apiece in 1996). In the same year, Western European ECAs supported an average of almost $10 billion of exports per annum, and North American ECAs covered an average of almost $46 billion. African ECAs covered an average of $881 million, Central and Eastern Europe (CEE)/ Newly Independent States (NIS) ECAs an average of $276 million, and South American ECAs an average of only $50 million in 1996.

(Gianturco 2001: 5)

The market size is thus great, while the subsidy to notionally 'free trade' internationally is quite astounding, helping to explain why poorer countries find it so difficult to join the exporting club. Yet ECAs in the most part have no developmental mandate or obligation, despite their accounting for, in 1996, some 24 per cent of total debt and 56 per cent of developing country official debt, after increasing their new commitments from about $26bn in 1988 to $105bn eight years later (ECA Watch 2001).

The International ECA Reform Campaign asserts that while the WTO (World Trade Organisation) and World Bank have become increasingly visible, the more secretive ECAs 'have as big, if not bigger, impacts on the process of globalization', since they are the world's biggest class of public IFIs, collectively exceeding the size of the World Bank Group (ECA Watch 2001a). In recent years ECAs are estimated to have been supporting between $50 and $70 billion annually in 'medium and long-term transactions,' the majority of which are large industrial and infrastructure projects in developing countries (ECA Watch 2008). These are often transactions in the dirtiest industries, which even the World Bank Group are reluctant to support because of likely bad publicity.

Crown Agents

The Crown Agents is the oldest organisation in the British frontier state, with precursors to its modern form and name going back to 1749, when:

> some agents were additionally authorised to receive and account for British Treasury grants to the colonies they acted for. Those agents were appointed by the Crown on the recommendation of the British Treasury, and came to be known (unofficially) as *crown agents*.
>
> (Crown Agents 2008a, author's emphasis)

From the mid-nineteenth century:

> the Agents General/Crown Agents were increasingly called upon by their principals to manage the construction of ports, railways, roads and bridges that accelerating colonial development and trade made necessary. The Office raised loan capital, engaged consulting engineers for the design work, procured and shipped the necessary materials and machinery, and project managed the work to its conclusion
>
> (Crown Agents 2008b)

Thus the Crown Agents were established to reduce costs and increase efficiency in the procurement of goods and services to the Crown Colonies, including in the raising of development finance before the modern 'aid' era was born. By the Second World War, for example, Crown Agents had already raised over £450 million for its principals through more than 200 loans (Crown Agents 2008c). After the Second World War Crown Agents greatly expanded due to the project of 'reconstruction and development' in the areas of engineering consultancy, turnkey projects, credit finance and fund management. They also engaged on their own account in the secondary banking and property markets. The global collapse of the mid-1970s resulted in substantial losses for Crown Agents and led to a 1979 Act which provided for the incorporation of Crown Agents as a statutory corporation, monitored by and reporting to the Minister for Overseas Development on behalf of the Secretary of State, who also appointed members of its board. Crown Agents has since concentrated on agency procurement; shipping and inspection services; advisory services, principally in the fields of economics, infrastructure and natural resources; banking and fund management; and human resource development.

In the late 1980s privatisation was being talked about, and an early institutional change was to create, in 1989, Crown Agents Financial Services Ltd (CAFSL) as a separate subsidiary company to act as bankers and financial services providers for Crown Agents as a whole, its other subsidiaries and clients. CAFSL was a bank regulated by the Bank of England and later, when regulatory powers changed in the UK, by the Financial Services Authority (FSA). In 2006 CAFSL's name was changed to Crown Agents Bank Ltd. Finally, in 1997, ten years after a change of status was first suggested, Crown Agents was fully privatised, changing from a statutory corporation into a private limited company, The Crown Agents for Overseas Governments and Administrations Limited, wholly owned by The Crown Agents Foundation, a newly created holding company. Members of the Foundation include

NGOs, charities, large companies and even university departments such as the School of Oriental and African Studies, the Institute of Development Studies at Sussex and Leeds Metropolitan University as academic members. When it was privatised, not only was it a going concern as a consultancy company with an impressive market share, but it also owned assets, such as the remnants of ships, ports and vehicles, and so forth, left over from the Empire.

In terms of the functions of the Crown Agents, its evolving structure of ownership facilitated its successful journey into the business of aid finance. During the 1980s and 1990s Crown Agents, as a non-departmental public body, was consistently encouraged, with the CDC and Natural Resources Institute (NRI) to increase business conducted with other multilateral and bilateral agencies (HC 1994a: 4). In this it was successful, embedding itself in the global aid architecture for derivative business in supply and logistics (see chapter 7). By 1994:

> The Crown Agents have increased their income from the providers and recipients of multilateral aid to nearly 20 per cent of their global turnover. Income from World Bank projects has trebled in the last two years.
>
> (HC 1994a: 4)

Indeed, Crown Agents has proved adept at riding the wave of successive policy fads and agendas. Following closely the developing aid agenda on both privatisation and transparency and accountability, in the early 1990s Crown Agents became a main provider of consultancy services in terms of the New Public Management (NPM) agenda, providing advice on public sector modernisation and revenue management. Specific interventions were made in customs reform, public revenue modernisation and nuclear safety. For example, in 1996 Mozambique out-sourced the running of its customs service to Crown Agents. These interventions, and particularly the wave of privatisations, saw Crown Agents expand, and by 2001 it was working for multilateral and bilateral donors and involved in projects with an estimated annual value of $6 billion (Crown Agents 2001). By 2007, it had operations in 25 countries, many through locally incorporated companies, 'agents in a further six, and project offices in many more' (Crown Agents 2008d).

It now has country offices in London, Japan and the United States, and has, since 1987 when it became a 'procurement agent' under Japan's Non Project Grant Aid Programme, managed over 130 projects with a total value of 189 billion yen for the Ministry of Foreign Affairs, Japan International Co-operation Agency, Japan Bank for International Co-operation and Japan International Co-operation System (Crown

Agents 2008e). In a rather ironic full circle, Crown Agents has recently become a market leader in debt management, and was named the Large Consultancy Firm of the Year 2006 in the annual British Expertise International Awards, for its role in helping Nigeria towards achieving debt cancellation worth $18 billion. In this role, DfID funded technical assistance from Crown Agents, working 'closely with the Commonwealth Secretariat' to establish and then assist a Debt Management Office in Nigeria from 2000, which then became a 'world-class debt management office', whose 'credible database and improved transparency, efficiency and professionalism in debt management provided vital technical support to negotiations with its creditors', efforts which were then 'largely' responsible for Nigeria being the 'first African nation to settle its dollar Paris Club debt' (Crown Agents 2008f).

Neoliberalism and the frontier institutions

The Conservative Government from 1979 was keen to increase the commercial benefits to the UK of the activities of all the frontier institutions, although obviously not theorised as they are here. The Overseas Development Administration-conducted Policy Review of the CDC in 1980 reduced CDC's targets for poorer countries and renewable natural resources, while the 1986 Review recommended more funding to be carried out with the private sector. In 1991, the CDC was referred to the Monopolies and Mergers Commission (MMC) for a review of its efficiency and effectiveness with a view to potential privatisation. It was not privatised, with a CDC official citing inadequate profitability as the reason (interview, London, 1993) although MMC did recommend more commercial lending rates (MMC 1992). The ECGD did not, however, escape privatisation of its short-term export insurance operations in 1991, as the Conservative Government's privatisation agenda was extended to them in order to reduce the Treasury's liability in this area, with a major part of the ECGD portfolio privatised to a Dutch company, NCM, in 1991. However, the demand for ECGD's remaining services in long-term bilateral trade insurance, where the private sector 'will not go', did not subsequently diminish, as illustrated by the high rates of ECGD activity in the 1990s and 2000s. The Crown Agents, as we saw above, was privatised in 1997 and CDC eventually (partly) followed in 2000 to 2004. Thus, all the major institutions of development finance were moved into the 'frontier state' of pseudo-private mediators in the 1990s.

The privatisation of the CDC was the most shocking from a developmental perspective, since it was an institution which, until 1993 at least, enjoyed about half of the entire UK bilateral aid budget, recycled from DfID (formally ODA) accounts. The CDC has an incredible post-war history, where all statistics about it appear grand. For example, in 1993, 350,000 people were employed in enterprises in which CDC had a stake, plus about 700,000 farming families were attached to CDC agricultural projects, and the CDC's own 30 directly managed companies (worth £355 million) were directly employing a further 40,000 people in 18 countries (CDC 1993: 10). At the time of privatisation it employed 17 per cent of the whole Swazi workforce in sugar plantations and related industries, and owned most of the world's palm oil, and so on. In fact, the CDC can be viewed as a principal global conduit for managing the investment flows associated with the post-war development project, and for dragging a significant number of the South's workers into circuits of wage labour, at least in the Anglophone ex-colonies and in the agricultural sector. The CDC was constituted to act as a backstop institution, an intermediary between the (un)credit worthy and the rich, but with some nonetheless very profitable enterprises in its portfolio. On privatisation, its historical commitment to development was diluted to a *Code of Business Principles and Prohibited Activities* (CDC 2008b).

Its privatisation resonated with a growing concern about a shift in development financing from public (and, therefore, potentially at least, democratic) control to private initiative, through processes of privatisation (for example, Soederberg 2004 and 2005, summarised in Storey and Williams 2006). Mosley (2001) wrote that the privatisation (or transformation into a public–private partnership) of the CDC in 1997 in the UK was a significant example of this process. Meanwhile, Cammack (2001) viewed CDC activities as part of the overall process of development promoting capitalist profit expansion at a global level, regardless of poverty reduction, while we have previously suggested that DFIs promote the interests of the already powerful at the expense of the global South (Bracking 2003). Apart from privatisation of itself, however, the effect of the neoliberal economic hegemony which was to emerge in the 1980s also changed the functionality of the CDC, what it did and who it did it with. Indeed the CDC was often given the job of rearranging corporate structures, commercialising parastatals and public companies under structural adjustment, and making the corporate governance changes necessary for privatisation in a myriad of different settings in countries across its portfolio. In this sense it became a Trojan horse for the widespread process of privatisation which has beset Africa since the 1990s, a process which has reduced public accountability over basic utilities in most cases, as Bond's work on South Africa so illustrates (see for example, Bond 2002).

Berthelemy et al. in an OECD publication noted that:

The privatisation process used most in sub-Saharan Africa has been the sale of shares (directly or through competition), followed closely by liquidations and sales of assets. Other methods are used much more rarely: leases, public flotation, transfers, management contracts, buyouts, joint ventures, concessions, trustees and swaps.

(2004: 43)

Indeed, the vast majority of privatisations recorded in their book were by selling shares to private individuals, a fact which the authors implied meant that local elites are as culpable for the outcome as external institutions, since there was, nominally, a choice about the implementation method for privatisation. The authors continue: 'what is achieved by privatisation is essentially a clarification of the role of the state' (2004: 12), which underscores their point that it was a deci-sion of local elites, in association with their advisors, which has led privatisation processes to be, in the main, supportive of widening inequality and personalised wealth creation. While the CDC cannot be singularly held responsible for this, the sale of shares model which has predominated, has also held sway in many arrangements involving DFIs, although the OECD authors maintain that the IFIs did not 'push' just the share option. Case study evidence and material the CDC produced in line with its role of preparing governments for privatisa-tion do indicate, however, a clear preference in this direction. In practice, donor agendas – for a secure and profitable investment envi-ronment – and the priorities of local elites – domestic accumulation and wealth – may converge around this outcome (see Craig 2000 for an excellent case study of Zambia).

For example, at a seminar at the University of Leeds in 1992, Alistair Boyd, a senior CDC executive, produced a slide of the CDC model of privatisation where a company would move from a monopoly market, through a stage of deregulation, to working in the context of a compet-itive market, with the privatisation process moving from left to right, through these three types. The firm is first commercialised, then corpo-ratised, then sold off by government. I have reproduced this slide from my contemporary notes in Figure 5.2 below. Boyd noted that it was very difficult to get the 'price right' to sell. To 1992, the CDC had carried out nine privatisations, including the East Usambara Tea Company Ltd in Tanzania, with Boyd explaining that while the World Bank and IMF 'preached' this, it was up to the CDC to work out how to do it. At this time, the privatisation of Zambia Sugar Company Ltd, a sugar production company with a mill managed by Booker Tate, was imminent. It needed $50 million to expand but was confounded by 'continual interference' at the board level and the problem of no one wanting to lend to (even productive) parastatals. The solution, according to Boyd was to move it out of government control. Meanwhile, The Companhia Do Buzi Sarl, a cotton and sugar production unit in Mozambique – in a 'terrible state and worth nothing' – the Kariba North Bank Co. Ltd electricity generating unit in Zambia, and the Botswana Power Corporation were also slated for privatisation. Boyd spoke of the problem of raising sufficient private sector finance to buy large public utilities, although moving them into the hands of the IFC could be an option, as in the last case of electricity in Botswana. Other obstacles to privatisation he listed as: retrenchment of excess labour and management; a resulting concentration of ownership, with Lonhro named as a company which could end up owning 'everything'; the sensitive issue of foreign ownership and control in an economy; the loss of strategic enterprises, although Boyd saw no productive asset as potentially strategic; and established interests and loss of privileges, where government appoints senior board members and wishes to continue to do so.

Since the World Bank and IMF have often imposed conditionality which makes financial assistance dependent on the execution of privatisation, there is then no surprise that a 'strong correlation between privatisation and international aid' (Berthelemy et al. 2004: 65) has been the outcome. For example, Guinea signed a lease with the private sector in 1989 for water, which resulted in a $102.6 million

Monopoly market ⟶ Deregulated ⟶ Competitive market

Government	Commercialisation	Corporatisation	Divestiture
-ownership	Government department	State-owned corporation	Private-sector company
-management	User charges	Restructuring	
-finance	Self accountability		

Figure 5.2 CDC's privatisation model
Source: Note that this is reproduced from the author's notes and thus may contain errors.

transfer to the Government for water sector investment. In Mozambique in 1999, the Government signed a contract with Bouygues for water provision for seven cities, and the World Bank and other donors granted $117 million for rehabilitation of the water infrastructure (Berthelemy et al. 2004). The amounts have also been large in support of privatisation relative to other funds. For example, in 2005, a year of famine in Niger, the World Bank was spending $14.8 million on the 'Financial Sector Technical Assistance Project', and $18.6 million on a 'Privatisation and Regulatory Reform Technical Assistance Project'; initiatives to privatise the water and make Niger fit for Western companies to invest in and exploit (World Bank 2005a). Yet the combined governments which own the World Bank couldn't initially find the $15 million the Government of Niger, through the UN, said it needed for famine relief until many had died. Up to 2 August 2005, DfID had provided $5.25 million matched roughly by the United States and the European Union (DfID 2005): too little too late, and not in the same league as the amounts spent on technical assistance to capitalism.

These are not, moreover, accidental correlations of funds around the same time as privatisation processes: a clear policy link remains between the resource flow and the change of ownership. Moreover, the culpability of the CDC and other IFIs grows if one considers that this was not an unpredicted result: that privatisation might lead to a concentration of ownership and control in the hands of some of the world's largest multinational corporations (MNCs) was recognised at the time. In 1994, the regional CDC Officer for southern Africa remarked, echoing Alistair Boyd, that 'The trouble with privatisation down here is whether we want Lonhro to own everything' (Fieldwork Interview, April 1994). At its worst, this process of concentration of ownership has allowed 'aid-spoilt' elites to adopt a particular style of exclusionary politics alongside MNCs, particularly in critical extractive enclaves (see Ferguson 2005 and 2006). MNCs, donors and local elites have then jointly managed a system of accumulation embedded in state authoritarianism and political kleptocracy (on Kenya, see Murunga and Nasong'o 2007; Browne 2007; Murunga 2007).

A more recent emphasis on public–private partnership (PPP) has not stopped privatisations, but has covered the process with an ideological fig leaf. While some projects genuinely combine public and private money in the supply of a good, such as mosquito nets or school text books, others combine public technical assistance in support of a private sector buyout. The PPP model describes both and is ubiquitous. By 2007, the US Agency for International Development (USAID), for example, was claiming that 'International development has entered a new era of public-private partnerships' and referred to a dramatic increase in private financing in 2003–05 from the United States to developing countries (apparently a threefold rise, large enough to provide 80 per cent of their capital funding), which offered a 'profound and promising change in the way international development is financed and conducted'. USAID has 'embraced this change' and adopted the 'Global Development Alliance (GDA) business model' to cultivate more than 600 alliances with 1,700 partners, using \$2.1 billion in public funding to leverage \$5.8 billion in private money (USAID 2007: iii, 1), including global level partnerships with Intel, Starbucks, Microsoft and Cisco (USAID 2007: 1). Whether this rise in financing is a permanent one, or capital rushing to escape the Northern epicentre of the credit squeeze by buying up Southern assets, is an open question. What is probable, however, is that the public money used to leverage the private has been used as subsidy or technical assistance, and does not result in profit-carrying assets, whereas the private money will result in wealth-creating assets for some time, long into the future.

Conclusion

The promotion of financial regulation and coordination has been a feature of the Bretton Woods settlement since the Second World War, and alongside this role of regulation there have always been contested spaces of power: between a bounded national sovereignty on the one hand and the imperatives of a global capitalist economy on the other. In this the British market makers are no exception, as an early row in 1949 between the Commonwealth Development Corporation (CDC) and the newly formed International Bank for Reconstruction and Development (IBRD) illustrates. In this prescient case the management of liquidity in the overseas territories of the British imperial state was at issue, in an early situation of 'credit crunch' following the war and a general shortage of dollars in the 'sterling area'. The negotiations concerned 'American investment in the Colonies', since at this point in time, the IBRD was seen as a conduit solely for US money. Negotiations broke down since the board of the CDC were 'convinced that the standard procedures of the International Bank are inappropriate in the case of this Corporation', rejecting a level of conditionality they considered only appropriate for less developed countries than Britain (CDC 1949: 6–7), since the:

> security offered for the loan was not and could not be challenged. Apart from the fact that the assets of the Corporation amounted to many times the amount of any loan contemplated, the capital and interest and the transferability of both were to have been guaranteed by His Majesty's Government.
>
> (CDC 1949: 47)

To the CDC this amounted to 'impregnable security', such that they express shock that the International Bank proposed:

> [a] loan conditional upon the Bank's being able to exercise a documentary supervision over the numerous undertakings in which some part of the equipment purchased might at some time be used.
>
> (CDC 1949: 47–8)

The CDC was unprepared to contemplate an early IBRD show of conditionality given the power and status of a British Government guarantee! Dismissing US investors' fears, the CDC concluded that growth of the Corporation would lead to a 'demonstrably economic institution through which American dollar investment in various forms can be canalized' (CDC 1949: 49). In chapters 7 and 8 we see how this took place, such that the Bretton Woods era, despite its technical demise with the US inconvertibility announcement in 1971, remains one in which IFIs learned how to collectively manage the allocation of liquidity to poorer countries. It was in solving these 'problems' facing the American investor that the current global system, characterised by the collectivisation of the management of development finance and the socialisation of risk in the markets of the South, emerged.

This chapter has given an historical review of the frontier institutions of the British state and an account of the changing role of the CDC in managing investment and liquidity. The case study shows how one dominant core lender in the global interstate system, Britain, worked within the Bretton Woods system to make its bilateral development finance work in the private sector of Southern countries, alongside British firms. In this process it also made a profit for the British Treasury. Over time, the needs of the 'American investor' combined with the development aspirations of the Southern populations to render a collectivised system with attendant rules and codifications of entry and behaviour. Together, the bilateral lenders institutionalised financial leadership within more truly multilateral organisations: the World Bank, IMF and IFC. The British case is specific in that it is bound up with the closing history of territorial empire. However, the experience of the CDC within empire, in particular, became an important catalyst of how post-colonial institutions were structured, and in that sense, the post-colonial structures directly carried relationships of power, of command and subordination of Southern populations into the 'post' colonial era. The system of financial management of liquidity is the materiality behind wider relationships of unequal power. Because of this, it is no surprise that institutions such as the CDC were perfectly placed to lead the neoliberal privatisation agenda. It is also within similar institutional contexts that the bilateral system emerged in other European countries. Tensions arose between and within the Anglophone, Francophone and Lusophone (Portuguese-speaking) zones which came to be managed within the EU as it developed a 'competition' policy for aid projects, a collectivised market which nonetheless continues to privilege European companies and financiers relative to those outside.

Notes

1. A metaphor borrowed from Gallagher and Robinson (1953: 1), who used it in a related context. They claimed that judging the size of empire merely by territories under direct control missed the 'informal empire', the submerged part of the iceberg.
2. And its liberal nature must not be overstated, since, as one example, it still blames labour shortages on the 'reluctance of backward people [sic] to enter regular employment, [and their] limited use for cash wages' (CDC 1950: 40)!
3. Sir William Rendell joined the Corporation in 1952, was appointed the first General Manager in 1953, retired in 1973 and is credited with successfully carrying out the Reith reforms from 1950 to 1959 of management streamlining and decentralisation through Regional Controllers, and subsequently of developing an efficient management structure (CDC 1972: 8). He also wrote a rare history on which much of this section is based.
4. Between 1951 and 1955, 20 earlier ventures closed, although direct management had to be used, 'thus breaching a most sacred principle of the time', which demands private management (Rendell 1976: 36, 38).
5. Geoff Tyler was a CDC employee from 1983 to 2000, and then a retained consultant from 2000 to 2004.
6. In the case of coffee, the Authority only paid 20–30 per cent of the sale price to growers but still accumulated a debt of 40 million kwacha by 1999, when it was privatised and bought by growers. (*New Agriculturist* online, March 2004: www.new-agri.co.uk/04-2/develop/dev04.htm)
7. The relationship of Actis to CDC is described in a CDC press release as: 'The firm was formed following a demerger from CDC in July 2004 when it assumed all direct investment activity and operations previously overseen by CDC'. In May 2008 it had US$3.5 billion funds under management (CDC 2008).

6 Poverty in Africa and the history of multilateral aid

This chapter presents an overview of poverty in African countries and then explores the role of the multilateral aid architecture that has grown up in the last 60 years in ostensibly ameliorating widespread poverty. That majority populations in African countries in particular, as compared to their European, Asian or Latin American counterparts, suffer from acute poverty, is not generally contested. In the United Nations Development Programme's (UNDP), 'human development index' (HDI) for 2007–08, the lowest ranking 24 countries were in Africa, and of the lowest 50, 38 were African. In 2005, incoming private investment was in single figures or negative (Angola) in all of the bottom 20 African countries by the ranking (except Chad, where it was 12.9 per cent of GDP), and in the table of African countries as a whole, foreign direct investment (FDI) was in double figures in 2005 in only five – Seychelles (11.9%), Equatorial Guinea (57.6%), Congo (14.2%), Gambia (11.3%) and Chad (12.9%).[1] In a further HDI category covering 'other private flows' – which are 'non-debt-creating portfolio equity investment flows, portfolio debt flows and bank and trade-related lending' – 22 were negative in 1990, with eight not recording any value, and Eritrea and Namibia not existing, and a further twelve remained negative in 2005, with seven not recording. In other words, there was considerable disinvestment of 'free-floating' portfolio holdings within Africa in both these years, and presumably most of those in between. Meanwhile, the aid dependence of the countries at the low end of the HDI ranking is reflected in the high figures of Official Development Assistance (ODA) receipts as a proportion of GDP.

These figures are significant because without adequate fiscal resources social spending to alleviate poverty is undermined: if the government, and by extension the country as a whole, has no money, it can't be expected to fund social welfare. In other words, intuitive logic would suggest that the debt burden requires to be lifted and aid needs to increase, to allow the theoretical chance of government revenue and then its passage to those needing social welfare and protection. This is not to argue that the availability of aid and finance is the only factor which affects the quality of social services in Africa, far from it, since there is a complex relationship between the state of fiscal balance in a country and the quantity and quality of social, health and educational services. For example, the oil-rich Angolan elite have managed to run up a debt of $11 billion despite oil-related earnings of $8 billion a year (Global Witness 1999: 6, cited in Ferguson 2006: 198–9), and despite the borrowing, had only managed a paltry 162nd place on the HDI by 2007. Also, how far these aggregate figures translate to people's lived experience of poverty is difficult to deduce, although the difference between contemporary poverty and traditional frugality and scarcity is to be found both in the context of increased global inequality, which renders relational context more extreme, and in people's knowledge and perception of that inequality, which has also been enhanced, not least because of sustained contact with development discourse and practice.

Thus economic deprivation is not, as Mbembe reminds us, a simple story for contemporary Africans, but involves:

> an economy of desired goods that are known, that may sometimes be seen, that one wants to enjoy, but to which one will never have material access.
>
> (Mbembe 2002: 271, cited in Ferguson 2006: 192)

Indeed, global inequality has been increasing rapidly (Easterly 2001), and the economic gap between the rich and poor is extreme and seemingly unbreachable, discouraging the once fashionable talk of developmental convergence in income or quality of life and encouraging the view that socio-economic status and income are just a matter of place within a de-temporalised hierarchy (Ferguson 2006). In other words, there is no improvement envisaged in order to progress to where others are: those with the desired goods. Many African countries are even worse off in absolute terms than they were 20 or 30 years ago, which adds to the cruelty of appreciation of one's poverty: not only are you worse off than your parents, but other people have become richer in the meantime and you are unlikely to have a change in status over the course of your lifetime. The current hierarchy is de-temporalised in the sense that the modernisation paradigm has decomposed, and while culture has enjoyed a consequent move to coeval pluralities and 'alternative modernities', socioeconomic inequality is left with nowhere to go, no evolutionary promise of betterment: countries are no longer 'behind' they are 'beneath' or 'somewhere else' (Ferguson 2006: 183–92).

What we can say with some certainty is that some of the reason why many African economies fail to provide for their populations is provided by the aggregate data on total available finance, and that this is then compounded or ameliorated by political contexts and fiscal policy. Getting the balance of explanation right is important: too much emphasis on the former issue of finance 'framing' causality lets elites off the hook, while too little on the former and too much emphasis on domestic politics serves only to pathologise African elites and political systems. However, in an absolute and relational context it remains clear that the outcome of these two sets of processes is, in most African countries, both exceptionally cruel and unprecedented, given other people's contemporary wealth. For example, the extent of service delivery failure for poor Africans is acute, as this example from the health sector illustrates:

> Africa currently loses over 8 million people a year mainly to TB, HIV, Malaria, maternal mortality ... this tragic loss which is the equivalent of whole countries dying out and greater than losses from all modern conflicts combined is a result of weak or collapsed public health systems.
>
> (Africa Public Health Development Trust, cited at Abdul-Raheem 2008)

In the case of HIV/AIDS, for example, of the estimated 6.5 million people in need of antiretroviral (ARV) treatment in June 2006, only 1.65 million people were reported to have had access to ARV treatment in low- and middle-income countries (UNAIDS 2008, citing World Health Organisation (WHO), June 2006).[2]

This has made many wonder that African lives can be deemed so expendable, including Stephen Lewis, the UN Special Envoy for HIV/AIDS in Africa, who asked:

> What is it about Africa that allows the world to write off so many people – to make people expendable – when all the money needed is found for war on Iraq? Is it so overwhelming? Have wealthy countries simply washed their hands of Africa? Is it too far away? Is it subterranean racism?
>
> (*Mail* and *Guardian*, 29 November to 5 December 2002, cited in Jones 2004: 385)

This problem of distance is at the centre of the political and cultural problem of relational poverty. As Mayer summarises, again in terms of the HIV/AIDS pandemic:

> the real problem remains one of political will on most fronts, of social and political isolation of first world countries from the realities and tragedies of HIV in sub-Saharan Africa, and of their continuing perception that the African epidemic is still far away.
>
> (Mayer 2005: 12)

This isolation, or distance, confines African people to expendability, as it contributes to profound chronic relief failure. This is not to say that African people are distant from each other, far from it. Rather, a plausible explanation for why rich people and their governments fail to assist is that they feel distant and act somewhere else. Also, efforts to help, when solidarity is expressed, have not worked for a series of reasons, some of which we explore in chapter 10.

Contemporary development research and poverty

The extensive statistical lows of poverty across Africa have led to a veritable cottage industry in recent years of poverty research, much of which addresses the likely (non) achievement of the Millennium Development Goals (MDGs) agreed in 2000 and set for 2015. Woolcock summarises this recent poverty research as having established a number of related propositions, namely that:

> poverty has many dimensions, that among these dimensions income is centrally important, and that inclusive ("pro-poor") economic growth policies are necessary but insufficient for reducing it.
>
> (2007: 1)

He notes that 'poverty traps' has become the 'policy shorthand for the microeconomics of poverty', while 'inequality traps' (citing World Bank 2005) are the equivalent for non-economics perspectives. In its simplest form, inequality traps refers to 'durable (compare Tilly 2000) structures of economic, political, and social difference that serve to keep poor people (and by extension, poor countries) poor' (Woolcock 2007: 4). Much chronic poverty is intergenerationally transmitted, and affects women, children, sick people and those with disabilities disproportionately to others. Those who are identified as most vulnerable, through vulnerability analysis, are those most affected by adverse life chances and shocks, generally those who are also members of lower social classes and/or suffer social stigma (CPRC 2004; see also Oppong 1998 on HIV and vulnerability).

However, while a great deal of research has confirmed what was already known intuitively about who is poor – the weak, sick and vulnerable, and those who are unable to work – there has been comparatively little research to establish why this might be the case in a relational context (Green and Hulme 2005). A promising central theme though is the theorisation of distance referred to above – cultural, structural and spacial – which serves to facilitate an absence of empathy for the poor. As Woolcock puts it, 'distance reduces elective affinity and sense of shared interests' (2007: 4) between rich and poor, such that the rich, citing Skocpol (1990), live in a different 'moral universe', with political characteristics and liberal democratic mores that are often starkly different to the political contexts in which poor people live, such that political solutions which are advocated, and which rely on these mores, often don't fit the place they are intended for (Bracking 2005). In short, the poor are often confined to discrete cultural and social networks, which nonetheless form the basis of their survival (compare Fafchamps 2006), and are often found in spatially remote places, where their social exclusion is secured from the relatively wealthier not least by political systems that exclude them. This is first and foremost a relationship of space, ordered by the political economy of development globally, itself configured by structures of power globally and locally.

Place, poverty and culture

Ferguson in *Global Shadows* has written an extremely pertinent book on culture and aspiring to global place in the context of relational poverty. It is worth quoting at some length. He notes that:

> [It] is not that analysts of Africa ought to focus on "political economy" instead of "culture" (as if economic inequalities were somehow non-cultural or cultural differences were somehow immaterial or apolitical). It is, rather, that the question of cultural difference itself is (everywhere, no doubt, but perhaps especially in contemporary Africa) tightly bound up with questions of inequality, aspiration, and rank in an imagined "world".
>
> (2006: 19)

In other words, people frame, understand and 'feel' poverty through culture and not being 'like' richer people. Moreover, the resulting African aspiration to 'likeness' 'forces an unsettling shift from a question of cultural difference to the question of material inequality' (2006: 20), such that:

> yearnings for cultural convergence with an imagined global standard ... can mark not simply mental colonisation or capitulation to cultural imperialism, but an aspiration to overcome categorical subordination. The persistence of cultural difference, meanwhile (however inventive and hybrid it may be), can come to appear as the token not (as it often appears to the anthropologist) of brave cultural resistance, but of social and

> economic subjection (where a "traditional African way of life"
> is simply a polite name for poverty).

(2006: 20–1)

This is an important corrective to both an overactive academic political correctness which sees just cultural difference when there is economic poverty, but also a corrective to a residual and popular reading of 'African life' which suggest that poverty does not impact as much as 'we' in the West would suspect, because areas of rural Africa are uncommodified or enjoy a 'traditional way of life' where $1 a day 'goes a long way'.

Ferguson's argument also impacts greatly on efforts to tackle African poverty, since he is pointing out the neglect of economic inequality which has become permissible because of the 'cultural turn' in social science. Thus, while it was an achievement to recognise contemporary African culture as 'modern' rather than 'backward', African views of everyday life and culture as signifying their low socioeconomic ranking have been simultaneously occluded. This then demotes economic justice from development agendas. The political consequences of Ferguson's corrective is that:

> the most challenging political demands go beyond the claims
> of political independence and instead involve demands for
> connection, and for relationship, even under conditions of
> inequality and dependence.

(2006: 22)

In other words, economic hierarchy needs to be foregrounded again, not least because, as Mbembe (2002) reminds us, aspiration for inclusion and connection relates to an acute and accurate knowledge of what global inequality means on the part of the poor themselves.

We can turn the question around somewhat and ask not 'what makes some people poor' but 'what makes some people allow poverty and what prevents them from forming relationships and empathy with their fellow humans'? On this question, which has been much less researched, we can only note some tentative possibilities as to what that relationship is prevented by: racial 'othering'; clumsy and popular accounts of cultural difference that suggest the poor are responsible or culpable for their own circumstances, perhaps because of inappropriate consumption of alcohol or drugs; blaming people's cultures for 'irrational' behaviours which undermine the (otherwise) 'scientific' interventions of aid workers; an overly 'cultural turn' that occludes poverty and insists on plurality of experience (Ferguson 2006); and the simple logistics of poverty which prevent poor people from doing 'recognisable' things that prompt relationship, like going to town on the bus (fieldwork, Chivi, 2005). There are also various excuses for non-intervention which mirror the TINA ('there is no alternative') argument in economics, that nothing can be done because, to cite a current trope, 'their' own elites are 'too corrupt' and aid money won't reach them anyway.

There is also the possibility that Ferguson (2006) can be misread, and that the argument risks a romanticisation of African aspiration which overemphasises 'culture' in the sense of global inclusion being won through iconic global goods, cell-phones, designer jeans and so forth, an aspiration which overemphasises this in relation to more mundane desires for basic commodities, school fees and the like. Ferguson's case study of a Zambian internet magazine illustrates the scenario of the young searching for and using the technology of the modern, but equally there is a greater majority who would want bread and meat as a signifier of inclusion. Whatever the finer points here, the problem of distance does not deter the transnational epistemic aid community from passing resolution after resolution aiming and promising to reduce poverty, themselves largely absent and critically distant from the subjects of their policy. Abdul-Raheem at the NGO Justice Africa called this the process of 'resolutionism' in his 'Tajudeen's Thursday Postcard' (Abdul-Raheem 2008).

Thus, the African Renaissance, New Partnership for African Development (NEPAD), the Commission on Africa, the Millennium Challenge Account and the poverty reduction strategy (PRS) process, all share the paradigmatic coordinates of an African crisis supposedly 'made in Africa' by irredeemable and intractable failures and inappropriate behaviours, which re-renders Africa as failed, intractable and (inaccurately) uniformly poor and needy. Corrupt elites are given a particularly nefarious central agency. But corrupt government and rapacious elites in Africa did not make the current crisis of African economies and welfare states, they are a symptom of it, although their behaviour can, and often does, make it more intractable. What is being made, instead, in these keynote transcripts and dominant cultural practices (aid conditionality), is not an accurate, empirically grounded and historically informed analysis of African 'reality'. It is instead a narrative that says more about the writers and promoters, and the wider beliefs of the 'development community', than about the avowed subjects. It is a culturally embedded understanding of African socioeconomic processes and cultural life, written largely by people who don't live there, which denies historical connectivity (slavery, colonialism, debt peonage); contemporary connectivity (internet communities; the World Social Forum; shared coeval history; diasporas; 'modern' middle classes;

educated, urban and professional Africans; debt peonage); and future connectivity (without a better policy response than this, Africans will feel, rightly, demonised and forsaken, and will seek autarchy, while a number who are chronically poor and sick will die). Waiting around for the MDGs to not be met is also a tedious intellectual milieu in which conservatism in human objectives – who said we only wanted to half the proportion of people in poverty, rather than eliminate it altogether? – has been written into policy to 2015, regardless of other more radical proposals which could have been attempted in the meantime.

Resolutionism also discourages historical evaluations of what has been tried to date in favour of a future which is always just around the corner, with a bit more effort and research in the present. This tends to conservative prescription and practice, again, because those very political economy processes that have made poverty in the present are not examined. Poverty was not made in the absence of efforts in the area of development 'aid', but in spite of it, and alongside it, and sometimes because of it, as the analysis in this book argues. Bearing this in mind, the rest of this chapter, and the next two, will explore the suggestion that the process of the political economy of concessional relationship and development finance might not be helping, might not help to attain the MDGs in the future, and indeed, might be a process in which poverty is, in a counterintuitive proposition, embedded and produced. So what is aid, how does it work, and why might there be problems with it?

The theoretical contribution of multilateral development assistance

One of the earliest arguments for multilateral activity to reduce poverty is that foreign assistance can provide a much needed global public good: not only can it help poor people, but it provides a shared infrastructure for international trade and finance, and helps to maintain peace and political stability (Krueger 1986). The public good nature of aid, particularly from multilaterals, 'springs from its unique ability to overcome global market failures in international trade and finance, particularly adverse selection and moral hazard in international credit and insurance' (Mellor and Masters 1991: 505), thus, in conventional economic terms, increasing the efficiency of global resource allocation. In other words, official development finance helps to raise the availability of credit for poorer countries. As we saw in chapter 4, official creditors have more recourse to powerful states should a risk of default occur, have broad portfolios with a high diversification of risk, and can lower the initial cost of capital through economies of scale in bulk borrowing. In addition, currency and exchange rate swaps lower the cost of loanable capital, while retained earnings from successful ventures have been impressive. For example, by 1985, the World Bank had accumulated $5.2 billion in retained earnings from its operations, more than the total paid-in capital from donors of $5.1 billion (see Blitzer 1986, cited in Mellor and Masters 1991: 507). In June 2007 'retained earnings and other equity' for just the International Bank for Reconstruction and Development (IBRD) (not including the International Development Association (IDA)) were valued at $27,127 million, calculated on a current value basis (World Bank 2007: 7), a figure repeated elsewhere as a 'fair value', but slightly larger at $28,440 million on 'carrying value' terms (World Bank 2007b: 93). While there can be problems surrounding the funding of global public goods, the free rider scenario being the most obvious, in neoclassical accounts, at least, development finance encourages the banks and the market to work more efficiently. In our terms, it extends capitalist markets and regulates dependent development.

To summarise arguments made earlier, aid in our terms is referred to as development finance – rather than 'aid' which suggests an uncritical benevolence – which is the provision of liquidity through public institutional frameworks. Only a small component of this is worthy of the 'benevolent' signifier; that tiny grant element spent directly on social welfare. Development finance is a category of second-line liquidity, the vast majority of which is borrowed rather than given, as low interest, long term (mostly) government to government lending, through either direct multilateral payments to international financial institutions (IFIs), or payments channelled through bilateral financial institutions. It is conventionally organised, particularly so since 1997, to reduce poverty. But some further definitions of 'aid' are required here. Official Development Assistance involves flows to developing countries and multilateral institutions from official government agencies, flows which have 'economic development and welfare as [their] main objective' with a grant element of at least 25 per cent, which excludes export credit used solely for export promotion (OECD 2008). 'Official Development Finance' (ODF), is defined as Official Development Assistance (ODA) combined with all development-oriented multilateral flows, while 'Other Official Flows' (OOF), is everything else vaguely developmentally inspired. To be development-oriented can mean flows which are non-concessional since these are, by increasing convention, included in the statistics for 'multilateral aid', with the major exception of IMF credit.[3] Mellor and Masters explain that this convention was increasingly used by the Development Assistance Committee (DAC):

because they judge that interest rates and payment structure (which determine the 'concessionality' of aid) do not fully describe multilateral aid. In particular, nonconcessional multilateral aid is additional to what would be otherwise available at that interest rate, is often targeted toward public goods, and may be accompanied by valuable technical assistance. It may also serve as a catalyst for other funds .... For these reasons, it functions more like bilateral ODA than like a nonconcessional bilateral flow.

(Mellor and Masters 1991: 504)[4]

We are, therefore, analysing flows of money disbursed by multilateral institutions which can be more expensive than commercial rates, but which are deemed concessional by those who lend them, because they project a positive developmental light on their institutional context. So the Commonwealth Development Corporation (CDC), International Finance Corporation (IFC) and other bilateral export and multilateral disbursers of aid can view their flows as concessional, despite transactions at 'market' interest rates or above. Inflated generosity can further be suggested when the agencies' own figures are reported in the media, such as in World Bank press releases, because far and away the largest element of resource transfer of the IFIs takes the form of nonconcessional loans, which therefore falls outside even this conservative OECD definition of aid (ODA), but people assume that they are referring to aid because of the organisation which is doing it. In other words, an impression of generosity is exaggerated by the inclusion of commercial flows, when the CDC or IBRD announce a commitment. While a proportion of these non-concessionary funds is channelled to ODA-qualifying countries and used to support development projects, a large part is not but rather, for example, used for export credits for military equipment sales or to fund a new port for a timber exporter, or some such.

Indeed, Riddell makes the point that there are three different types of multilateral agency – the group of IFIs, which are the principal subject of this book; the UN agencies; and a growing collection of 'others', such as the Bill and Melinda Gates Foundation or the Global Fund to Fight AIDS, Tuberculosis and Malaria (GFATM) established in 2002 – which collectively disburse about one-third of all ODA (Riddell 2007: 77, citing Rogerson et al. 2004: 29–31). The developmental value of the two latter types is more easily demonstrated in direct transfers of life-saving resources. However, the IFIs' activities are larger than the other two types, accounting for 44 per cent of total net multilateral ODA disbursements in 2004 and 71 per cent if the EC aid is excluded (Riddell 2007: 78). But, this actually underestimates their activities since that proportion of money disbursed by IFIs which is strictly counted as ODA – with the grant element, and which is used for this statistic – is generally a small proportion of their total turnover. For example, Riddell gives the example of 2004, where the IFIs together provided just over $9 billion in ODA (net disbursements) to ODA-qualifying countries, but their total spend in these countries was nearly five times that figure at just over $34 billion (Riddell 2007: 80, citing OECD 2006: 200). A quite astonishing statistic is that 'Excluding EC aid, the IFIs accounted for almost 90 per cent of all gross concessional and non-concessional funds channelled to ODA-qualifying developing countries, the UN's development and humanitarian agencies accounting for only 8 per cent of the total' (ibid.). These differences have also widened over time, with a similar figure for the early 1990s being that the UN agencies contributed 17 per cent of flows. In total, the IFIs provide twice as much official ODA as all the aid provided by the UN agencies in 2003, and in addition, their gross disbursements were ten times as large, at $36.5 billion compared to $3.5 billion.

In other words, the official statistics record a lower figure than actual disbursements, meaning that 'the reach and influence of the IFIs is far greater than the official statistics would suggest' (Riddell 2007: 80). For those commentators who view IFI activities as an unqualified success, this extra commercial reach will be considered a welcome bonus. Thus, the income and expenditure figures recorded by most multilateral agencies are 'considerably and consistently' higher than the equivalents recorded in official statistics, because the bulk of their spending – such as money to countries which are not poor, or ODA-qualifying, or which is tied to particular projects and therefore classified as bilateral – do not count within the stricter official statistics. Most of it is commercial loans to the private sector, and this gap between official 'aid' and agency recorded business can be wide. Riddell reports, for example, for the less commercial United Nations Children's Fund (UNICEF), that in 2003 its worldwide expenditure was nearly $1.5 billion, while the OECD recorded its net ODA disbursements at only $629 million (Riddell 2007: 78). Therefore, it is possible to read the figures promoted by the organisations themselves and get an inflated view of their actual grant-making or developmental character, because one might reasonably but erroneously assume that they are reporting ODA rather than turnover, which is generally the norm. While in the case of UNICEF, this might not be such a big problem, because their other expenditures which are not ODA are probably pretty much spent on welfare, staff and overheads in any case, for other institutions this difference is more misleading. For example, in the case of IFIs, the official figures hide the actual larger extent of commercial activity, a tendency which is exacerbated by the habit of their publishing 'net disbursements' rather than balance sheet 'profits': this underplays the amount which is paid back. For example, in 2003 a gross transfer of about $26 billion of non-concessional flows was 'wiped out' by a reverse flow of $33 billion in repayments from previous loans, making a balance of $7.2 billion in the IFIs' favour (Riddell 2007: 80). These repayments scuppered the apparent generosity of 'new' ODA for that year of $10.8 billion, reducing the combined net flow of concessional and non-concessional to only $3.6 billion (ibid.). Needless to say, it tends to be the former 'new aid' figure that hits the news headlines or is announced by development ministers, not the net figure with profits included.

Another error of reporting is also common. This is where authors inflate the developmental character of the monetary flows of IFIs, by talking about concessional provision, without putting it into the context of all the flows that are counted when total figures are announced. For example, Calderisi (2006) argues that there are a number of 'excuses' which are used to shift the blame for African development failure to agents outside Africa – slavery, imperialism, former colonialists and so forth – illustrating his (dubious) point with a summary of development assistance that portrays it as exceptionally generous. Calderisi writes:

> since 1985, most new assistance for Africa has been in the form of grants or near-grants. All World Bank assistance has come from a special fund that allowed it to offer 40-year loans, without interest. The European Union, which controls the other large multinational fund for Africa, provides total grants rather than soft loans. Other countries would be pleased to have such help rather than lament the way the world is treating them.
>
> (2006: 29)

While he is correct about these particular vehicles of assistance, the remark is not contextualised relative to all flows, which leaves the reader with the impression, and ubiquitous misunderstanding, that the big numbers often quoted on 'aid' apply to grant assistance of these types. The truth is more qualified, as we see below, since most assistance is commercially oriented, bilateral and relates to export credits, leaving these types of special concessional funds a much smaller proportion of all accounted development assistance.[5]

A short history of multilateral development finance

With these definitions and the consequent problems of reporting in mind, Table 6.1 shows the flows of Official Development Assistance

(ODA), Official Development Finance (ODF) and Other Official Flows (OOF) to developing countries in aggregate, and then the latter to Africa, from 1960 to 2007. ODA rises steadily over the whole period, but starts to climb quite rapidly from 2002 to 2003 onward, reaching a new plateau of over $100,000 million from roughly $50,000 million in constant prices. This very recent hike in ODA is illustrated for its effect on African flows in Figure 6.1, and looks impressive. However, other flows compromise this story.

Multilateral assistance, as opposed to bilateral flows, is roughly one-third of the total, and rises proportionately to bilateral aid, although payments to the IFIs are quite sporadic. The total bilateral OOF includes export credits, and during the years 2000 to 2006, six of the seven entries were quite sharply negative, with only the single positive year of 2005 which is shown in Table 6.1, indicating that flows were returning back to DAC members in repayments and liabilities, rather than being donated. Indeed, in 2006 the figure was a significantly negative $9,774 million! In terms of the two lines for Africa in particular, the OOF figures were negative in five of the seven years since 2000, and were only positive in 2002 and 2003. The ODF flows remained healthily positive, but as the definitions indicate, these include finance transferring at non-concessional rates. Thus, official aid, or ODA, might have been rising, but other related flows have compromised the net resource transfer.

In the early 1970s, in a period of rapidly growing total aid, both bilateral and multilateral lenders increased the share of funds to the least developed countries influenced by the 1970s emphasis on helping the poorest. While members of the OECD DAC's bilateral flows

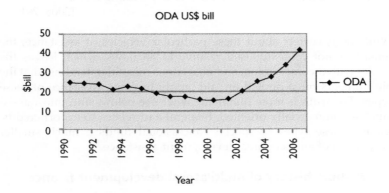

Figure 6.1 Official Development Assistance to Africa, 1990–2006
Source: African Development Bank (2008), *Group Financial Presentation*

[104]

Table 6.1 OECD members' aid to developing countries, 1960–2007

US$ mill.	1960	1970	1975	1980	1985	1990	1995	2000	2005	2007
ODA, total [1]	4,676	6,713	13,254	26,195	28,755	54,264	58,780	53,749	107,099	103,655
Bilateral ODA	4,094	5,672	9,808	16,983	21,190	38,462	40,481	36,064	82,445	71,666
Multilateral ODA	582	1,277	4,046	9,212	7,566	15,802	18,299	17,685	24,653	31,988
OOF, [2] to all developing	300	1,122	3,912	5,037	3,144	8,648	10,070	−4,326	1,430	
OOF, to Africa, total [3]		55	233	1,050	1,182	851	3,577	−333	−494	
ODF, [4] to all developing	4,412	7,806	21,140	40,480	43,483	73,778	70,964	55,393	115,684	
ODF, to Africa, total [4]	1,418	1,766	6,870	12,098	14,594	27,773	26,210	14,800	37,114	

Notes:
OECD (Organisation for Economic Co-operation and Development), ODA (Official Development Assistance), ODF (Official Development Finance), OOF (Other Official Flows). In millions of current US$, various years.
(1) From 'ODA by Donor', Table 1, at OECD.StatExtracts:
http://stats.oecd.org/wbos/Index.aspx?DatasetCode=TABLE1
(2) From DAC1, 'Official and Private Flows', at:
http://stats.oecd.org/wbos/Index.aspx?DatasetCode=ODA_DONOR#
In the years 2000–06 only two years were positive.
(3) From DAC2b, 'Other Official Flows', at:
http://stats.oecd.org/wbos/Index.aspx?DatasetCode=ODA_DONOR
OOF are defined as 'official sector transactions which do not meet the ODA criteria, e.g.: i.) Grants to aid recipients for representational or essentially commercial purposes; ii.) Official bilateral transactions intended to promote development but having a grant element of less than 25 per cent; iii.) Official bilateral transactions, whatever their grant element, that are primarily export-facilitating in purpose. This category includes by definition export credits extended directly to an aid recipient by an official agency or institution ("official direct export credits"); iv.) The net acquisition by governments and central monetary institutions of securities issued by multilateral development banks at market terms; v.) Subsidies (grants) to the private sector to soften its credits to aid recipients [see Annex 3, paragraph A3.5.iv)b)]; vi.) Funds in support of private investment.'
(4) From DAC ref_Reference Total ODF, at:
http://stats.oecd.org/wbos/Index.aspx?DatasetCode=ODA_DONOR#
ODF is defined as 'the sum of their receipts of bilateral ODA, concessional and non-concessional resources from multilateral sources, and bilateral other official flows made available for reasons unrelated to trade, in particular loans to refinance debt.'

Source: OECD, statistics databases online for DAC country members.

shifted away from the least developed countries in the late 1970s, they shifted back a few years later, although toward the Middle East, North Africa and sub-Saharan Africa at the expense of Asia (Mellor and Masters 1991: 343). There was a rapid increase in ODA to multilaterals in the earlier period, and shown in Table 6.1, but also in bilateral and multilateral portfolio investments, with the latter in particular rising from $204 million in 1960 to $6,204 million in 1985 (Mellor and Masters 1991: 336–9). In 2005, of total ODA available ($107,099 million), 77 per cent was bilateral and 23 per cent multilateral, as opposed to 69 per cent of ODA being bilateral in 1995 and 31 per cent being multilateral (using figures in Table 6.1). In 2007, bilateral aid was again 69 per cent of total ODA, and it was also 67 per cent in 2000, suggesting that 2005 was not a representative year, containing as it does a jump in bilateral expenditure, probably attributable to the once-off debt cancellation agreements with Nigeria and Iraq. In short, there has been a fairly constant one-third/two-third split between the two over the last 20 years or so.

In the mid-1980s bilateral and multilateral assistance constituted 26 per cent and 8 per cent respectively of total resource flows to all developing countries. Ten years earlier the share of multilateral assistance had been only 0.05 per cent of total resource flows, which illustrates both the amount it had grown in absolute terms, but also the process of multilateralisation of aid finance which took place in the years following the onset of the debt crisis in the context of a dropping off of private finance (Lele and Nabi 1991: 8). Of total resource flows in 2005 (in Table 6.2, of nearly $320,000 million), multilateral aid from all donors remained at just over 8 per cent, while bilateral aid from all donors, as a proportion of total financial flows available, has risen slightly since the mid-1980s figure, to over 29 per cent (using OECD figures as outlined in Table 6.2). Table 6.2 also shows the difference between DAC members' ODA and the total for all donors, which includes new donors (but not the more critically important India, China and Russia) such as the Czech Republic, Hungary, Iceland, South Korea, Poland, the Slovak Republic, Turkey, Latvia, Lithuania, Estonia, Slovenia, Kuwait, Saudi Arabia, the United Arab Emirates, Israel, Thailand and Chinese Taipei. It shows that while new donors have been accused of undermining Northern conditionalities on governance and human rights, in actual fact aid from these new donors at least remains a small percentage of total aid.[6] Using these figures, a full 88 per cent of ODA in 2007 originated from DAC members, down from nearly 90 per cent in 2000 but relatively stable and high. What remains striking is that both ODA from DAC members and from all donors has been the subject of a large rise since 2000, nearly doubling, with the contribution of other donors more than doubling from $6,041 million to $13,757 million (using figures from Table 6.2).

Table 6.3 illustrates this long-term increase in multilateral lending by a selection of DAC members. The drop in the percentage shares for multilaterals for a number of countries in 2007 is due not to falls in

Table 6.2 OECD members and all donors' flows of ODA and OOF, 1990–2007

	1990	1995	2000	2005	2007
Total 'Official and Private Flows', all donors	81,324	172,755	139,725	319,806	
ODA, DAC	54,264	58,780	53,749	107,099	103,655
ODA, all donors	57,188	65,133	59,790	120,394	117,412
Bilateral	41,092	45,965	41,262	94,140	84,098
Multilateral	16,096	19,169	18,529	26,254	33,314
OOF, DAC	8,648	10,070	–4,326	1,430	
OOF, all donors	9,035	10,811	–4,532	4,140	

Notes:
DAC (Development Assistance Committee of the OECD). At current prices in US$ millions.

Source: From OECD, dataset DAC1: 'Official and Private Flows', at:
http://stats.oecd.org/wbos/Index.aspx?usercontext=sourceoecd

monies to multilaterals per se, but to a large rise since 2000 in the overall ODA, which seems to have been concentrated in bilateral channels or not been absorbed yet into multilateral contributions. Thus, the aggregate figures for Canada, France, Germany, Sweden, the UK and the United States have all more than doubled, with only Japan declining in the 2000 to 2007 period as shown in Table 6.4, but the flows to multilaterals haven't risen by as much proportionately.

Table 6.3 Percentage of total ODA to multilateral agencies: selected countries, selected years

	1960	1970	1980	1990	2000	2007
Australia	13.1	10.2	26.9	21.2	23.2	14.5
Canada	25.9	20.5	38.9	31.6	33.5	21.6
France	7.7	14.0	24.3	21.7	31.1	36.6
Germany	26.4	22.2	34.9	29.1	46.6	34.2
Japan	24.7	18.9	40.1	25.2	27.7	24.2
Sweden	85.1	46.1	25.7	31.3	31.0	31.8
UK	23.3	17.8	28.4	44.1	39.8	47.7
United States	9.3	15.9	38.8	26.6	25.6	13.1
All DAC countries	12.4	19.0	35.2	29.1	32.9	30.9

Source: Percentages derived from data on ODA and multilateral ODA from the OECD, dataset: 'ODA by Donor', at: http://stats.oecd.org/wbos/Index.aspx?usercontext=sourceoecd

Table 6.4 Selected countries' total ODA and ODA to multilaterals, 2000 and 2007

	2000 ODA total Multilateral ODA	2007 ODA total Multilateral ODA
Canada	1,744 583	3,922 849
France	4,105 1,276	9,940 3,641
Germany	5,030 2,343	12,267 4,200
Japan	13,508 3,740	7,691 1,858
Sweden	1,799 557	4,334 1,376
UK	4,501 1,792	9,921 4,731
United States	9,955 2,550	21,753 2,858
DAC total	53,749 17,685	103,655 31,988

Note: In US$ millions in current prices.

Source: Derived from data on ODA and multilateral ODA from the OECD, net disbursements, dataset: 'ODA by Donor', at: http://stats.oecd.org/wbos/Index.aspx?usercontext=sourceoecd

There are a number of features of ODA which are fairly consistent when considered in the longer term, as far back as the official inauguration of international development assistance in President Truman's 'Point Four Program' in 1948:

- a steady growth in all forms of foreign aid combined with unstable private flows to developing countries
- increasingly large flows channelled through multilateral agencies, including private portfolio investment in development banks
- an increasing number of donors and aid channels
- large changes in aid allocations among countries, including reversals in the direction of some flows (see Mellor and Masters 1991: 331)
- a more recent increase in flows from private equity funds and private charitable foundations.

However, it is still important to note that these are not large amounts of money relative to private market funds per se, they are large only in terms of other types of comparative benchmarks, such as large relative to the size of the markets in which they are spent, or large once combined with the additional finance they often 'leverage in' such as more strictly private fund managers who are happy to add money in to a fund once they know that the public institutions are already involved.

It remains an open question as to whether the current global 'credit crunch' or recession will prompt a similar multilateralisation of funds as the crisis of the early 1980s did, although early signs suggest a similar pattern of winners and losers emerging with some developing countries experiencing a boom from rising commodity prices, particularly from oil, while non-oil producing developing countries are being hit worst in 2008 by rising food prices. The World Bank in May 2008 announced a new $1.2 billion 'fast track' facility to address the food crisis (World Bank 2008). Thus, just as the rapidly rising price of crude oil led to hyper-inflation and indebtedness for developing countries in the 1970s it can be expected that the current price hikes in 2008 will lead many non-oil producing developing countries back to the IFIs in need of further emergency assistance.

Conclusion

The aggregate data on poverty in Africa are quite shocking. Although the figures for unnecessary deaths from illness and malnutrition were not reviewed here, the headline figures for income per head and available finance are enough to show that African governments have very little money to buy food and medicine, should they choose to. Of course, there is another economy in Africa which is informal and possible quite large, but the official one reviewed here shows increasing inequality and income poverty for the majority. Adding in to the picture more qualitative ways of looking at poverty gives an even worse scenario, one in which the relative place of the poor is situated in a highly unequal world, one in which distance does not prevent people knowing how other people live, although it does prevent some from doing anything about it.

Multilateral and bilateral aid are theoretically seen as a global public good, and are supposed to both reduce poverty and increase growth, assisting Africa with its external payments position and investment levels. Reviewing the quite complex means by which these figures are accounted showed that only a small proportion of total aid is highly concessional, that is existing in the form of untied grants, and much of the rest is of dubious vintage. Money alone can't solve the cultural and social problem that is inequality and poverty, but spent wisely it could help a lot. So, what can we expect the recent hike in ODA to be spent on, and how do the other flows contribute to reducing or reproducing poverty? The next two chapters review the economy and set of activities that these wider development expenditures actually fund.

Notes

1. Mostly oil and minerals related investments, 'hopping' into the enclaves for extractive industries in not-so democratic countries noted by Ferguson (2006: 40–1).
2. This is in despite of strong rhetorical commitment, in March 2006, to the Commitment to Scaling up Towards Universal Access to HIV prevention, treatment, care and support in Africa by 2010, agreed in Brazzaville, Republic of Congo.
3. ODF includes '(a) bilateral official development assistance (ODA), (b) grants and concessional and non-concessional development lending by multilateral financial institutions, and (c) Other Official Flows for development purposes (including refinancing Loans) which have too low a Grant Element to qualify as ODA' (OECD 2008) 'Glossary of Terms' available at: http://stats.oecd.org/glossary/detail.asp?ID=1893
4. They cite Kharas and Shishido (1991), as showing how such non-concessional multilateral funds can act as a catalyst for other funds.
5. In regional development banks Riddell puts the proportion of concessional to non-concessional funding at roughly half for the ADB and the AfDB, but at less than 10 per cent for the Inter-American Development Bank (Riddell 2007: 81–2).
6. These figures do not include, however, Russian, Chinese or Indian ODA. As Ann Zimmerman for DAC Contact clarified by email: 'DAC1 is a reporting table meant principally for the DAC Members. However, aggregate aid figures from bilateral donors who are not DAC Members are also reflected in Table DAC1. For 2006 flows (the latest available data set) the non-DAC bilateral donors who reported their aid flows to the DAC Secretariat were: OECD DAC OBSERVERS – Czech Republic, Hungary, Iceland, Korea, Poland, Slovak Republic, Turkey; OTHER BILATERAL DONORS – Latvia, Lithuania, Estonia, Slovenia, Kuwait, Saudi Arabia, United Arab Emirates, Israel, Thailand, Chinese Taipei.'

7 Derivative business and aid-funded accumulation

This chapter explores the role of the Great Predators, the bilateral, regional and multilateral development finance institutions (DFIs), in directly sponsoring and underwriting an economy and set of activities in supply and procurement which delivers goods and services to the development industry. In other words, if a country borrows money from the World Bank to fund the construction of a port facility, this in itself then generates contracts for technical assistance, supply of cement and steel, supplies of soft infrastructure such as customs systems, as well as a set of contracts for its actual construction. All of these go to consultants and firms, and we explore in this chapter who gets the contracts and the business. Perhaps unsurprisingly, the answer in general is those countries who own the development banks, alongside other countries who are just undeniably competitive in their pricing, such as China. In the early 1990s, the pattern of beneficiaries was more overwhelmingly the core creditor states, whereas now newly industrialised countries and India and China have joined in as major recipients. This suggests that the new cycle of increased expenditures to the private sector will not be merely a close iteration of the last, but will distribute benefits more widely, and potentially add to the trade deficits of Europe and North America. However, allowing some new countries to come to the feeding frenzy has not changed the pattern profoundly, particularly in the high skill consultancy and supply sectors, and African business people are still largely excluded from the feast, despite their populations adopting the contracted costs as sovereign debt. In short, this chapter explores that part of the 'global Keynesian multiplier' (see Figure 4.1) where core states decide where to place their funds (Box 2) and how this relates to where (Box 3) the money borrowed as sovereign debt (alongside that smaller part lent as equity straight to the private sector with or without government guarantee) is on-lent to companies (Box 4). In chapters 8 and 9 we take a closer and longitudinal view of bilateral ODA, which still outweighs multilateral development finance despite the global characteristics of the industry. Overall, we are examining aid to the private sector, and exploring the beneficiaries of the system and the pattern of risks and rewards entailed.

Objectives for development finance

We can theorise that official development assistance (ODA) has had three objectives historically, and is used for three not entirely complementary purposes in different proportions at different times:

1. the commercial objective, to promote and expand exports (in, for example, the dumping of excess food to generate taste transfer by consumers and drive local producers out of business, such as in the case of the post-war use of Public Law 480 by the United States);
2. a geostrategic objective (the best way to attract ODA from the United States in the post-war period was to be Israel or Egypt, the worst was to be Cuba from 1959); and, finally,
3. the developmental objective, which is of course the one which is the subject of the most publicity.

Under the category of geostrategic motivation, we can add aid to change the direction of political ideologies, such as to promote capitalism or socialism during the Cold War, an important reason why the Asian Tigers emerged as a bulwark against the spread of communism, significantly because of very large injections of US ODA. Private sector development instruments, or PSD instruments in the jargon, are more likely to be used in pursuit of the first two of these three objectives, while grant funding and social welfare spending through the public sector is more often targeted at the third. This is not an exclusive association, however, and there is a current focus on PSD as a supposedly efficient way to do 'pro-poor' growth in pursuit of poverty reduction (OECD 2007).

Multilateral aid does not display the aid to per capita extremes and apparent misallocations of bilateral lending, since the latter is more likely to follow both the short-term security, geopolitical and ideological concerns of lenders, and the commercial priorities advised to governments by powerful industrial constituencies in their home countries. This is not to say that multilateral lending is more concerned with welfare and development per se, since the multilateral International Finance Corporation (IFC) is the largest PSD lender, rather that at this level individual nation states' priorities are somewhat weakened since they are pooled with those of other lenders. Also, some multilateral agencies have singularly welfarist missions, such as to support refugees (UNHCR) or children (UNICEF), and to a slightly less 'welfarist' extent, food and agriculture (UNFAO) or development (UNDP), which make the pursuit of profit less dominant in their behaviours. For this reason, multilateral aid has traditionally been of particular importance to the poorest, who have high ratios of aid to GNP but who often have little strategic or political importance to bilateral donors, a central reason why they are probably poor in the first instance. Thus, the stability of multilateral aid, relative to bilateral aid, is seen to contribute significantly to its effectiveness, particularly for poor countries.

In addition, the macro public-good benefits which derive from multilateral aid are constructed through the policy instruments and goals which dictate how it is spent. That is, programme aid in support of structural adjustment, in particular balance of payments support, trade and foreign exchange liberalisation, and the efficiency benefits to capital of the various good government and technical assistance instruments, contribute to the construction of 'free' market economies benefiting in turn the greater accumulation of capital in its present core areas. These are what are currently termed 'investment climate' effects, as opposed to the more direct 'market making' instruments in PSD, which we return to in the next chapter. The policy instruments in place under the Highly Indebted Poor County Initiative (HIPC) and PRS are comprehensive and economy-wide, and affect the way other government spending is allocated, even when this is not money which comes from donors. It is the complete package that has prompted critiques of the poverty agenda to the effect that it principally promotes the greater accumulation of capital on a global scale and disciplines labour to succumb to the capital relation (Cammack 2002). We explore further the avowed advantages and types of PSD instruments, principally designed to assist bilateral investments in the private sector, in chapter 8.

The policy leverage that ODA obtains for its 'donors' has been the subject of quite heated and extensive debate over the years, particularly as international financial institutions' (IFIs') remedies and commitment to neoclassical economics has proved singularly unpopular across the global South. Periodic food riots, rent strikes, labour disputes, 'IMF riots' and pilfering of services from utilities, since people cannot often afford to pay, has marked the era of permanent adjustment since the early 1980s as one replete with social conflict. This globalised struggle from the yoke of debt peonage has sponsored a wave of international social movement events and struggles, although sustaining the energy of an iconic occasion, such as the 'Battle at Seattle', the riot at the WTO Ministerial Meeting in 1999 in Seattle, has proved as notoriously difficult as coordinated class organisation has in previous historical periods, such as within the First International (1848–64) and Second International (1889–1916), when such struggles seek an international arena.

Patterns of multilateralism, domestic constituencies and national shares

Throughout this period of ideological and social dispute one aspect of the power of IFIs has remained relatively constant: their continued and regular profitability, in and of themselves as institutions, outside of any consideration of whether their policies work or don't work, are imposed or advised. The institutions make money and so do (mostly Northern) consultants and firms. This aspect of development finance garners very little attention. We saw in chapter 4 how the IFIs are owned by the creditor states, a relationship which serves to institutionalise and collectivise the risk of doing business in distant places. At this level, the global public good which they are said to confer on populations in general looks very much more bounded, as an oligopolistic source of supply of contracts for the companies of creditor states. In other words, creditor states pay in money, which is ostensibly lent to developing countries, in the sense that they are encouraged to adopt sums of it as sovereign debt, and then the money is organised into a pool of investment funds which Northern companies can access in order to pay for their overheads and investment costs for plant, material, new factories and the building of infrastructure. The firms might benefit directly from these contracts as contractors, or indirectly from them, as they use the infrastructural goods provided in connection with their own plant and factories, such as roads or electricity. Simply put, the workers of the global South are buying, through their debt repayments, the means of their own exploitation.

Thus, the greater multilateralisation of aid since the mid-1980s has led to vast derivative business, many of the contracts of which are enjoyed collectively by the creditor states; a list of beneficiaries which more latterly includes some newcomers. The volumes of derivative contracts in the early 1990s are shown in Table 7.1 below.

At an aggregate level, the difference in the economies and international articulations of core creditor states are clearly present with respect to where they choose to invest their money (or 'donate' in the vernacular); while the distribution of benefits deriving from the (aggregated) expenditures of the multilateral agencies in turn reflects the pattern of who is paying in to the kitty. We will explore these in turn. In terms of choices over where money can be placed, creditor states have differing expectations which relate to domestic constituencies, both public and corporate, although the latter of these has a more powerful voice in regard to PSD instruments since it organises into a multiplicity of industry-based lobby groups. The result of these national influences at an international level shows up in differences in holdings in the DFIs, and preferences over which funds individual

Table 7.1 Multilateral development agencies' expenditures in 1992

Agency	Works	Supplies/ equipment	Consultancy/ tech. assist.	All contracts
World Bank	422.2	4,400.0 3,469.7	564.2	9,174.4
ADB		885.5	132.2 88.8	1,007.3
EDF V	699.3	733.9	567.4	2,001.0
EDF VI	743.8	884.4	595.3	2,223.5
IADB				1,264.7
AfDB				2,166.7
Total	1,865.3	10,373.5	1,947.9	17,837.6

Notes:
ADB (Asian Development Bank), EDF (European Development Fund), IADB (Inter-American Development Bank), AfDB (African Development Bank). In US$ million. Figures aggregated from UK figures and proportions of total to one decimal place.

Source: This table is reproduced with permission from Bracking (1999: 221), adapted from DTI World Aid Section, *Multilateral Development Agencies – UK Procurement*, leaflet G17 (October 1992).

states contribute to. For example, the United States has both a low bilateral contribution to net Development Assistance Committee (DAC) aid flows relative to GNP, and one of the smallest proportions of its total aid channelled through multilaterals in recent times (see Table 6.3), although in an earlier period, from the mid-1960s to the late 1970s, the United States and Sweden had accelerated the build-up of multilaterals with larger contributions.

This relatively low input to multilateral aid is probably due to the United States having a relatively low proportion of international trade to GNP, and few historic colonial ties to create the linkage to domestic constituencies which would provide support and motivation for increased multilateral flows of a welfarist nature. The US public has a greater proclivity, relative to Europeans, for charitable expenditures within private foundations and a culture of private philanthropy, such that the two principle expenditures within official US ODA that have enjoyed a constituency of support from the 1970s have been more commercial: first, the large amounts spent on food aid under Public Law 480, because of domestic subsidies which produce perverse surpluses and the power of the agribusiness lobby; and second, on security-related aid, which creates exports related to the military and security sectors, again a powerful domestic commercial lobby, recently epitomised by the Halliburton contracts in Iraq. Security-related aid has historically been concentrated in Israel and the wider Middle East, particularly Egypt, where the United States seeks geopolitical influence. The Bush administrations have also been marked by a retreat from multilateralism – epitomised by withdrawal from the Rio Convention on the Environment and non-membership of the International Criminal Court – to 'Fortress America' under neoconservative doctrines.

However, the United States still enjoys exceptional influence within key multilaterals such as the World Bank and IMF due to geographic, cultural and political ties linked to its post-war role as world hegemonic power, such that current expenditure on these institutions to maintain or increase influence within them is less necessary relative to other, structurally more distant countries and to newcomers. For example, Germany, as a core European country without substantial ex-colonies, most often spends a larger proportion of ODA multilaterally relative to the French and British, as illustrated in Table 6.3. Meanwhile, Japan, a more recent major power in the international economy and with less historic influence in international financial and trading affairs, spent until very recently a large proportion of GNP in aid, with a high proportion channelled through multilaterals. It has the second highest contribution to the International Development Association (IDA), the more concessional wing of the World Bank (relative to the International Bank for Reconstruction and Development (IBRD)), with over $28.8 billion committed (World Bank 2007a).[1] Japan also leads the funding of the Asian Development Bank (ADB), and spends a higher proportion than other major donors on large-scale capital projects in the utilities sector, reflecting its industrial strength. Interestingly, Japan, as a new creditor, uses the British Crown Agents as the vehicle to manage the worldwide logistical services and procurement needs of its bilateral programme, thus involving the institutional advantages and global reach of the British state's imperial past. In effect, Germany and Japan are still buying in to a club where their political influence does not do justice to their relative industrial strength, as a consequence of the post-Second World War settlement.

Thus, the nature of a creditor nation's articulation to the world economy, and the configuration of its industrial sectors, shapes multilateral funding patterns. These nationalities and industrial configurations are then, our second consideration, clearly correlated to the distribution of derivative economic benefits in the expenditure of funding, relative to who paid it in. In other words, the respective nationality of firms successful in winning contracts is weighted to the nationality of key contributors, while the firms which get most work tend to be sited in the most competitive (or well connected) industrial sector from that particular country. For example, as can be seen from Table 7.2, in the early 1990s the United States spent the lowest proportion of multilateral aid relative to GNP, but it still enjoyed 14.4 per cent of all derivative procurement business arising from the expenditures of the World Bank, leading the ranking of recipients. This reflected its global power and predominant influence in the Bank, as well as it being the largest shareholder. The numbers in parentheses in Table 7.2 are the rank order in which countries' companies benefited from derivative business emanating from contracts when the aid monies were spent for various regional banks, the EU and the World Bank. EDF V and EDF VI refer to two successive tranches of aid money through the EU. France was ranked first in contracts received from the EU with an impressive 30 and then 26 per cent of all the business generated, while also leading the ranking of recipients from the African Development Bank (AfDB). Meanwhile, the United States managed to monopolise more than half of all derivative business from the Inter-American Development Bank (IADB) in 1991–92! Germany came second in winning contracts from the World Bank, IADB and AfDB.

Japan leads funding of the Asian Development Bank (ADB), but in this example from the early 1990s the benefits it garnered were commensurate, as Japanese firms enjoyed 33.5 per cent of the derivative benefit, with the United States second at 30.6 per cent. Taken as a whole, just five core creditor states, the UK, United States, Japan, Germany and France, accounted for a massive 96.8 per cent of all derivative contract business of the ADB, while, with the addition of Italy, they also account for 96.5 per cent of business from the IADB.

Table 7.2 Multilateral development agencies: comparisons between creditor states in derivative procurement business in 1991–92 (all contracts)

	World Bank [a]	ADB [b]	EDF V [c]	EDF VI [d]	IADB [b]	AfDB & Fund [b]
UK	8.6 (4)	8.2 (4)	20.5 (2)	16.2 (2)	3.4 (7)	3.6 (5)
United States	14.4 (1)	30.6 (2)			51.5 (1)	3.9 (4)
Germany	11.1 (2)	7.9 (5)	19.8 (3)		13.2 (2)	5.8 (2)
Japan	9.0 (3)	33.5 (1)			8.7 (5)	
France	8.4 (5)	16.6 (3)	30.3 (1)	26.4 (1)	9.5 (4)	6.8 (1)
Italy				16.1 (3)	10.2 (3)	5.0 (3)
Total (%)	51.5	96.8	70.6	58.7	96.5	25.1

Notes:
The first figure in the columns represents the percentage share of each country of the contracts resulting from multilateral development agencies' expenditure. The figures in parenthesis are the relative ranking of each country.
(a) Fiscal 1 July to 30 June 1991, (b) Fiscal 1 January to 31 December 1991, (c) Cumulative to 31 December 1989, (d) Cumulative to 31 December 1991.

Source: This table is reproduced with permission from Bracking (1999: 221), adapted from DTI World Aid Section, *Multilateral Development Agencies – UK Procurement*, leaflet G17 (October 1992).

The low proportion of AfDB funds of only 25.1 per cent to the five listed in Table 7.2, in comparison to the concentration of funds of the other multilaterals that accrued to core creditor states in the early 1990s, is due in part to the presence of more competitive tenders from middle-income industrial countries. The AfDB noted in 1994 that while the UK has historically been one of the four major beneficiaries of procurement contracts generated by projects funded by the bank, along with France, Germany and Italy:

> Further analysis has shown that whereas countries like Italy, France and Germany have a strong presence in Africa in the field of construction, the UK's presence in that sector is rather on the decline. It would appear that the gap created is being filled by construction companies from countries such as China, the former Yugoslavia and Korea which became members of the Bank precisely in order to sell their construction skills through projects financed by the Bank.
>
> (HC 1994: 35)[2]

The relationship between being a member of a multilateral development finance organisation, as a creditor that is, and acquiring derivative business, is therefore clear both empirically and through the known intentions of members. The AfDB also noted in 1994 that in the early 1990s while Japan and Germany consistently exported capital goods based on supply contracts throughout Africa, they perceived:

> a decline in the presence of UK-based companies in the supply of goods for projects financed by the Bank. This is usually an indication that the manufacturing base of the supply country is experiencing difficulties in competing on the open market for contracts where they are required to meet high standards of technical specification for various types of goods and machinery that are subject to international competitive bidding.
>
> (ibid.)

So, the relative decline of UK manufacturing in relation to its competitors is reflected in the derivative procurement it receives from the AfDB. The UK retains a 'strong presence' in engineering and consultancy services, but the bank warned of strong competition from Canadian and US companies in the same Anglophone African countries for language reasons, as well as from Scandinavian engineering firms and French and German firms whose employees are increasingly multilingual (ibid.). The multilateral organisations can thus be seen as the intermediaries in an institutionalised market which manages the competition between the core states in terms of the business which their contributions create.

In general, UK plc, an historic creditor state with sectoral strengths in supply, merchant and international banking and consultancy, favours relatively large contributions through multilateral channels, not least because it benefits from business related to the spending of those funds, particularly in terms of consulting services through technical assistance budgets. The ADB statistics illustrate this consultancy strength but also the high rankings for European Development Fund (EDF) monies in Table 7.2., which were related to UK derivative benefit from the supplies and equipment (ranked first for both programmes) and consultancy and technical assistance (ranked third and second, respectively) expenditures within those two programmes. More recently, the Crown Agents have developed their emergency response function for supplies and equipment, which can meet supply expectations of development institutions rapidly in the event of natural disasters. The UK also supports greater untying of programme aid and balance of payments support, again because it expects to enjoy a large 'natural share' of the run-off business related to these funds.

UK multilateral contributions lead primarily to opportunities in the areas of consultancy and technical assistance as well as supply. As Table 7.3 shows, in 1992 the UK was receiving a higher share of derivative procurement contracts in consultancy from the World Bank than any other country, while in the ADB the UK was ranked second for consultancy business and first for technical assistance contracts. The figures available for works contracts from multilateral development agencies show that the UK receives proportionately less business in this area. The high ranking for supplies and equipment contracts from the European Community (EC) development funds probably reflects the role of the Crown Agents in providing logistical services, and managing consequent supply contracts for the EC. Indeed, multilateral development agencies, regional development banks and the United Nations in financial year 1990–91 were disbursing more than $30 billion (Tate's 1992: 1). The Head of the World Aid Section (WAS)[3] of the UK's DTI Overseas Trade Services noted that:

> At present the United Kingdom holds about 7.5% of business funded by the agencies, behind the United States, Japan and Germany. As an example, contracts to a total of US $875 million were awarded in 1990-1 by the World Bank alone to British companies. However, there is clearly room for British companies to take a larger share of this business.

> (ibid.)

Table 7.3 shows the amounts, proportionate shares and ranking of the UK in the various categories of programme expenditures of some selected multilateral development agencies in 1991–92.

By 2007, the proportion of derivative contracts by value which were accruing to the largest owners of the World Bank had fallen, and particularly in civil works contracts were reflecting instead the new competitive edge enjoyed by China and India globally in terms of industrial manufacture. In tables 7.4 and 7.5 below, all those countries receiving 4 per cent or more of contracts are listed. In Table 7.4, for those countries heading the list in terms of contracts for goods, China and India have joined the traditional beneficiary Germany. Meanwhile, in derivative contracts in the area of consultancy services, the UK in 2007 still enjoyed 7 per cent of all contracts by value, but Indonesia and Russia had joined the list of countries at the top (Table 7.5), ranked by percentage, and the UK and United States had lost market share proportionately. These figures are not accurate of all World Bank contracts,[4] but are of a cumulative lesser value since the database they are from excludes a plethora of small contracts which are not subject to prior review.[5] These figures do indicate that the population of recipients has grown since 1992 and the share of each has been diluted.

So, by the 2000s, the share of contracts collectively won by the major creditor states and owners of the Bank had dropped from its 1980s and early 1990s high. The following tables, 7.6 and 7.7, show the nationality of consultants who have partially displaced them. These tables list all the countries that appear in the top five by volume of goods contracts, and (this time) civil works contracts, received in any of the years 2002–07 in percentage form. If a cell is blank it is because that country does not appear in the top five in the year in question. The figures are the percentage of that year's business taken by that country, and their ranked place is in square brackets. Again, as we saw above, the pattern of goods contracts supplied (Table 7.6) reflects the global industrial strength and competitiveness of China and India, although Germany has maintained a place at the table. The Russian Federation has emerged quite recently as a major contender.

In the area of civil works contracts (Table 7.7) the dominance of China and India is even more striking, although Brazil emerges in a strong third place. In 2002, for example, China and India took over half of all the value of derivative business from World Bank civil works contracts between them, with China winning singularly $1.3 billion worth of contracts from a total budget of $4.2 billion. In fact China was the largest supplier in all six years, except in 2006 where it was just overtaken by India, although by so little they still have 20 per cent of the business each on rounded percentage figures. The percentage of the total value of contracts awarded to the top three suppliers is given in the 'total' row,

Table 7.3 Multilateral development agencies and derivative UK procurement business

Agency	Works amount	% (a)	R (b)	Supplies/Equipment amount	%	R	Consultancy/Tech. Assist. amount	%	R	All contracts amount	%	R
World Bank (c)	19.0	4.5	5	440.0	10.0	4	101.0	17.9	1	789.0	8.6	4
				229.0	6.6	3						
ADB (d)				48.7	5.5	5	19.7	14.9	2	82.6	8.2	4
							14.2	16.0	1			
EDF V (e)	104.9	15.0	4	207.7	28.3	1	97.6	17.2	3	410.2	20.5	2
EDF VI (f)	66.2	8.9	3	192.8	21.8	1	101.2	17.0	2	360.2	16.2	2
IADB (d)										43.0	3.4	7
AfDB & Fund (d)										78.0	3.6	5
Total	190.1			1,118.2			333.7			1,763.0		

Notes:
In US$ millions.
(a) percentage share of total expenditure by agency, (b) R means 'ranking' as compared to other countries' shares, (c) Fiscal 1 July to 30 June 1991, (d) Fiscal 1 January to 31 December 1991, (e) Cumulative to 31 December 1989, (f) Cumulative to 31 December 1991.

Source: Adapted from DTI World Aid Section, *Multilateral Development Agencies – UK Procurement*, leaflet G17 (October 1992).

Table 7.4 Top countries receiving contracts from the World Bank for goods in 2007

Supplier country	Amount (US$ mill.)	%
Germany	399.7	17
China	336.3	15
India	202.1	9
Russian Federation	161.8	7
Turkey	96.1	4
Total	1,196.0	52 [51.67]*
Total for all countries	2,314.8	100

Notes:
Rounded to 1 decimal place in US$ millions. This table includes all countries with 4 per cent or more of the total. Countries with 3 per cent, which are listed in order of most (actual amount) first, were Vietnam, World and France.
* Because of cumulative rounding errors the actual figure is given in brackets.

Source: World Bank, 2008, Prior Review Contracts under Bank-finances Projects, Contract Detail Report by Supplier Country, for goods, FY2002-2007, at: http://siteresources.worldbank.org/INTPROCUREMENT/Resources/Bankwide-Goods-FY02-07.xls

while the second 'total' row is the value of all the contracts in this World Bank spreadsheet, which includes contracts subject to prior review but not a mass of smaller contracts, for all countries. In three of the six years in the table China singularly won more than 30 per cent of all contracts by value; in four of the six years, just three countries won more than half

Table 7.5 Top countries receiving contracts from the World Bank for consultancy services in 2007

Supplier country	Amount (US$ mill.)	%
Indonesia	71.0	8
United States	64.4	7
United Kingdom	61.6	7
World	51.2	6
Russian Federation	50.7	6
France	36.6	4
Total	335.5	38 [36.63]*
Total (global for countries)	916.0	100

Notes:
Rounded to 1 decimal place in US$ millions. This table includes all countries for 2007 which received 4 per cent of contracts or more. DRC, Germany, Brazil, Canada and Turkey followed next with 3 per cent each.
* Because of cumulative rounding errors the actual figure is given in brackets.

Source: World Bank, 2008, Prior Review Contracts under Bank-finances Projects, Contract Detail Report by Supplier Country, for consultant services, FY2002-2007, at: http://siteresources.worldbank.org/INTPROCUREMENT/Resources/Bankwide-Consultants-FY02-07.xls

Table 7.6 The 'top five' suppliers to World Bank goods contracts, 2002–07

Country (%)	2002	2003	2004	2005	2006	2007
China	16 [1]	17 [1]	10 [1]	11 [2]	10 [2]	15 [2]
India	9 [2]	9 [2]	6 [5]	22 [1]	7 [3]	9 [3]
Germany	6 [3]	6 [3]	8 [3]	4 [5]	6 [4]	17 [1]
France	6 [4]					
Brazil	5 [5]					
World		6 [4]	8 [2]	7 [3]		
Turkey		5 [5]			6 [5]	4 [5]
Argentina			6 [4]			
Russian Federation				5 [4]	10 [1]	7 [4]
Total	42	43	38	49	39	52
Total for all countries (US$ mill.)	2,122	2,327	2,179	2,647	2,196	2,315

Source: Compiled from Prior Review Contracts Under Bank-financed Projects, Contract Detail Report by Supplier Country, for goods contracts, FY 2002-2007, at: http://siteresources.worldbank.org/INTPROCUREMENT/Resources/Bankwide-Goods-FY02-07.xls

of all contracts, while just three countries – China, India and Brazil – were the top three in four of the six years listed, winning more than 47 per cent of all contracts in each year.

Table 7.7 Top suppliers to World Bank civil works contracts, 2002–07

Country (%)	2002	2003	2004	2005	2006	2007
China	31 [1]	32 [1]	19 [1]	28 [1]	20 [2]	32 [1]
India	21 [2]	19 [2]	13 [3]	13 [2]	20 [1]	
Brazil	6 [3]	4 [3]	15 [2]		10 [3]	
Argentina				11 [3]		7 [3]
Italy						8 [2]
'Top 3' % of total	58 [57.8]*	55	47	52	50	47
Total contracts for all countries (US$ mill.)	4,213	3,983	4,846	5,008	4,225	3,626

Notes: In US$ millions.   * Because of cumulative rounding errors the actual figure is given in brackets.

Source: Adapted from Prior Review Contracts under Bank-financed Projects, Contract Detail Report by Supplier Country, for civil works contracts, 2002-07, at: http://siteresources.worldbank.org/INTPROCUREMENT/Resources/Bankwide-Works-FY02-07.xls

Derivative business at the Asian Development Bank

This opening up for business, particularly apparent in this civil works sector, was not as large in all the regional development banks. The distribution of derivative contracts from the ADB in 2007 had a similar distribution to that in the early 1990s, although the UK had increased its share of derivative business from 8.2 to 12.1 per cent (Table 7.8, see also Table 7.3). The UK is currently the fourteenth largest shareholder in the ADB (fifth of 19 non-regional members) and has contributed $1.14 billion in capital subscription and $1.23 billion to special funds since joining in 1966, while companies and consultants from the UK have enjoyed $2.29 billion in procurement contracts on ADB-financed projects since 1967 (ADB 2007). In 2007 the UK owned just over 2 per cent of total shares in the ADB: its contribution to 'funds' is larger than to the share base. Table 7.8 shows the UK's share of goods and works and consultancy contracts from the ADB in the years 2006 and 2007 and for all the years since 1966.

Two recent Memorandums of Understanding (MOUs) between the UK and ADB illustrate well the UK's historical and contemporary interests. The first MOU in 2001 (extended in 2005 to cover administrative arrangements) provided finance for poverty-focused and technical activities in India of £20 million (2001) and then a further £30 million (2005), which together led to 48 projects in India. The second MOU in 2002 of £36 million was a contribution to a multi-donor Poverty Reduction Co-operation fund for poverty-related studies and technical assistance in selected member developing countries, leading to 106 projects. Co-financing of projects between the UK and ADB, from 2003 to 2007, also added another eight investment projects, co-financed to $296.65 million and comprising of five grant packages in rural infra-

Table 7.8 The UK's share of procurement contracts at the Asian Development Bank (ADB) 2006–07

Item	2006 Amount (US$ mill.)	2006 % of total	2007 Amount (US$ mill.)	2007 % of total	Cumulative (as of 31 Dec 2007) Amount (US$ mill.)	% of total
Goods and Works	52.34	0.85	80.00	1.18	1,473.84	1.68
Consulting services	21.95	6.12	23.69	6.56	820.07	12.12
Combined UK total	74.29		103.69		2,293.91	

Source: ADB (2007).

structure (Bangladesh), health (Bangladesh), water services and health (Indonesia), education (Bangladesh) and social services (Pakistan), and three commercial co-financed projects in cellular telephony (Afghanistan, Roshan Phase II expansion), municipal natural gas infrastructure (China) and hydroelectric (Laos) and a further 58 technical-assistance projects co-financed to $90.55 million (ADB 2007: 3). Given the type of co-financing provided and the overall policy objectives of the MOUs it is not surprising that the actual contractors and suppliers from the UK who have benefited from contracts from the ADB between January 2002 and December 2006 for loan projects are mostly in the education sector (seven companies) but also in the water supply, sanitation and waste management sectors (three companies).

By 31 December 2007 the ADB had approved a cumulative total, since its inception, of $133.3 billion in loans for 2,080 projects in 41 countries, a further $3.27 billion for 221 grant projects and $3.26 billion for 6,347 technical-assistance projects. These totals generated procurement contracts for goods and works and consulting services by 31 December 2007 worth $94.37 billion, with $6.49 billion awarded in 2006 and $7.13 billion in 2007 (ADB 2007: 4). ADB further noted that 'most contracts were awarded on the basis of international competition' (ADB 2007: 3–4), at least to firms and individuals from ADB member countries, both regional and non-regional. Table 7.8 summarises the UK share of the $94 billion (for consulting services), cumulatively at $820 million, or over 12 per cent of the total in that sector, while for goods and works the total was nearly $1.5 billion or 1.68 per cent of the cumulative total for the sector. Overall, the UK has paid in $2.37 billion but UK companies have received contracts for $2.29 billion, such that the ADB is recycling funds in a type of subsidy from the UK state to UK business. The rate of return is not bad, particularly when it is considered that it is not the 'paid in' amount of $1.14 billion in 'overall capital subscription' which changes hands, but the 'paid-in capital subscription' of only $79.87 million, leaving the rest as an accounting liability on UK national accounts.

From 1 January 1985 to 31 December 2007 ADB loan projects generated $3.08 billion in contracts for consultants, with UK consultants contracted for $276.57 million of the total or just under 9 per cent. During the same period ADB technical-assistance projects were worth $2.14 billion, and UK consultants took $295.8 million of the business or just under 14 per cent (ADB 2007). Top consultants for ADB loans between January 2002 and December 2006 were Roughton International (three contracts worth $13.99 million), Scott Wilson Kirkpatrick & Company Ltd (three contracts worth $13.69 million), Halcrow Group Ltd (five worth $11.28 million), Mott Macdonald Ltd (four worth $10.69 million), WSP International Management Consulting (two worth $9.35 million); and another four companies with contracts of between \$4.88 million and \$1.39 million. Of the consultants involved in technical-assistance projects, individual British consultants together were contracted 388 times to a total cost of \$26.43 million, while many recognisable firms were contracted a handful of times each with contract values of between \$4.28 million (GHK International Ltd) and \$1.71 million (Maxwell Stamp plc) (ADB 2007).

Derivative business at the African Development Bank

In 1994, when the House of Commons Select Committee on Trade was preparing for the post-apartheid feast that South African business was predicted to represent, it was predicting that South Africa would join newer industrial countries in the displacement of the traditional European suppliers at the AfDB, becoming both a major shareholder and major borrower: 'It will, therefore, be in a position to absorb internally most of the procurement contracts that are generated through international lending activities to South Africa' (HC 1994: 35). The AfDB stressed that the competitive position of South Africa would mean that, in a regional context:

> in addition to absorbing all procurement contracts relating to projects financed in South Africa, it will displace many European and North American firms that have been active in the southern Africa region.
>
> (HC 1994: 35)

British firms 'stand to be among the major losers' in the region, and are urged to make direct investments in establishing South African subsidiaries, and to:

> weld strategic alliances with relevant local partners ... to become more competitive in the procurement activities in other southern Africa countries North of the Limpopo River.
>
> (ibid.)

With hindsight, advocating increased business in Zimbabwe might have been foolish, but strategic deals were done, particularly by the Commonwealth Development Corporation (CDC), through Actis, with emerging South African firms in infrastructure (the N4 toll road, Trans-African Concessions), hotels, paper (Peters Papers), packaging (Lenco), finance (\$1.2 billion leveraged buyout for Alexander Forbes in 2007), transport and logistics (Fuel Logistics in 2007), electrical equipment (Savcio), platinum (through its Actis stake in Platmin Ltd) (Actis 2008). In particular, UK plc has attained strategic continental influence in power through the Globeleq company, which, as we saw in Chapter 5, contributed greatly to the success of the newly privatised Actis and to the bulging of senior staff's pockets.

In chapter 5 we saw how CDC, through its Actis fund company Globeleq, was heavily involved with power and energy assets in Africa, including, from May 2004, a consortium known as Umeme which was set up to distribute electricity in Uganda. CDC, through its firm Globeleq, holds a 56 per cent stake in Umeme, while Eskom (the publicly owned integrated South African electricity utility) holds the minority 44 per cent (Hall 2007: 12). Umeme is significantly unpopular in Uganda for price hikes and disconnections.[6] However, this case illustrates well the recycling potential of the Great Predators, such that money paid in to them can seem to be of a multilateral origin but nonetheless ends up supporting a bilateral interest, funding firms of the same nationality. In Umeme's case, the World Bank, through the IDA, provided a further loan of $11 million to back up the CDC/ Actis/Globeleq investment (Hall 2007: 10), while Eskom (Globeleq's partner) then received a further $500 million loan from the AfDB (HC 2008: 14), a regional development bank in which the UK heads the list of bilateral non-member contributors. Interestingly, Globeleq also own 30 per cent of Tsavo Power in Kenya and 70 per cent of Songas Power in Tanzania (Hall 2007: 11). In short, an agglomeration effect can be observed, whereby a grouping of DFI loans supports key assets in favour of a private sector interest, in this case Globeleq, with a significant national embeddedness, in this case British.

By 2007–08, UK funding to the AfDB was standing at an historic high, with the UK doubling its previous level of support in the eleventh replenishment of the African Development Fund (ADF11) 2007–09, from approximately £200 million for 2005–07 to £417 million for 2008–10, making the UK the largest single contributor to the AfDB, overtaking France for the first time (HC 2008: 5). This rise was in accordance with both the recent rise in UK ODA expenditure overall, and the increased proportion – over 40 per cent – through multilateral institutions, of which the regional development banks (RDBs) are the chief beneficiaries. The AfDB receives more than double the amount from the Department for International Development (DfID) than any of the other RDB (DfID 2007: 117), although the International Development Committee was concerned that the board structure was not giving DfID sufficient 'leverage' commensurate with this level of contribution (HC 2008: 3).[7] The UK is part of a 'constituency' of the UK, Germany, Netherlands and Portugal, with one seat on the board, rotating between Germany and the UK. The constituency as a whole contributed one-third of all donor funds to ADF11, with Germany increasing its previous contribution by nearly 80 per cent, and the

Netherlands and Portugal by 50 per cent (HC 2008: 6). However, votes are based on share capital held – the UK has 1.676 per cent – placing it in sixth position among non-regional shareholders, not on fund contributions, where the UK heads the list.

The priorities of ADF11 include a 60 per cent spend on building and upgrading infrastructure, following a 2007 High Level Panel Report which advised the AfDB of its comparative advantage in this area (HC 2008: 8, citing High Level Panel Report 2007: 1). The AfDB was given a mandate by the New Partnership for Africa' Development (NEPAD), formed in 2001, to lead the NEPAD agenda on regional integration, including the critical contribution of 'hard' and 'soft' infrastructure (such as roads, water pipes and border and customs procedures respectively) (ibid.). Commensurate with this, DfID identifies four objectives for the AfDB in its 2006 joint constituency strategy paper,[8] of which reinforcing the AfDB contribution to infrastructure is one (complimented by a five-year Technical Co-operation Agreement worth £13 million from 2007); improving bank effectiveness at headquarters level and in-country are two and three; and 'sharpening AfDB's contribution to good governance in African countries' is four (HC 2008: 22). Interestingly, the poverty agenda is not emphasised as a strategic priority, but private sector development features prominently. Indeed, private sector development is a 'growth area' within the AfDB, with lending to private companies, which began in 1991, growing seven-fold since 2004, and identified as a priority area for ADF11 with activity set to rise again (HC 2008: 14). Apparently, AfDB staff viewed the AfDB's competitive edge as residing in private sector work because of its '60% ownership by African Governments. This ensured that the Bank was seen as "one of them"; an "honest broker"'(reported in HC 2008: 14).

The AfDB reports that in 2004,[9] $585 million of goods and services were contracted to regional member countries, while $1,580 million were contracted to non-regional members, a factor of roughly 1:3 in favour of non-regional members (AfDB 2008). The UK has enjoyed a very small share of the contracts awarded by the AfDB in recent years, 0.49 per cent in 2007 and 0.59 per cent in 2006, with the majority of this figure – expressed as a proportion of the UK total – in goods (65 and 82 per cent, respectively), with services second (32 and 17 per cent, respectively) and the remainders in civil works (3 and 1 per cent). The figures for all countries are instructive, reproduced in full and online by AfDB in a laudable show of transparency (see AfDB 2008a). Of 70 countries receiving contracts in the period 2003–08, worth $1,220 million in 2007, the top recipient was China. Removing the countries with less than 1 per cent of the business in the period 2003–05, average figures leave 29 countries with more than a 1 per cent share of the business, collectively representing 88 per cent of the total, which means in converse that 40 countries shared 12 per cent of the budget.[10] Removing those countries with less than 2 per cent of the total derivative business, calculated on this five-year average basis, leaves 14 countries (which does not include the UK, which is deleted at 1.29 per cent) that share 67 per cent of the total. These are reproduced in Table 7.9 below. The figures are for 2006 and 2007, with the percentage of total contracts, and then the cumulative share for the 'average over 6 years' 2003–08 to April 2008.[11] Following China, with a cumulative average of 12 per cent of all derivative business, but a striking 18 per cent for 2007 alone, is a group of middle-income African Francophone countries – Mali, Morocco, Tunisia – and France. What is perhaps most striking is the countries missing from this list, those which might reasonably be expected to be there as African economic powers, such as Nigeria, Kenya or Egypt. China's success here is relative to a small shareholding. It is fifteenth in the list of non-regional members with voting rights and a reportedly low engagement with AfDB activities; a fact which is bemoaned by the UK's International Development Select Committee, which, citing the High Level Panel Report on the AfDB (2007), wants the AfDB to influence China to increase its engagement, join the Infrastructure Consortium for Africa – since it is Africa's third largest investor and trade partner (High Level Panel 2007: 35) – and become more transparent in its engagement, so 'that development partnerships are easier to form and manage' (HC 2008: 21).

Crony networks and closed procurement

Despite some dilution of benefits, what empirical evidence exists in the public domain still suggests that Northern creditors can advocate competitive bidding, and so claim the apparent moral high ground, safe in the knowledge that it is disproportionately of benefit to them. Also, in a similar manner to their advocacy of liberalisation in financial and trading regimes, creditor states can retain important caveats and detractions from the high principle buried in technical procedures. Thus, just as with international trade policy, which makes only limited impact on the protectionism of 'Fortress Europe', advocacy of international competitive bidding does not prevent the World Bank from using other systems in practice itself, as we see in this section.

In general, the high concentration of derivative business which the core states enjoy from multilateral development finance is due to their technical, spacial and financing advantages relative to poorer countries. While regulations in DAC ensure controlled competition among members, opportunities to maintain a competitive edge nonetheless remain in place since the funding of research and consultancy relating to tendering for bids can be financed completely by the

Table 7.9 Distribution by country of African Development Bank contracts, 2003–08

Country	2006 Amount in US$ mill.	2006 % share	2007 Amount in US$ mill.	2007 % share	Average 6 years (to April 2008) Amount in US$ mill.	Average 6 years (to April 2008) % share
India	0.95	0.11	32.32	2.65	15.71	2.08
Senegal	30.04	3.41	22.80	1.87	16.75	2.22
Mozambique	12.33	1.40	14.84	1.22	17.34	2.29
Italy	11.79	1.34	41.86	3.43	17.56	2.32
Burkina Faso	49.53	5.62	6.76	0.55	20.07	2.66
Uganda	14.60	1.66	65.72	5.39	22.39	2.96
United States	130.12	14.76	1.45	0.12	26.45	3.50
South Africa	29.35	3.33	8.90	0.73	27.02	3.58
Germany	20.54	2.33	99.27	8.13	35.60	4.71
Mali	15.82	1.79	11.93	0.98	42.57	5.64
Morocco	31.54	3.58	148.89	12.20	48.32	6.40
France	91.32	10.36	53.43	4.38	53.82	7.13
Tunisia	80.10	9.08	107.79	8.83	72.34	9.58
China	70.27	7.97	223.16	18.29	91.31	12.09
Total	588.3	67	839.12	69	507.25	67
Total, all countries	881.73	100	1,220.22	100	755.37	100

Notes:
To April 2008, converted from the original amounts, which were in UA at 1 UA = $1.58025. In US$ millions and rounded to two decimal places.

Source: AfDB, *Procurement Statistics*, Procurement Summary by Country from 2003 to 2008 (April 2008), at: www.afdb.org/portal/portal/page?_pageid=473,9696658_dad=portal&_schema=PORTAL, accessed 13 June 2008.

bidding company's government. This partly explains the proportion of the British aid budget assigned to 'technical assistance'. Other technical and spatial advantages are enjoyed by companies from richer states: for example, the Commercial and Aid sections of the British High Commissions can send sensitive information about potential contracts to registration-only services in London, coordinated from the UK Trade and Investment website and involving proactive alerts to subscribing companies of opportunities which 'match' their business. By contrast, a domestic company in the country in which the contract is generated may need to rely on surface mail services in the context of a limited bidding time and limited information (interview, Zimtrade, Harare, 1994). Currently, the UK has The Aid-Funded Business Service, which was 'set up to help British companies get ahead in aid-funded business' (UK Trade and Investment 2008). A coordinated effort involving Whitehall and overseas embassies provides a range of services to help companies access the system, including subsidised participation at selected trade fairs, outward missions and bespoke market intelligence, such that, as UK Trade and Investment services summarise, 'we can help you crack foreign markets and get to grips quickly with overseas regulations and business practice' (ibid.).

The Aid-Funded Business Service summarises that

> Aid Funded Business is about win-win. British companies win the business, the aid agency funds a sound project and the developing country gains a sustainable asset.
>
> (UK Trade and Investment 2008a)

Pointing to global annual spending of $60 billion per year, they continue that:

> Aid Funded Business offers real opportunities .... **But you need to know – and be known by – the right people**, in the right places, to break into this market. UK Trade & Investment's Aid Funded Business Team can help you through this process.
>
> (ibid., emphasis in original)

This UK Government website estimates UK companies receive:

> between 4–17% of multilateral aid-funded business. The most sought after expertise is in the healthcare, construction, consultancy, ICT, environmental, and transport sectors.
>
> (ibid.)

These advantages are legitimated through the language of efficient business and are upheld in general for core states as a group relative to companies from poorer countries, by the discursive practices and procedures of the multilaterals themselves. For example, consultancy contracts derivative of aid projects funded by the EDF have tradition-ally been distributed to short-listed, registered companies via a complex qualification procedure (World Aid Section (WAS) 1991).[12] These provisions for procurement from the early 1990s set a pattern: as more projects were subsequently opened to more 'untied aid', allowing apparently competitive environments and open tendering to become the norm, the qualifying technicalities of registration continued to work against companies from more distant places, including those where the project would actually be constructed. The large and iconic projects of contemporary African development – such as the Lesotho Highlands Dam, the Chad–Cameroon pipeline, the infrastructural developments at Cabinda in Angola and so forth – have continued to be the exclusive preserve of large Northern companies. The European Commission has also preferred large size, to 'deal with companies which are fully capable of completing projects, most of which require multidisciplinary inputs, which weighs against the use of very small consultancies (eg. one, two or three men [sic])' (WAS 1991: 3). Argu-ments that only large companies will do occur repeatedly, since size is seen to relate to efficiency. This obviously benefits established compa-nies from core states in the attraction of derivative business generally. Indeed, the use of open tendering, which would allow new companies to join these elite networks, is not practiced as a general principle by multilateral organisations.

An interrogation of the World Bank procurement database[13] gives a snapshot of how procurement has developed since the era of the effec-tively closed business communities of the 1980s and 1990s, and since the arrival of more donors and economic heavyweights such as India and China. The World Bank qualifies the use of its database by pointing out that it does not contain details of all bank-funded projects, which result in the award of about 20–30,000 contracts worth about $20 billion each year, but only about 7,000 of these, although these do include 'major contracts financed under investment lending' which were reviewed by Bank staff before they were awarded. The bank explains that 'The thresholds for prior review vary from loan to loan, and country to country' (World Bank 2008a). There were 503 contracts in total for UK businesses in all sectors, in all African countries, between 2000 and 2007, of which 262 are for consultants and 241 are for 'Goods and Works'. The 262 consultancy contracts were collectively worth over $144 million, and when those projects are disaggregated to include smaller proportions directly given to other subcontractors or, in most cases, UK firms registered in other countries such as Scott Wilson Kirkpatrick & Co. in France and Ivory Coast or Pricewater-houseCoopers Consultants Limited in Senegal and South Africa, the result is 277 contracts in total, distributed as outlined in Table 7.10. The corresponding figures for successfully won contracts from all supplier countries carried out in Africa for the World Bank in the area of consultancy services between 2000 and 2007 is 6,215,[14] which to a supplier amounts to nearly $2,253 million. The distribution of type of procurement selection is given in column one. The table shows the type of selection that can be viewed as most 'competitive': 'quality and cost-based selection' was used in 57 per cent of cases where British consultants won contracts and in 49 per cent of cases overall, and in the rest of the cases it wasn't.

When a company bids for a contract funded under EU authority it is expected that the procurement office of the country borrowing the money will assess the applications. Indeed, following the recent initiatives to improve aid effectiveness after the Paris Declaration, a move to untie aid has led, according to the OECD, to all 39 HIPC countries having completely untied aid, to 'buy goods and services locally at the best price' (OECD 2008a). However, the process of procurement itself is still regulated by 'standards' of competition which privilege companies 'in the know', and it remains to be seen whether these new initiatives can successfully confront vested interests. Previous similar initiatives suggest not, as do the current statistics, which remain

Table 7.10 Types of procurement selection and UK contracts from the World Bank, in consultancy services for Africa, 2000–07

Type of selection	Number of contracts awarded to UK consultants	Number of contracts to all consultants
Quality and cost-based selection	158 [57.0%]	2,959 [48.5%]
Single source selection	65 [23.5%]	1,505 [24.7%]
Selection based on consultant's qualification	27 [9.7%]	606 [9.9%]
Individual	17 [6.1%]	596 [9.8%]
Quality-based selection	10 [3.6%]	290 [4.8%]
Least-cost selection		65 [1.1%]
Selection under a fixed budget		25 [0.4%]
Service delivery contracts		54 [0.9%]
Total	277* [100%]	6,100 [100%]

Note: *This figure includes twelve subcontracts to other countries where the parent in the bid is UK domiciled.

excessively high, of the proportions of business which goes to Northern consultants.

In general, a successful company must be proximate and, under EU regulations, use marketing resources to extend relations with both the national authorising officer in-country, usually the minister who is responsible for issuing calls for tender, supervising appraisal and awarding contracts with the EC delegate, up to certain financial limits, and to the Commission, which regulates the process and relevant financial ceilings for negotiation with beneficiary states. Both functions can be costly, even if legality is strictly adhered to, such that enclaved networks emerge and the language of business expertise is required to rebuke any whiff of cronyism or corruption (see Bracking 2007). The importance of proximity was recognised by Crown Agents when it opened an office in Washington D.C. as long ago as the Second World War, from which to lobby the emerging structures that would become the World Bank (interview, Crown Agents, London, 1994). However, close but not too close, is the watchword. For example, the World Aid Section UK Representative in 1991 urged consultants with 'good relations with government' in the poorer countries to avoid displaying evidence of preferential access at the Commission, particularly when a consultant might have both helped to initiate the project and assisted the government in preparing the application to Brussels for funding. Here the UK Rep notes:

> It is important here to recall that project definition studies can preclude the consultant from participating in the main study work. Therefore it could be helpful tactically to play down the extent of any earlier input.
>
> (WAS 1991: 5)

Thus, 'good relations' and proximity to key political figures in the borrowing countries, and an ability to furnish them with resources in order to make a bid to the Commission, are seen as assets of the companies concerned, but not assets to necessarily be made public within the Commission. The rationality of such behaviour is related to the requirement on the part of the Commission to institutionally manage the competition between each member state's consultants in an apparently fair manner.

Meanwhile at the AfDB in 2008, anticipated new business is systematising procurement to a degree that hasn't been reached before. Increased procurement opportunities in general can be expected at the AfDB because of both the historic rise in funds and the renewed emphasis on private development, but the distribution of these depends on procurement procedures. The UK is supporting the AfDB's move to procurement arrangements under the provisions of the Paris Declaration on aid effectiveness, namely aid untying and using in-country procurement systems, and harmonisation with the other multilateral development banks led by the World Bank (HC 2008b: Evidence (Ev.) 33). This may be because the UK gets very little derivative business when the procurement system is run by the bank itself. In a memorandum of evidence by the Institution of Civil Engineers (ICE) and Engineers Against Poverty (EAP), whose conclusions are supported by DfID (HC 2008b: Ev. 31), it was concluded that in these objectives of using in-country procurement systems the AfDB had 'not yet progressed very far', and that while the Water Department is taking the lead with International Competitive Bidding in Uganda and Tanzania, in other departments the bank 'retains considerable control over procurement' and ICE and EAP want this delegated to in-country authorities (who would be mostly regulated by the World Bank but also by the DfID under Poverty Reduction Budget Support interventions). In other words, preferences at the AfDB would be replaced by in-country dynamics as the key determinant of winners and losers.

This displacement away from the AfDB would not, however, solve the critical issue of whether foreign or domestic businesses win the funds. With regard to this, ICE and EAP recognise that:

> AfDB was very concerned that much of the funding invested in African infrastructure flows straight out again in the form of contracts awarded to foreign contractors and suppliers.

In fact, ICE and EAP, rather surprisingly on the face of it, support the case for the developmental benefits of local supply in increasing capacity and contributing to economic growth and poverty reduction (HC 2008b: Ev. 32). The AfDB reportedly also asserts that the widespread use of foreign contractors did not ensure quality, and implementation of projects was often poor, with initial social policies not carried into tender and contract documents and thus not implemented. ICE and EAP suggested that AfDB change its procurement focus from 'lowest price' to 'best value', but AfDB has its hands tied to some extent by aid harmonisation commitments to multilateral development bank (MDB) procedures, which generally insist on International Competitive Bidding and acceptance of the lowest evaluated bid. New procurement regulations in many African countries reflect this move, since they are 'reforming their procurement procedures under the direction of the World Bank' (HC 2008b: Ev. 33). However, while the World Bank sells this change as an anti-corruption policy, the ICE and EAP conclude that:

Corruption is rife under the current regime and lowest price does not necessarily offer the best value for money with a detrimental effect on the quality of the infrastructure asset.

(HC 2008b: Ev. 34)[15]

In an interesting footnote, they note that:

For many years there has been some expectation among the major donors that benefits in the form of contract awards will be commensurate with the size of donations and donor country firms. That there is still some connection between contributions and awards would seem to be borne out by the fact that the United Nations supports purchasing from developing countries but still has to include on tender lists firms from 'Under-utilised major donors countries'.

(ibid.)

While anti-corruption policy might be the conduit of reform in this area, it might not be the driver; instead we can test the proposition that, just as in 'free markets' and liberalisation policy, often it is the market leaders and market makers who disproportionately benefit from the introduction of 'competition' in any case. Or, at the least, the loss to their business is not as much as you would expect. Certainly, free trade, when at all in evidence, has tended to benefit the already economically strong. In this instance, the AfDB retains a preference for African businesses built into the system, whereby 'all else being equal, African businesses that fell within a 10–15% margin of competitor bids would be successful', within the limits set by the competitive tender system and an 'over-riding concern' with 'quality' (reported in HC 2008: 10). However, in a potentially telling caveat, the AfDB also reported that 'ensuring that companies could prove they were entirely locally-based was not straightforward' (ibid.). There seems to be a policy fudge at work here, on two levels. First, a fudge that while local is seen as best for development, open competition is also seen as best for efficiency. For example, the IDC conclude that local procurement 'creates more sustainable outcomes and helps generate skills, income and employment', but then go on to urge the AfDB to 'ensure it is doing all it can' to promote local business 'whilst continuing to harmonise its procurement processes with other donors in line with the Paris Declaration on Aid Effectiveness' (HC 2008: 10–11). The actual distribution of contracts by value between regional and non-regional members of the AfDB is given in Table 7.11, with a fairly even overall split between the two. The second potential fudge is that nationality can, in any case, be hidden

Table 7.11 Distribution of contracts among regional and non-regional member countries of the African Development Bank

	Goods	Works	Services	Others	Total
Regional member countries					
2006	66.40	214.97	74.81	0.13	481.04
2007	75.27	312.47	67.24	0.52	636.79
Non-regional member countries					
2006	115.63	236.45	44.48	0.03	396.60
2007	96.35	438.05	46.25		580.65
All member countries*					
2006	182.01	576.16	122.55	0.63	881.73
2007	172.25	931.83	115.63	0.52	1,220.22
Proportion of contracts for regional members (2007) %	43.70	52.99	58.15	100	52.19

Notes:

Figures have been converted to US$ million from UA million at the rate of 1 UA = US$1.58025, pertaining in 2007, according to AfDB (2008). Figures rounded to two decimal places. Figures may not entirely match totals due to rounding errors.

* These figures are not simply the sum of the two categories – regional and non-regional members – since there is a third group of contracts deemed 'multinational'. In 2006 the total for these was 2.59 (services 2.06, others 0.53). In 2007 these totalled 1.77 (goods 0.41, services 1.36).

Source: AfDB Group (2008), *Procurement Summary by Regional and Non Regional Members Countries from 2006 to 2008* (April 2008) at: www.afdb.org/portal/page?_pageid=473,969665&_dad=portal&_schema= PORTAL, accessed 13 June 2008.

by complex inter-firm relationships, nationally incorporated subsidiaries applying as domiciled locals, sub-contracting and so forth. If the second fudge promotes vertical linkage and access to markets it might not be wholly negative, but it certainly can confound indigenisation and capacity building within the African private sector as well.

Conclusion

The activities of the Great Predators are not just for other people who 'need developing', for development and poverty reduction, they also act to create economic opportunities in and of themselves, or for themselves in the shape of opportunities predominantly reserved for the firms of the countries providing the credit. The Great Predators – the bilateral, regional and multilateral development finance institutions – underwrite and regulate a global market in development goods and services; a growth-enhancing injection of liquidity which has characteristics of a public subsidy to the already privileged firms of the Northern private sector; an institutional system of support for a Keynesian multiplier, which we modelled in chapter 4. In so far as the projects actually produced are profitable, the money paid back to the DFIs by the borrowers would be, ideally, only a small part of an additional flow of funds produced by the activities of the project once completed and functioning. However, this ideal scenario is rare, since many projects are infrastructural, and thus have no obvious income stream produced; some are just unproductive; while others are in zones where overly generous profit repatriation is in place for the controllers of the resulting asset, most of whom are foreign. Some DFI-funded 'assets' are simply white elephants, and the history of development is littered with abandoned projects, failed projects, and 'virtual' projects, or projects which never even existed at all, due to corrupt persons taking the monies at the inception stage. Thus, in so far as borrowed money has been paid back with interest, but relates to these failed projects, the Southern tax payer foots the bill: the public subsidy to the firms is actually coming out of the pockets of the world's poor, those who the 'aid' was ostensibly there to help in the first instance.

Notes

1. In US$ million, the subscriptions and contributions committed on 30 June 2007 – the financial year end – for the top five members were: US, $38,981.03; Japan, $28,858.06; Germany, $19,734.68; UK, $18,275.67; and France, $12,612.15 (World Bank 2007a).
2. In a memorandum of evidence written by the AfDB and submitted to the Committee.
3. The World Aid Section (WAS) was part of the Projects and Export Policy Division (PEP) of the then DTI.
4. The 1991–92 data came directly from WAS in the then DTI. My best efforts to acquire an updated equivalent table were unsuccessful; such data services are reserved for the private sector.
5. The World Bank (2008) summarise: 'Since the reports on this site do not list all contracts awarded by the Bank, they should be viewed only as a guide to determine the distribution of major contracts among the Bank's member countries. The Procurement Policy and Services Group does not guarantee the data included in this publication and accepts no responsibility whatsoever for any consequences of its use.'
6. Even having its own online opposition in the form of a Facebook group: 'I bet I can find 100,000 who hate Umeme'.

7. The AfDB is the seventh largest source of aid to Africa, behind bilateral donors such as the Netherlands. Even with these increases, ADF11 amounts to half the World Bank's current IDA replenishment-round spend in Africa, IDA15, totalling approximately $20 billion (HC 2008: 5–6).

8. Governments of Germany, the Netherlands, Portugal and the UK (2006) *Working in Partnership with the African Development Bank: Joint Strategic Framework for Partnership with the AfDB*, p. 7.

9. The figures in this section have been converted from the AfDB unit of account, the UA, into US$ at a rate of 1UA = 1.58025 (2007) (AfDB 2008: 36).

10. One cell is for 'multinational' but it is less than 1 per cent.

11. The figures for 2008 are unfinished.

12. From a World Aid Section hand-out: EDF 08, *European Community-Funded Aid Projects in Developing Countries: Consultancies*, compiled by the UK Permanent Representation to the European Communities, January.

13. I would like to thank Sithembiso Myeni for assisting me with the online searches.

14. For some reason, the database reports 6,215 hits, which downloads to 6,100 records.

15. They encourage the use of UK Office of Government Commerce guidelines for 'Achieving Excellence in Construction' and the UN 'Commission on International Trade Law (UNCITRAL) Model Law' instead (HC 2008b, Ev. 34).

8 Private sector development and bilateral interventions

Bilateral finance institutions taken together make investments across the developing world and manage foreign direct investment (FDI) from within their institutional structures, using umbrella guarantees which cover their private sector partners. In relation to investment and finance capital per se, they have a very distinctive role, all under the auspices and organising fulcrum of the directly multilateral International Finance Corporation (IFC), of regulating liquidity. In this, the role of linking up businesses in the North and South, as well as consumers and trading partners, is a central effect of bilateral interventions. This chapter examines the theoretical benefits of private sector development instruments, and then explores the effects of these interventions in practice. This is not to suggest that bilateral institutions have a monopoly in the private sector, while multilateral aid goes to the public. Since both types are spent in both areas, it is rather that bilateral aid to the private sector plays a particular role in building trading and investment relations between national economies, and thus has an important effect on reproducing and remaking older relationships of inequality and power between nation states.

Benefits of private sector development instruments

Private sector development (PSD) instruments are policies and resources aimed at developing and expanding the private sector. There are generally two broad types: first, direct interventions and subsidies at the firm or sector level, and second, macrointerventions at the level of the market and economy as a whole, or 'market development and investment climate approaches', respectively (HC 2006: 1). Together they are intended to generate growth by improving the investment climate, which, according to the British Government, would then provide opportunities for 'poor people to participate in markets' (ibid.). More specifically, PSD instruments are said to work best when they are strategically used or, as these Overseas Development Institute (ODI) researchers summarise, when they:

> target resources where maximum impact can be leveraged …
> on business models with high potential for replication and
> demonstration, on pump-priming expansion of domestic

commercial financial services, or investment climate reform to complement direct business support.

(Ashley et al. 2005: 1)

Policy makers have been advocating the use of both types of instrument in a complementary and holistic fashion to encourage private sector growth and, in turn, capital accumulation.

In the last 30 years or so there has been a general movement away from direct intervention by governments and direct subsidies to individual firms, to more enabling or facilitative approaches, at least rhetorically. Within this general trend there have also been regular exceptions to the rule for powerful groups, such as the 'liquidity backstops' or payouts of public money to banks in the wake of the credit crunch. The current consensus, summarised by the Organisation for Economic Co-operation and Development (OECD), is on tackling 'coordination failures' concerning investment, innovation and R&D (OECD 2007: 9). Governments are charged with 'enabling' business, providing public goods, mitigating 'externalities' (which means the pollution and other side effects of capitalist production), and promoting trade (OECD 2007: 11). In the 'Enhanced Private Sector Assistance' (EPSA) programme launched at the Group of Eight Summit Meeting at Gleneagles in July 2005, PSD was put centre stage for African development, with five areas outlined for intervention:

creating an enabling environment, strengthening financial systems, building competitive economic and social infrastructure, promoting the development of small and medium sized enterprises (SMEs) and promoting trade and foreign direct investment.

(OECD 2007: 11)

Pretty comprehensive stuff! The OECD reviews these initiatives and then proposes an approach targeted at remedying 'co-ordination failures', which involves 'building well-functioning institutions and appropriate incentive mechanisms', in order to try and avoid 'direct interventions' in favour of 'indirect inducements' (OECD 2007: 14), a 'whole-of-government' approach to provide that ever-elusive 'stable macroeconomic environment', with safe property rights and reliable contract enforcement (OECD 2007: 17).

The central attributes of aid to the private sector, which are said to make it 'developmental', are that it opens new and otherwise unavailable markets; reduces country risk in the process, including for other companies in an agglomeration effect; and can be organised to promote and solidify recipient governments' commitments to wider improvements to the market architecture and macroeconomic policy environment, not least because bilateral money is often used as a reward for 'good behaviour'. The development finance institutions (DFIs) themselves employ a number of concepts to elaborate and explain these effects; the main ones are summarised in Table 8.1. A principal concept is the 'demonstration effect', whereby they seek to promote a project with the expectation that others will see how successful it is and copy their example, either in a previously under-developed industrial sector, or because the risks have proved surmountable. An accompanying concept is the 'augmentation of capital flows', where private effort is critically helped along its way by the DFIs, both by their pecuniary and non-pecuniary contributions; this latter being principally the application of technical expertise and experience. A third would be 'the catalytic effect', again where public money is used to encourage a mimetic response by more private actors. If we return to the ODI summary of the benefits of PSD instruments, we learn that they are supposed to have a demonstration effect, a multiplier effect to crowd in investors, and a wider developmental impact. Additionally, assistance is variously advertised by DFIs as leading edge, strategic in the development of industrial sectors or markets overall, as helping to catalyse and 'crowd in' new and otherwise unwilling investors, and as helping to select and promote the most adept and skilful local entrepreneurs and fund managers – and so forth.

Assisting accumulation – but development?

This long list of very general policies, instruments and principles belies the commonality of intervention in practice, which remains predominantly equity and development finance purchases that privilege certain constituencies over others. Also, the effect of macro policies is not to equally privilege all, since neoliberal 'free' markets have a tendency to help the already strong and exacerbate inequality (Pieterse 2002). The ODI researchers warn of the risk of an '"escalator" of donor-assisted instruments, resulting in donor dependency' (Ashley et al. 2005: 1) on the part of African entrepreneurs and enterprises, although as our analysis shows, there is also a risk of 'dependence' for large equity funds and their managers, a process outlined more generally by Larry Elliott and Dan Atkinson in their recent book, *The Gods That Failed*. In this reading, private investors are happy to parrot free market truisms in boom times, before exercising indiscreet haste in rushing to central banks for bailouts once the economic weather turns bleaker! (Elliott and Atkinson 2008). In short, and as is common for many public policies, PSD creates a constituency which becomes accustomed to the

Table 8.1 Summary of concepts in private sector development interventions

DFI objective or principle	Explanation	Instrument
Demonstration effect	A successful project encourages imitation by other firms	• Setting up a unique commercial venture • Providing equity, loans and management (E, L & M) • 'Infant industry' investment
Augmenting capital flows	Public funds can provide critical weight to other investors' efforts	• Moderating investment risks • Improving capital market efficiency • Being the owner-operator of its managed companies • E, L & M
Enhanced developmental effect	IFIs have singular interest in project, not a trading interest	• Leadership • Provision of hard infrastructure • Technical assistance, E, L & M
Moderating investment risk	Expertise and standing in relation to domestic government and the capital markets provides insurance against investment and political risk	• Providing a 'Seal of Approval' • Providing an 'umbrella role' • Negotiating with government and partners • Designing and planning project • Raising funds in capital markets
Adding value	Proving capital which would not otherwise be available or suitable	• Modifying the risk-reward relationship • Design, experience, expertise • Raising capital
Catalytic principle	Proving minority stake to catalyse others' crowding in	• Leveraging equity by providing core stake • Providing direct management function • Securing political 'go-ahead'
The business principle	Funds are transferred under market disciplines to ensure profitability	• Making up acceptable rates of return
The principle of special contribution	To supplement, complement but not displace market operators	• Declaring that others not willing to participate without IFIs

Source: CDC and IFC Annual Reports, various years.

subsidy, which then has a broader effect on shoring up the constituency's relative economic and social position.

There are also other contradictory and adverse effects of PSD instruments, not least that they are somewhat covert and opaque. For example, the effort to appear in a secondary or supplementary role is critical to the success of private sector development, not least because many international finance institutions (IFIs) are bound by stature to avoid displacing the private sector. For example, the IFC is bound by its Articles of Agreement, which state that 'the Corporation shall not undertake any financing for which in its opinion sufficient capital could be obtained on reasonable terms [elsewhere]', or the 'non-displacement provision'. In other words, 'its participation must make things happen that otherwise would not happen in a timely way'; a 'special contribution' which doesn't substitute for but 'supplements or complements the role of market operators' (IFC 1992: 3), preferably in economies and sectors where a 'demonstration effect' of a successful IFC project encourages imitation (IFC 1992: 5). Thus, augmenting capital flows must be assessed relative to a counterfactual caveat, difficult logically in any context, that if DEG, AFD or IFC and so forth hadn't been there, it wouldn't have happened. Since this is impossible to prove, investment decisions in practice are open to cronyism and abuse: when other people quickly show up, it can be attributed to the 'demonstration effect' which has 'augmented flows' rather than to the fact that the businesses were waiting in the wings for a public sector subsidy to materialise, after their initial protestations about insurmountable risk were met with promises of assistance.

This is particularly a problem when full commercial profitability is expected, historically from about the mid-1980s, and prompted many conceptual elisions between the discourses of development and business. For example, by the early 1990s the IFC and Commonwealth Development Corporation (CDC) were defining their roles as in parallel to 'real' market processes: 'the essence of IFC's role is to combine the object of profitability with that of development' (IFC 1992: 3). Both the CDC and the IFC extended this 'principle' of profitability to one where 'development' becomes synonymous with capitalist profitability itself (IFC 1992: 2; CDC 1993). The IFC explained this forced complementarity in terms of the 'business principle', where funds transferred under 'market disciplines' are then subject to 'full commercial risk' which in turn means they 'are more likely to be efficiently used' (IFC 1992: 2). In this respect the Articles of Agreement precluded the IFC from accepting government guarantee of repayment for its own financing since this could subvert the business principle by displacing some of the full commercial risk (ibid.). Explained in full the IFC continue that:

> By functioning as a business and seeking to ensure that its own bottom line is healthy, IFC in effect converts funds from official sources (its own capital, subscribed by governments) into

market-like funds. The Corporation's primary goal is development, not profits, but the aim of profitability should be seen as consistent with the development objective, not in conflict with it. IFC's profits depend on the success of the client companies that it finances: private companies that operate in private markets where profitability is the essential test of success.

(IFC 1992: 2)

Thus, capitalist profitability and 'development' became one and the same, a shotgun wedding which ideologically served to legitimate the effective privatisation of much development finance from the mid-1980s in bilateral and multilateral development finance institutions.

In the case of the CDC, it sought to achieve private sector levels of profitability, partly to avoid accusations of distorting the market place. But this full commerciality meant it entertained some quite contradictory situations, where it was outbidding rival private companies to win newly privatised concerns, and citing its 'value-added' attributes in explanation. As Tyler summarises:

It was not clear what the public policy justification was for CDC (mandated to promote the private sector in developing countries) outbidding genuine private sector companies during the privatisation (of) some African agricultural ventures:

(Tyler 2008: 25)

Similarly, the IFC spoke of its 'special contribution', arguing that the difference between itself and the private sector proper was that it was the:

only party interested solely in the success of the project itself; other parties frequently have other objectives (for example, a trading objective) that are linked to the project's success but that, in the end, take priority over it.

(IFC 1992: 4)

Although not expanded upon, this illustrates the divergence of interest that different external groups may have in a project, only a part of which is developmental in terms of the public good. In the case of plantation agriculture, companies have a strong 'trading interest' in the supply of upstream processing and retail ventures, but have little interest in investing in sources of supply if at all avoidable. Thus, multinational agribusiness companies maintain thin equity bases in their plantation operations, often with the help of IFC and CDC who bridge the equity gap through public funds. But even if true, the argument only runs to suggesting that the IFC provides indirect support for the other more mercenary partners!

The Great Predators also seek to differentiate themselves and establish developmental credentials by claiming to be trustworthy and reputable, which in turn reduces risk for others. Their publications are replete with references to status, experience, expertise and worldwide contacts. They also claim to have important friends, not least the home 'creditor' government who can wade in to remind the hosts of their obligations, should the need arise. This has meant, over time, that DFI investments have become clustered in countries where purposive promises on the macroeconomic environment are in place, such as a structural adjustment programme or more latterly poverty reduction strategy (PRS), or in countries which have gone furthest in signing up to voluntary treaties and codes of practice which tie countries in to the governance modalities of the neoliberal order. An example would be the Financial Action Task Force recommendations, and the OECD 'Convention on Combating the Bribery of Foreign Public Officials in International Business Transactions' of 1999.

These more recent trends in the codification of neoliberalism illustrate some fundamental problems with the business principles as outlined above. Globally now, there is little new, embryonic or catalytic to be invented or discovered: frontiers to global capitalism just do not exist to justify the IFIs in their promise to not displace someone. In fact their habit of clustering investments in managed climates suggests just the opposite, that nice middle-income countries with a relatively advanced investment climate are preferred. Altenburg (2005) claims that public–private partnerships for development (and DFIs often head these) have three potential positive effects: increased resources; deployment of extra (private sector, often) expertise in development; and innovative approaches that would not occur to traditional aid organisations. However, Altenburg also notes the risk of public resources being wasted on viable projects which commercial banks would have financed anyway, which is sometimes termed the 'windfall waste' problem (as in Storey and Williams 2006: 12, who cited Altenburg 2005). Conversely, and in contradistinction to the windfall waste problem, is that the potential investment has no private interest because it is dumb or unprofitable.

Taking just one example from chapter 7 – the Asian Development Bank (ADB) fund support for mobile telephony in Afghanistan – illustrates how many of the benefits of development assistance to the private sector can be refuted. The telephone loan was an intervention in an already developing marketplace, where there were already two other mobile network suppliers and a government-run fixed line supplier, which suggests it might be a example of the windfall waste problem. In fact under European regulations which regulate 'state aid' such a subsidy would face problems in the EU as market distorting, privileging as it does just one participant. In this case the company in question was offering village phone services to meet the needs of the rural poor, and also cash transfer services through the network to allow Afghans to use the phones to make remittances, or cash transfers, to relatives (which, not uncoincidently, allows informal remittance transfers to be regulated and monitored) (ADB 2006). These elements of added value could be used in defence of public support, a 'public good value added', but the question doesn't go away of why this particular loan is 'developmental', or why this particular company is more deserving than its rivals and nor does the suspicion, in this particular case, that security interests also played a role in the selection. Storey and Williams's (2006) summary of the problems of DFIs remains: they either pick up losers in the market or they generate market distortions.

The European Development Finance Institutions

A Monopolies and Mergers Commission (MMC) report of 1992 provides an interesting exercise on measuring private sector development more widely, as well as a rare insight on the profitability of the Great Predators. The MMC ranked the profitability of the CDC and other bilateral equivalents in terms of the gross income that each organisation received on its investments, expressed as a percentage of its investments for the financial year 1990–91 (MMC 1992: 147). The German DEG (German Finance Company for Investments in Developing Countries) was the most profitable at 10.3 per cent, followed by 3i (10.3%); EDESA (Luxembourg, 10.2%); OPIC (United States, 9.1%); IFC (Bretton Woods institutions, 8.8%); SIFIDA (Luxembourg, 8.0%); EIB (Europe, 7.8%); IFU (Denmark, 7.8%); CDC (UK, 7.4%); FMO (Netherlands, 6.4%); SBI (Belgium, 5.0%); and CCCE (now AFD, France, 5.0%). Of the four organisations deemed most comparable to the CDC, DEG and IFC show a return, averaged over the two years, a little higher than CDC, and FMO (Netherlands Development Finance Company) and IFU (Danish Industrialisation Fund) somewhat lower (MMC 1992: 147). CDC had also accumulated a significant surplus to 1992 and had not incurred a deficit in any single year since the 1950s (MMC 1992: 4). All rates of return for DFIs in Europe and North America were respectable and over 5 per cent in both years, rising to 10 per cent in a number of cases (MMC 1992).

Evidence of large and persistent profits is in contradistinction to the representation that DFIs give of their work, where profitability is said to prompt exit and disposal, as the job has 'been done'. Of course, profits also accrue from the sale itself, while losses can be absorbed by the wider 'aid' budget of the creditor government. For example, in the 1980s, the CDC investment in Tanwat in Tanzania was a failure, but new money was nonetheless provided, such that losses were socialised. By comparison, the successful Usutu Pulp Company in Swaziland was sold off to the private sector proper, in Usutu's case to SAPPI of South Africa, by a first tranche in 1990 when Courtaulds sold its stake and then by means of CDC's remaining stake in 2000, after the issue of full South African ownership had been made more palatable to the Swazi Government following the end of apartheid (Tyler 2008: 9–10). Sufficient numbers of projects were successful, and sufficient amounts of bad debts were absorbed by sovereign Third World governments and by the Northern owners of the DFI clubs, to produce an excellent balance sheet over time. For example, in the Usutu pulp and paper success story, from 1950 to 2000, CDC committed nearly £18 million to Usutu (much more in today's values) and all loans were repaid with interest to make a compound return of approximately 13 per cent per annum in sterling terms on its equity (Tyler 2008: 11).

Table 8.2 summarises the scale of activities of the CDC and eleven comparators in 1991, compiled for the MMC Review, ordered by the balance sheet value of investments (the largest, the European Investment Bank (EIB), heads the table) (MMC 1992). As can be seen from the table, nine of the twelve organisations are wholly or partially owned by governments, while the three private groups (EDESA, 3i and SIFIDA) were owned by consortia of banks and large US and European industrial companies (MMC 1992: 146). Most of the organisations were making investments in the form of equity and loans, with EIB and OPIC investing in only loan form, and the French CCCE, now AFD, being predominantly loan-orientated. It is only later through the 2000s that the grant component of, for example, EIB money was increased. The CDC and other DFIs were making investments entirely in poorer countries, while the EIB was predominantly focused on the EC (90 per cent of loans), but also provided financing outside the EC in the 69 African, Caribbean and Pacific (ACP) countries, twelve Mediterranean countries and several in Central and Eastern Europe (MMC 1992: 146–7; EIB 1992). This profile is interesting in that current debt cancellations can be traced back predominantly to development finance extended in this model, at near market rate loans, and as such the future failures through the 1990s and 2000s must be contextualised within the commercial risk model with its attendant provisioning. In other words, any full value write-offs suggest a greater generosity on the part of creditors than the actual book value of the debt would justify, since this would have been written down against its relevant provisioning many times in the years that followed.

At the time of the MMC review, the organisations were looking healthy. The size of the US contribution is confusing, however, since while the Overseas Private Investment Corporation (OPIC) is ranked ninth in the table, it also had extensive US Treasury securities at its disposal for the purposes of insurance and investment risk guarantees. The scale of US export credit and investment insurance is also severely underestimated here since there were also other quasi-public and private organisations in the United States with similar functions: the Export–Import Bank (Eximbank), the chief government agency; the Foreign Credit Insurance Association (FCIA), which is an unincorporated association of private commercial insurance companies operating in co-operation with Eximbank to provide export credit insurance; and the Private Export Funding Corporation (PEFCO) (Eiteman et al. 1992: 539–41). Eximbank is the US equivalent to the UK's Export Credit Guarantee Department (ECGD) (see chapter 5). It was established in 1934, primarily to stimulate and facilitate trade to the Soviet Union, and was rechartered in 1945 to provide for its present global reach. Eximbank facilitates the financing of US exports by insuring export loans extended by US banks to foreign borrowers, and by a direct-lending operation with private partners (to ensure it compliments with, rather than competes with them), to lend dollars to borrowers outside the United States for the purchase of US goods and services. At this time, Eximbank was also providing financing to cover the preparation costs incurred by US companies for engineering, planning and feasibility studies for non-US clients on large capital projects; a perk that, as we saw in the last chapter, helped to skew derivative business into the hands of creditor states. The US Government underwrites each institution. In the case of PEFCO, this provides a subsidy to a coalition of private interests with particular exporting interests since all PEFCO's loans are guaranteed by Eximbank, allowing PEFCO to undertake no (costly) evaluation of credit risks or appraisal of country conditions itself. PEFCO's stockowners are predominantly commercial banks, 49 in 1992, dropping to 24 in 2008.

For the common affairs of the European bourgeoisie

When combined, the available value that these institutions can put into global liquidity is small compared to private markets in the core areas of the world system such as North America and Europe, but large relative to smaller markets in the poorest countries, and also large relative to the members' contributions. This is because the actual amounts members pay in are only tiny: the bulk of the money is then subsequently raised on capital markets using the reputation of the members. This reputation of members means that the risk of non payment is

Table 8.2 Financial performance of CDC and eleven comparable
organisations in 1990–91

Name of organisation[a]	Status	Country of origin	Balance sheet value of investments, 1990–91[b] (£ mill.)
EIB	Established under Treaty of Rome. Owned by member states of EU	EC	43,965
CCCE [c]	Public institution	France	6,151
IFC	Shareholders are the member countries	International, BWI	2,385
3i	Private company. Shareholders are UK banks	UK	2,312
CDC	Public corporation	UK	957
DEG	Limited liability company owned by government	Germany	304
FMO	Public limited company with government as 51% shareholder	Netherlands	216
IFU	Autonomous fund established by Act of Parliament	Denmark	64
OPIC	Government body	United States	33 [d]
SBI	Company majority government-owned with private shareholders	Belgium	25
SIFIDA	Private company	Luxembourg	22
EDESA	Private company. Shareholders are European banks and international industrial companies	Luxembourg	19
Total			56,453

Notes:
(a) Names of organisations in full: BWI (Bretton Woods institutions), CCCE (Caisse Centrale de Cooperation Economique), CDC (Commonwealth Development Corporation), DEG (Deutsche Investitions und Entwicklungsgesellschaft mbH), EDESA (EDESA SA), EIB (European Investment Bank), FMO (Nederlandse Financierings-Maatschappij voor Ontwikkelingslanden), IFC (International Finance Corporation), IFU (Industrialiseringsfonden for Udviklingslandene), OPIC (Overseas Private Investment Corporation), SBI (Société Belge d'Investissement International SA), SIFIDA (SIFIDA Investment), and 3i (3i Group plc).
(b) Year ends falling within the range July 1990 and 30 June 1991 as 1990–91.
(c) CCCE is now known as the Agence Française de Développement (AFD).
(d) Also has £833 million of US Treasury securities to back up its export credit insurance and investment risk guarantee activities.

Source: Monopolies and Mergers Commission (1992), *Commonwealth Development Corporation: A Report on the Efficiency and Costs of, and the Services Provided by, the Commonwealth Development Corporation* (London, HMSO), June. Compiled from Appendix 4.2: Financial performance of CDC and eleven comparable organisations, tables 1 and 2, pp. 145-6. From the published accounts of the organisations.

negligible, while investors are also reassured that profits from the banks are normally generous. For example, the EIB, similarly to the World Bank, IFC and AfDB that were examined in chapter 4, has only a small proportion of usable funds provided by member states in the form of an interest subsidy and 'risk capital' drawn from the European Development Fund or Community budget resources. The bulk of its resources are borrowed from capital markets, mainly through public bond issues, where it has been regularly endorsed by the 'Triple-A', or 'AAA' rating awarded to its securities. There are currently 17 European members in the European Development Finance Institutions (EDFI) organisation, with a consolidated portfolio for all EDFI members at year end of 2007 of €15.1 billion (euros) (EDFI 2007) or $24 billion (dollars),[1] while members make new commitments every year to the value of about one-third of their portfolios (EDFI 2006). Furthermore, since 2004, ten members of the EDFI have formed a joint venture company – European Financing Partners (EFP) – with the European Investment Bank (EIB) to support projects in ACP countries with which the EU has a special relationship under the Cotonou (formerly Lomé) Agreement (Storey and Williams 2006: 2). Table 8.3 shows further DFIs not included in the MMC review; a table which owes a great deal to the work of Storey and Williams (2006). These EDFIs illustrate how collective membership of states, which cannot go bankrupt, create credit resources for other poorer states, which also theoretically, if not de facto, cannot go bankrupt, using global capital markets.

Table 8.3 shows how most of the European DFIs have a special responsibility for their own national firms, often having to be in a partnership with them, or privilege their interests. Also, however, the set of institutions often work together. There was, after the onset of the debt crisis, a sharp growth in the co-financing of projects between the Bretton Woods institutions, EC bilateral finance companies and regional development banks, creating a system of finance from a reactive response to crisis. Private funds dried up and DFIs expanded rapidly. For example, the CDC had long worked with the World Bank and IFC, mainly on infrastructural projects, but during the 1980s and 1990s increased this co-operation through venture capital and finance companies, and in the early 1990s, in terms of Africa, by involvement with the IFC-conceived Africa Project Development Facility (APDF)[2] and Africa Management Services Company (AMSCO) (CDC 1991: 15). By 1993, some 18 and 20 per cent of CDC's portfolio was co-financed with the World Bank and IFC, respectively (HC 1994: 5). The CDC also expanded alongside other European DFIs under the auspices of the Interact Group, which initially had been set up in 1972, pending Britain's accession to the European Community, as a 'joint working group' to structure co-operation and 'anonymously entitled the

Table 8.3 A wider set of European development finance institutions

Name of organisation[a]	Status	Country of origin	Value of investments	Comments
AWS	Wholly owned by government	Austria		Austrian Council for Research and Technology Development provides recommendations for companies and researchers to support. The focus of the bank is explicitly on supporting Austrian firms to expand overseas, primarily in new European member states.
BIO	50/50 public-private partnership between government and Belgium Corporation for International Investment	Belgium	By end-2004, BIO had a committed portfolio of €49 mill.	The bank provides equity to private companies and financial institutions, taking a minority stake (generally not more than 35%). Untied to the involvement of Belgian firms.
SBI-BMI	Semi-public investment company	Belgium	SBI-BMI's equity capital currently amounts to €33 mill.	Major shareholders include Belgian public institutions, the Federal Investment Company and the Central Bank of Belgium as well as private companies. The bank's main objective is to co-invest with Belgian companies..
COFIDES	Majority-owned (61%) by government	Spain		Ownership through three public institutions: the Spanish Institute for Foreign Trade, the Institute for Official Credit and the National Innovation Enterprise. The remaining 39% ownership stake is held by the three largest commercial banks in Spain: BBVA, SCH and Banco Sabadel. Spanish Government trust funds used to support Spanish investments abroad.
Corvinus International Investment Ltd	State-owned	Hungary		Co-investments with Hungarian industrial investors in foreign countries as a minority stakeholder. The bank and its investment partner must together control a majority stake in the target company.

[152]

Table 8.3 continued

Name of organisation[a]	Status	Country of origin	Value of investments	Comments
DEG	DEG is a subsidiary of KfW, a state-owned German bank	Germany		The board of supervisory directors of the parent bank KfW largely appointed by the Government, including the chairman and deputy chairman. Aid is untied.
Finnfund	Majority government-owned	Finland	At end 2004, portfolio valued at €91 mill.	The state of Finland owns a 79.9% share in Finnfund. Finnvera, the state-owned official export credit agency of Finland, owns 20% and the Confederation of Finnish Industries owns 0.1%. If a project sponsor is not a Finnish parent company, it must be some other link to Finnish interests.
FMO	Majority government-owned	Netherlands	Investment portfolio of almost €2 bill.	The Dutch State holds 51%; large Dutch banks hold 42%; the remaining 7% of shares are held by employers' associations, trade unions, some 100 Dutch companies and individual investors. Untied aid, but must conform with government development cooperation policy.
IFU	Wholly state-owned	Denmark	The total equity capital for the two funds amounts to €379 mill.	For OECD DAC list of development aid recipients (and with the exception of South Africa, GNP per capita less than $2,604), IFU/IØ participation conditional on presence of Danish co-investor.
IØ	Wholly state-owned	Denmark		Focuses on countries in Central and Eastern Europe. Officially independent, but Minister for Foreign Affairs appoints the Supervisory Board and the Managing Director. Needs Danish co-investor.
Swedfund	Wholly state-owned	Sweden	At the end of 2004 had a total invested portfolio of around €55 mill.	Representatives of the Ministry of Finance and the Ministry of Foreign Affairs sit on the board of directors. The bank's terms of reference aligned to government development policy. Swedfund co-operates with the Swedish Trade Council; the Council seeks to make it easier for Swedish companies to grow internationally.

Table 8.3 continued

Name of organisation[a]	Status	Country of origin	Value of investments	Comments
SIMEST	State-controlled	Italy	At end of 2004 held equity interests valued at €157.3 mill.	SIMEST's private sector shareholders include major Italian banks and business organisations, but it is controlled by the Italian Ministry for Productive Affairs. Aim is to promote Italian investments abroad. Takes equity stakes in Italian firms and joins joint ventures.
Norfund	Hybrid state-owned company	Norway	At end 2004 capital of approx. €330 mill.	Board of directors is appointed by the Norwegian Parliament. Untied aid, but concentrates on priority partner countries of Norway's development co-operation programme.
PROPARCO	Majority state-owned	France	Bank's total lending is €497 mill.	The Agence Française de Développement (AFD, formally CCCE), owns a 68% share. The remaining shares are owned by IFIs, and French finance institutions and companies. The AFD has two permanent positions on the board of directors. The Ministry of Economic Affairs and the Ministry of Finance are also represented on the board. Untied.

Notes:
(a) Names of organisations in full: AWS (Austria Wirtschaftsservice Gesellschaft mbH), BIO (Belgische Investeringsmaatschappij voor Ontwikkelingslanden), COFIDES (Compañía Española de Financiación del Desarrollo), IFU (Industrialisation Fund for Developing Countries), IØ (Investment Fund for Central and Eastern Europe), PROPARCO (Société de Promotion et de Participation pour la Coopération Economique), SBI-BMI (Société Belge d'Investissement International S.A., Belgian Corporation for International Investment), SIMEST (Società Italiana per le Imprese all'Estero), and Swedfund (Swedfund International AB).

Source: Compiled from Storey and Williams (2006).

Interact Group ... a club rather than an institution', in order to 'harmonise procedures and to provide the means of co-financing' (CDC 1982: 11). There were eight members of Interact in the early 1980s, jointly responsible for £1.6 billion annually (CDC 1983: 10).[3] Interact is now incorporated within EDFI, with working groups that meet regularly and a CEO group that meets annually, all for the 'exchange of views on development topics' (EDFI 2007).

The European institutions had 'widely differing relationships overseas' which led to 'fruitful areas of co-operation' with, for example, the CDC specialism in agriculture used to provide 'know-how' to DEG, who 'had long wished to participate in agricultural development but lacked German partners', while the Caisse Centrale de Coopération Economique (CCCE) 'introduced CDC to the Ivory Coast' and in turn, by 1982 their funds were 'becoming available' for projects in Anglophone Africa (CDC 1982: 11). In Tyler's periodisation of the CDC – The Development Bank (1964–83); The Development Finance Institution (1984–94); The Emerging Private Equity Investor (1994–2000); and The Fund of Funds (2000–present) (Tyler 2008) – this cross-investment helped the CDC move from its first to its second model, with several large agribusiness ventures jointly promoted, acquired and managed, with CDC now the principal vehicle of British PSD, with private businesses as recipients and investments on or near commercial terms. By 1996, CDC was charged with placing 25 per cent of all new investment in equity (Tyler 2008: 18). Investments were even made in countries where governments had defaulted on their sovereign debt obligations to CDC, but where deals had been struck and CDC accepted debt service payments in local currency in order to reinvest them.[4] Agribusiness represented 54 per cent of CDC's total African investment portfolio in 1996 (Tyler 2008: 18).

However, Tyler summarises that 'generally, investing as a minority partner alongside private entrepreneurs was not a success', since some had little capital of their own, viewed projects as 'low stakes gambles', had little experience or were 'expert fraudsters' (2008: 19), such that 'CDC made a substantial loss on the African agribusiness investments that it made during this period, writing off over half of the capital invested' (2008: 20). This desire to support private-sector development left as its legacy an enriched state class of new equity owners and an impoverished capital account on the balance of payments of poor countries in so far as state guaranteed loans were implicated in the failures. Many parastatal agricultural development authorities also took stakes, such as ARDA in Zimbabwe, in Rusitu Valley dairy production, the Cold Storage Commission and South Downs Tea, and were then left with increased debt burdens when the project failed but no income streams when the project succeeded and was privatised, such as with the refurbishment of Hippo Valley and Triangle Sugar estates on CDC's 'exit'. In other words, this mode of investment has as a moral hazard, that private entrepreneurs can't lose and the public purse can't win. The least worst outcome in some countries is that a relatively honest ruling elite emerged with acumen in holding equity positions and accumulating through investment of capital: a key function of a capitalist ruling class. Thus, this development finance period helped facilitate the growth of finance capital and accumulation. All the high turnover African stock exchanges in Anglophone countries, for example (and the supreme example of this is now Ghana, following Zimbabwe's demise), were catalysed by the listing of DFI-sponsored large companies created with exchangeable equity. Pools of venture capital funds were created in this period, by CDC, IFC and other DFIs, to liquidate the new exchanges.

In the current period there is resurgence in private sector finance, alongside a spurt in growth in some private sectors, while the Great Predators retain a leading role in listing stock for companies, and·in sponsoring financial institutions and instruments. The IFC set up its Capital Markets Department back in 1971 and initiates a 'high proportion' of financial sector interventions itself, as an advisor and investor, and sees its role in the financial sector as transmitting efficiency to the economy as a whole, and of changing ownership conventions away from family firms to listed companies as a competitiveness measure. Meanwhile, the AfDB summarises that it made a sevenfold increase in private sector operations from 2004 to 2007 (AfDB 2008: 9), while Africa's GDP growth rate has exceeded 5.5 per cent since 2004, with 25 countries achieving GDP growth rates of above 5 per cent and 14 achieving GDP growth rates of between 3 and 5 per cent. The AfDB suggest that the 'drivers' are macroeconomic stability, debt relief and global expansion (AfDB 2008: 32). For example, debt relief initiatives have reduced debt service as a proportion of exports from 13.6 per cent in 2002 to 6.3 per cent in 2007, while external debt to GDP dropped from 55.4 per cent in 2002 to 22.7 per cent in 2007 (AfDB 2008: 33). Moreover, new investors in the shape of China and India are producing significant, large interventions such as $10 billion by Indian national oil companies (Naidu 2008: 118). However, growth in itself is not an unqualified positive. The argument of this book is that systemic reform is required to democratise the political economy of development before renewed indebtedness merely reaffirms dependent development.

Conclusion

In an interview in London in 1993, a senior representative at the CDC bemoaned the amorality of the new 'merchant bankers' who were replacing his generation at board level. He then gave a telling analysis of the political gain to the British elite of having the CDC, despite the erosion of its developmental role by commercialisation:

> I think it can be argued that it suits ... the current government, to maintain CDC, doing a bit of what its doing because it doesn't cost the government anything. If they cut the supply of funding, and let ourselves fend for ourselves from the turnover that we have, which is what they're doing, then unless we go into the red and they have to bail us out, and that hasn't happened, it costs us, it costs them nothing. And it, then, enables the government to say, to outsiders, that yes, we are providing ... money.
>
> (interview, London, 1993)

CDC investments are counted by OECD convention as either 'Official Development Assistance' (ODA), or 'Other Official Flows' (OOF), as we explored in chapter 6, depending on how concessional they are. But in either category they increase the UK's apparent contribution to international aid. The CDC official used the example of Sri Lanka, where 'just little dribs and drabs' of aid money were appearing but where CDC could invest and:

> they can then say, it's ... aid. So it's a political thing, and for political reasons I think they will keep the CDC doing what they would like to keep the CDC doing, what it does. To be called developmental in inverted commas. On the other hand, CDC is, there is a pressure by the government to make us behave like a merchant bank .... So, one side is the political benefit of having a tame organisation, that says it does development, and on the other hand turning this into a bank.
>
> (ibid.)

This official predicted that privatisation would cause the CDC to lose its 'mission' and he was correct; by 2008, the new generation of bankers had done their work. What is perhaps surprising is that the Government can still pretend to be doing its utmost for the private sector development of poor countries, despite such changes in the CDC's ownership. Therein lies the great power of the symbolic arsenal of the Great Predators. A critique of development assistance to the private sector, even 15 years on, is still a voice from the margins because of the structural ability of the powerful to confuse and obfuscate the material meaning of their activities using symbolic power and the moral language of development.

At a global level the Great Predators still effectively decide when a country is deemed to be acceptable to further injections of finance capital, overwhelmingly a position reached through adherence to neoliberalism. These resources in turn are marketed under the PSD brand and are supposed to develop local markets, industries and economies and fuel growth, development and participation. However, much of the froth of advocacy for PSD instruments has proved contradictory. It is good ideological cover for market intervention done on the Predators' own accounts, but the PSD instruments themselves are not the new, catalytic, cutting edge and superior policies that is pretended. Instead, they tend to support capital exports and agglomerations of their national and regional interests abroad, in the case of the European and North American DFIs at least.

The sheer size, scope and profitability of these DFIs justifies their being called the 'Great Predators', as they have collectivised the common interests of capital owners in Europe and North America, represent them through a pseudo-public institution and then roam global market places and the national stock exchanges of poorer countries looking for large national firms to invest in. In this, they fundamentally sponsor inequality. Much has been said of the 'missing middle' in African economies, that is, that there are a few large firms that dominate African economies, coexisting with a large number of micro and small enterprises, the majority of which exist in the informal sector, but a dearth of medium-sized firms (OECD 2007: 13; OECD and AfDB 2005). These Great Predators contribute to that problem. It is a consequence of the type of private sector development that they sponsor. That DFIs carry size and its attendant institutional supports in supplier credit, export insurance, market access, equity and government sponsorship, explains somewhat why there is now this super class of African large firms and then nothing beneath them save the micro enterprises.

Notes

1. Converted at US$1 = €0.629291 to 1 decimal place on 16 July 2008.
2. The APDF was established in 1986 and was also partly financed by the AfDB and UNDP, and received funding from the governments of 15 industrial countries (IFC 1992b).
3. From the 1982 Annual Report the eight can be listed as: the German Finance Company for Investments in Developing Countries (DEG), the Danish Industrialisation Fund (IFU), the Belgian Société Belge d'Investissement International (SBI), the French Caisse Centrale de Coopération Economique (CCCE), the German Kreditanstalt für Wiederaufbau (KfW), the Netherlands Development Finance Company (FMO), the British CDC and the EIB (CDC 1982: 11).
4. Tanzania, Zambia, Malawi, Ivory Coast and Cameroon defaulted.

9 Taking the long view of promoting capitalism

We saw in chapter 2 how poorer countries must rely on three sources of money: private investment, debt relief and 'new' aid, and that in general the poorer a country is, the more it relies on public finance. This chapter looks at a case study of British flows of investment, debt relief and aid, which go abroad to poorer countries. The case study shows, for Britain at least, that while recent noise about increasing the benevolence of the political economy of development has attracted much attention, when you look at the actual numbers involved, it is clear that the system of international economic relations has not changed substantively, and remains a system which serves the privileged capital owners in Britain the most. The numbers on the balance sheets have merely been tweaked. This chapter shows how the figures just don't add up to 'development' in our British case study, first by exploring the actual flows of money and then by assessing British interventions historically in the private sectors of Ghana and Zimbabwe in more detail. The data illustrate that ring-fenced pools of privilege were sponsored in these countries, much profit is made there, and that the debt relief that has occurred refers largely to write-offs of money given to British and African elites, to the general expense of both the British taxpayer and the African poor. In this conclusion, both the arguments of Teresa Hayter's *Aid as Imperialism* (1972) and Susan George's *The Debt Boomerang* (1991) are brought to mind, reiterated and updated with empirical evidence.

Post-colonial disinvestment

Bennell summarised of the 1980s, that in 'English speaking Africa ... chronic and persistent' shortages of foreign exchange meant that even when companies were making a healthy profit in local currency rates of return, the effective rate of return in sterling to parent companies was much lower, because subsidiaries had difficulty remitting (1990: 166). This shortage of foreign exchange in English-speaking African countries thus aggravated disinvestment in the 1989–94 period, as companies responded to these problems of getting their profits 'out' (Bennell 1994: 8). In fact, outward investment to selected sub-Saharan African countries to the mid-1990s did not recover from the low levels of the mid-1980s, a problem compounded by the high variance of year-on-year investment flows, and thus their relative unreliability (Central Statistical Office (CSO) 1996). In effect, while the pool of private lending had been growing globally, little was reaching Africa and in the case of UK private investment to Anglophone ex-colonies, there has been little overall recovery since 1982, but rather a long-run process of company withdrawal to date. Indeed, it is a sad irony that in 2005, the year of Prime Minister Tony Blair's Commission for Africa, there was a historic disinvestment from Africa by UK companies, despite it being something of a boom year of earnings elsewhere.

Thus, direct investment sent abroad by British companies during the single year 2006 rose to £49.4 billion (an increase of £4.9 billion on the amount invested in 2005), contributing to an International Investment Position (the overall level of foreign direct investment) at the end of 2006 of £734.7 billion, which then generated earnings of £84.6 billion, the highest level ever recorded (Office for National Statistics (ONS[1]) 2008: 3). However, despite increases in all other geographic areas, Africa showed a large decrease in net direct investment flow from £5.8 billion in 2005 to £0.3 billion in 2006, and a commensurate decrease in earnings of £2.3 billion (ONS 2008: 2–3).[2] At the end of 2006, Africa was home to just 2 per cent of the book value level of direct investment abroad of British companies, after a decrease of £5.3 billion in a single year (ONS 2008a: 2).[3] This paucity of funds can be seen graphically in Figure 9.1, where the destinations of UK investment flows in millions of pounds were Europe (£16.0), the Americas (£21.2), Asia (£8.3), Australasia and Oceania (£3.6) and Africa (£0.3) (ONS 2008).

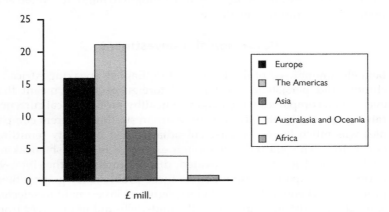

Figure 9.1 Net direct investment abroad by UK companies in 2006
Source: ONS (2008a)

Table 9.1 shows the relatively small amounts, in millions of pounds, of UK foreign direct investment (FDI) to selected African countries, including the 'big five' – Egypt, Kenya, Nigeria, South Africa and Zimbabwe – which have been in receipt of most investment from the UK historically, between 1997 and 2006. The Africa total is made up of the separate figures by country shown here, and also data for countries not included here, for all other African countries. The table entries comprise the sum of all the years 1997–2006 inclusive, and other areas are included in order to put these figures into relative perspective. The world total sum of net UK FDI flows abroad, for all the years 1997–2006 inclusive was over £646 billion, over £550 billion of which went to countries in the OECD and over £311 billion of which went to Europe (where a billion is 1,000 million). Africa received nearly £22 billion (a mere 7 per cent of the European total), but still more than Central and Eastern Europe at over £3.6 billion, China at just over £4 billion and Australia at nearly £10 billion. As can be seen in Table 9.1, investment flows to South Africa dwarfed all other investment flows to Africa in this period, being more than four times the amount of all the other countries listed put together, and singularly constituting over 71 per cent of the total for all of Africa.

The nearly £22 billion investment flow for the period 1997–2006 helped to generate an investment position in Africa worth around £15.5 billion at the end of 2006, up from just under £6 billion in 1997, with a high of nearly £21 billion in 2005 (see Figure 9.2). Investment positions differ from investment flows, as they represent the year end totals, or value, of investment overseas. The net investment positions for British investment in Africa reflects historical legacy, but also shows few enlarged investment stocks for the modern period, excepting South Africa. Recently, there has been some recovery in the overall investment position between 1997 and 2006 (as compared to the early 1990s), but again, just over half of renewed British investment in Africa can be attributed to South Africa. Investment in Kenya and Nigeria has remained stagnant. For Kenya, British investments were worth £361 million in 1997, and then they declined slightly to £315 million by 2006. In Nigeria, again there wasn't much change over these years, with an investment position worth £1,009 million in 2006, as compared to £1,060 million in 1997. Investment in Zimbabwe unsurprisingly declined over the period from £192 million in 1997, to £58 million in 2006, despite a large investment flow figure (in Table 9.1) of £378 million for the same years, much of which has, presumably, been lost or subject to local devaluation. Thus, the biggest jump, which is by far the largest contributor to 'Africa as a whole', is South Africa, where the value of British investment rose from around £2.5 billion in 1997 to over £8.6 billion in 2006, peaking at £13.7 billion in 2005. In other

Table 9.1 Some destinations of UK foreign direct investment flows abroad, 1997–2006

	1997–2006[a] (£ mill.)
Total Europe	311,365
Central and Eastern Europe	3,676
China	4,079
Australia	9,903
Africa	21,975
of which:	
Kenya	614
Nigeria	507
South Africa	15,697
Zimbabwe	378
Cameroon [b]	46
Egypt	1,760
Ghana	347
Malawi [b]	40
Mauritius [b]	−175
Tanzania [b]	70
Zambia	137

Notes:
(a) These are summary figures obtained from adding the totals for 1997–2006. Where a negative entry occurs (indicating a net disinvestment by the UK parent companies in their foreign affiliates), it is deducted from the cumulative total. Negative figures occur in Egypt 1998; Cameroon, 2004 and 2006; and Mauritius spectacularly in 2006 at −713.
(b) In the original ONS tables '..' appears in cells to indicate 'confidential data that cannot be released'. In nine of the ten years each, Sierra Leone and Swaziland had this type of embargoed data: in other words the cells were blank, marked '..'. These series have been omitted completely here. Cameroon had confidential data/non-recorded data in 1999 and 2001; Malawi in 1999; Mauritius in 2000, 2003 and 2005; and Tanzania in 2000. These countries have been included here, consequently without the data for these cells, such that there is an error relating to what happened in those years.

Source: ONS: *Foreign Direct Investment surveys* (Crown Copyright 2008).

words, over 55 per cent of all British investment held in Africa is in South Africa.

The ONS also has data on firms' destinations for investment by industrial sector, but much of this data for sub-Saharan Africa is incomplete to the public gaze, and is not released because of confidentiality considerations. These considerations arise principally because there are so few investors in these countries and sectors, perhaps only one company reporting for each cell category, and so they could be identified by a 'knowledgeable party',[4] and this is deemed unacceptable by current rules for the release of government statistics. From what is included for 'Africa as a whole', we can see that the financial services and retail and wholesale sectors are the largest earners, although the country-based data for the former is largely embargoed, with some large investments also in mining and quarrying, particularly in South Africa.

While these investment positions are comparatively small in global terms, are unevenly spread and are largely stagnant with the exception of South Africa, their profitability is still very high, absolutely and comparatively. If the earnings from these investment positions are expressed as a percentage of the value of the investment, the earnings for Africa as a whole represent over 22.5 per cent in the single year 2006. In other words, against an investment position of around £15.45 billion, earnings were just under £3.48 billion. The equivalent profit rates for Kenya, Nigeria, South Africa and Zimbabwe for British investments in 2006 were 27.9, 13.2, 18.7 and (even) 17.2 per cent respectively.[5] What these numbers add up to are investments in Africa that have not grown in the vast majority of countries, but have declined overall except in South Africa, but which remain highly lucrative to their owners. These types of returns are largely unheard of in more 'developed' countries, and while in business vernacular this would be explained by reference to high risk, a quick look at the data for all the years 1997–2006 shows that this is not an exceptional year, in fact in the boom year of 2005 profitability shot to 27.6 per cent for Africa as a whole. In other words, there is no evidence that the supposed 'high risk' translated into lower returns in any of the years examined. This raises the question of how poorer countries can be expected to fund adequate public services when they have to permanently surrender such large proportions of their efforts to capital owners. The rise of investment value premised on South Africa is illustrated in Figure 9.2, where the top line is the value of investments in 'Africa as a whole', while the second is the value of investments in South Africa, plotted for the years 1997–2006.

A review of the fairness of British economic relations overseas

The figures above reflect outgoing investments, but what is perhaps most critical to a judgement of fairness in international relations between states is the relationship between what one country puts in to another, in relation to what it takes out. Economists refer to this as the payments position, but when one country or group is supposedly developing it is more complex than merely comparing private flows, since ostensibly concessionary ones must be considered too. For the

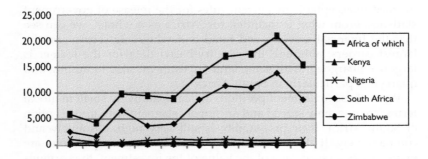

Figure 9.2 UK investment position in selected African countries, 1997–2006
Source: ONS (2008), Table MA4 3.1, in £ mill.

figures we have reviewed above, we can now compare the magnitudes of aid, debt and investment in relation to each other for our British case study: The Department for International Development's (DfID) bilateral assistance to sub-Saharan Africa was £1,107 million in 2006–07; while the net foreign direct investment position in Africa of UK companies in 2006 was £15,455 million (15 times more); and net earnings from foreign direct investment in Africa in 2006 were £3,479 million (three times more) (DfID 2008; ONS 2008). In other words, the payments position in this continental account appears to be well in the UK's favour,[6] despite rhetorical commitment to the Millennium Development Goals (MDGs) and the generalised perception that as a creditor country its benevolence is expressed by transferring resources overseas, rather than the reality of a situation where the flow is in the other direction in terms of many of the poorest countries and is in the UK's favour overall. So what about the much publicised debt relief?

Which institutions in Britain are owed debt?

States who default on intergovernmental loans may have their eligibility for renewed borrowing reduced for some time, while the actual debts they have accrued are accounted for over a longer period than in the creditor states' yearly balance of payments account. The frontier institutions are important here as vessels in which debts owed can be stored, to ameliorate their negative effect on short-term liquidity. In other words, many debts owed by African countries to the British state from the 1982 crisis and in the aftermath of the 1991 recession were transferred to the frontier institutions of the British state. It is interesting in this respect to note, for example, that much of the debt write-off by the UK Government in 2005 and 2006 referred to debts owed to the Export Credit Guarantee Department (ECGD) and Commonwealth Development Corporation (CDC) – rather than to the DfID directly – and we can speculate that these were of some vintage. Indeed, a House of Commons Library research paper notes that 'Most of the debt relief provided by the UK pertains to debts owed to the ECGD by low and lower-middle income countries under Paris Club debt rescheduling agreements' (2007: 25), amounting to more than $4 billion from 2004 to 31 January 2007. As we can see from Table 9.2, by far the largest cancellation was in respect of Nigeria, followed by Zambia, both of which must refer to debt acquired some time ago, since neither has been allowed to borrow such amounts in the 1990s.

If the debt stock held against the British state is broken down, the liabilities to ECGD are the largest, then CDC, with DfID coming a much smaller third, as illustrated in Table 9.3. Most of these historic

Table 9.2 UK debt relief on debts owed to Export Credit Guarantee Department, for low income countries, 2004–07

	Total debt relief [a] 2004–07 in £ mill.
Ivory Coast	1.0
D. R. Congo	2.4
Ethiopia	10.6
Ghana	82.7
Madagascar	24.1
Malawi	1.1
Niger	5.0
Nigeria	2,800.0
Senegal	1.0
Sierra Leone	2.7
Zambia	291.9
Total*	4,096.2

Notes:
In £ millions to one decimal place.
[a] Total debt relief includes flow and or stock relief.
* These totals include a further section of the table for lower-middle income countries omitted here.

Source: Derived from table 2, House of Commons Library (2007), at:
www.parliament.uk/commons/lib/research/rp2007/rp07-051.pdf, citing House of Commons Debate,
19 February 2007, c475-6WA.

liabilities relate to disbursements of development finance from the 1980s and 1990s. Thus, the debt cancellation from 2003–04 to 2005–06, granted for low-income countries in respect to ECGD was over £4,000 million, nearly two-thirds of which went to Nigeria, while the comparable figures for CDC were only £42 million and for DfID a paltry nearly £12 million, which are generous summary figures since some of the flow relief could relate to stock subsequently cancelled which is an indirect form of double counting if the debt is not performing (HC Library 2007: 36). According to a House of Commons Library paper, in 2005–06, CDC was still owed a total of £23.4 million by low-income countries, whereas DfID was owed £9.1 million and the World Bank, where DfID is a creditor, £26.3 million. So the Commonwealth Development Corporation is the tail wagging the proverbial dog when it comes to debt relief, with bigger transactions than the formal Department for International Development, who ostensibly oversee its affairs (HC Library 2007: 36).

What these figures illustrate is that aid to the private sector (and marginally to parastatals) has, for 30 years or so, been much larger than aid to the public sector and its social institutions in developing countries, and that much of current debt relief relates to liabilities generated there, in unpaid loans for ports, bridges, sugar processing mills and the like. By far the largest source of liabilities (roughly 74 times more, if the ECGD figures are compared to the sum of the CDC and DfID totals combined) relates to exported equipment though the ECGD, which includes military equipment where the purchaser simply didn't pay up, and the UK taxpayer was thus forced to pay out in insurance claims against the ECGD, which were then eventually written off. In this most common scenario, not only did the original 'aid' have a low 'developmental' value in the first instance, which hardly justifies its accounting as part of a sovereign development debt, but these non-payments were covered by British Government reinsurance cover in any case. Some dictatorship got the guns, British citizens paid, and then the bill was counted as debt relief![7]

Indeed, UK debt write-offs seem to be concentrated in a few strategic countries in terms of the large deals, and pertain to the long-running debts of the frontier institutions as mentioned above. For example, 'DFID debt relief through all channels amounted to £145m in 2006/07. Non-DFID debt relief (through CDC and ECGD) was £1,867m, £1,649m of which relates to Nigerian debt relief' (DfID 2008). Moreover, debt write-offs are also additionally counted as increases in Official Development Assistance (ODA) in the year they are affected, such that apparent generosity in the present can be portrayed and political capital is made by the British Government appearing as a good global citizen, while the bulk of the money actually goes to debt

Table 9.3 Debts owed and relief granted against CDC, DfID and World
Bank, 2003–06

	CDC	DfID	World Bank, where DfID a creditor
Debt owed, total for low-income countries	23.41	9.11	26.28
Flow relief (debt relief granted)	9.97	2.79	
Stock cancellation 2003–06	32.19	9.04	
Total debt relief (stock and flow)	42.16	11.83	

Notes:
CDC (Commonwealth Development Corporation), DfID (Department for International Development)
Converted from £ thousands to £ millions to two decimal places. Rounding errors will have occurred.

Source: Compiled from Appendix 1, House of Commons (HC) Library (2007), p. 36, table: 'UK Debts
owed and debt relief given to low income and lower middle income countries', citing HC Debate 15
January 2007, cm 743-8WA.

initially related to commercial transactions in the better-off countries.
Here, nearly all debt write-off goes to the ECGD for its past insurance
for commercial deals in Nigeria – where the UK supplier wasn't paid –
but because this figure (over £1,600 million) is subsequently added to
the general figures for all other countries (£145 million) a generalised
generosity can be portrayed.

Thus, a House of Commons research paper can summarise that the
UK has 'exceeded' its debt relief commitment by cancelling 100 per cent
of all bilateral debts for highly indebted poor countries (HIPCs) that
qualified for debt relief under the Multilateral Debt Relief Initiative
(MDRI) (HC Library 2007). As of February 2007 the UK had cancelled all
its outstanding sovereign claims for Cameroon, Ethiopia, Ghana, Mada-
gascar, Malawi, Niger, Senegal, Sierra Leone and Zambia, while the
Democratic Republic of Congo, Republic of Congo and Ivory Coast had
received 'full debt flow relief' and were waiting for 'full stock cancellation' once they reach HIPC completion point' (HC Library 2007: 25).[8]
This sounds impressive, but pertains to the smaller £145 million figure.
Meanwhile, and again in aggregate, between 2004 and 2005 UK ODA to
Africa reportedly increased from £1.3 billion to £2.1 billion, a rise of
nearly 60 per cent. However, when this debt relief is excluded the
amount of aid to Africa actually decreased slightly from 2004 to 2005.
Similarly, the increase in bilateral aid to sub-Saharan Africa was from
£2.1 billion in 2005 to £2.9 billion in 2006, a rise of 41 per cent, but when
debt relief is excluded it represents a smaller, but not insignificant 29 per

cent rise. Table 9.4 contains a further breakdown of debt relief figures. The top five rows are mostly intergovernmental loans, and the latter three previous loans to the private sector, for the earlier years 2003–06. Again, the predominance of write-offs to the commercial sector is in evidence, while the much publicised schemes – HIPC, MDRI – garner much fewer resources.

Even grants under the World Bank's Debt Reduction Facility have been handed straight back to the private sector, in order to reduce commercial debt:

> used to eliminate approximately $8 billion of low-income country debt by providing grants that enable those countries to buy back commercial debts at a 90 per cent discount (on average). This programme helps protect low-income countries from 'vulture fund' litigation, whereby their commercial debt is bought up at a discount and then enforced through the courts.
>
> (HC Library 2007: 27)[9]

Thus, not only are these payments to commercial banks counted under overhead 'increases in ODA', but so too is debt relief which comprises a write-down in ECGD liabilities, and, as we explored in chapters 4 and 6, CDC Group investments and the promissory notes deposited in respect of the United Nations, World Bank and regional development banks and funds. No wonder authors such as Bond (2006) refer to 'phantom aid'.

Table 9.4 Total DfID and UK debt relief, 2003–06

	2003–04	2004–05	2005–06
DfID debt relief	16	15	40
Bilateral HIPC	18	13	1
Multilateral HIPC Trust Fund	20	42	11
MDRI debt relief to IMF			14
Total DfID debt relief	54	70	65
CDC debt	12	35	18
ECGD debt	163	583	1,570
Total CDC and ECGD debt	176	618	1,588
Total UK debt relief	229	688	1,653

Note: In £ millions.

Source: DfID (2006) *Statistics on International Development 2001/02–2005/06*, October.

Where did the debt come from?

The CDC historically has often had a direct involvement in production in order to reduce risk, often owning or managing its largest commitments and so using the institution of the firm to enclose its investments more safely. Alone among DFIs, the CDC has owned and maintained a significant number of projects, nearly half of which were involved in African estate agriculture until the sell-off to Actis (14 out of 30 managed companies were in this category in 1993 (CDC 1993: 24)). Many dated from the earliest colonial plantation investments; most were in primary commodity production for export, such as in oil palm, cocoa, rubber, tea, coffee, sugar and forestry; and in most of them CDC remained the largest shareholder, such that the combined equity in managed companies represented 62 per cent of the portfolio in 1992 (CDC 1993: 24). The CDC claimed that all had a 'valuable demonstration effect in proving the viability of estate agriculture' (CDC 1993: 24).

However, this demonstration effect would appear stymied if the market conditions of the Zimbabwean investments are anything to go on: the critical CDC loans were in sectors, such as sugar and beef, where EU trading concessions under the Lomé Conventions guaranteed an export market in the 1990s, which would not be repeatable for others. Also, and again preventing 'demonstration effects', in Zimbabwe and other countries, local firms could not be 'catalysed' because CDC companies were of such a large size that output effectively saturated markets. This was particularly the case where CDC companies were large ventures in small economies, with, for example, the Soloman Islands Plantations Ltd, an oil palm and cocoa estate, responsible for all the islands' production of oil palm and 10 per cent of national export earnings in the early 1990s. Similarly, in Swaziland, a 50 per cent CDC-owned sugar complex, Mhlume (Swaziland) Sugar Ltd, milled one-third of national output in 1992, growing one-third of this itself, while a further third of mill throughput was provided by the Inyoni Yami Swaziland Irrigation Scheme, which was also 50 per cent owned by CDC. The Mhlume mill also processed sugarcane cultivated by out-growers involved in the Vuvulane Irrigated Farms Scheme, whose general manager was provided by CDC (CDC 1993: 25–6). In forestry, similar large estates crowd out, rather than in, other firms: Tanganyika Wattle of Tanzania (established in 1956), and Usutu Pulp of Swaziland (established in 1948 and then sold out to SAPPI, a South African firm, in 2000) are both significant exporters in their host countries, and the latter was the largest block of man-made forest in Africa in the early 1990s, producing 10 per cent of Swaziland's export earnings (CDC 1993: 30). Actis still owns forestry assets which are market dominant, such as Shiselweni in Swaziland and Kilombero Valley Teak in Tanzania.

It is also difficult to take even a cursory glance at the Actis portfolio now and suggest that they have any interest in infant industries or demonstration effects. For example, a relatively recent acquisition (in May 2003) was of a 14 per cent stake in Flamingo Holdings with a $16 million equity stake, a fully integrated horticultural business involved in growing, processing, packaging, marketing and distribution of flowers and fresh vegetables, with a wholly owned subsidiary in Kenya, Homegrown, Africa's largest exporter of vegetables and flowers to the UK and owner of a 15 per cent market share of Kenya's horticultural exports (Actis 2008a; Actis 2008c). Also, Flamingo has processing, distribution and marketing operations in the UK, and is the UK's leading supplier to supermarkets, including Marks & Spencer, Tesco, Sainsbury and Safeway. As Actis summarises:

> CDC's investment will be used to support the company's growth plans, which include the acquisition of other horticultural businesses in Africa and the UK to strengthen its supply chain and expand its capacity and product range.
>
> (Actis 2008a)

Flamingo also sources from Zimbabwe, South Africa, Guatemala, Thailand, Spain and the Netherlands, and had a worldwide annual turnover of $250m when Actis bought its stake (Actis 2008a). Michael Turner, CDC's East African director, reportedly commented:

> Flamingo is exactly the type of business CDC is looking to invest in – an integrated business with control of the entire supply chain, managed by an excellent team of experienced and committed professionals with a successful track record. Its position as an innovator and supplier of the highest quality products means that it has exciting growth prospects.
>
> (ibid.)

While Flamingo, we are told, meets CDC's benchmarks on social and environmental standards, none of the 1990s arguments for the role of CDC capital as augmenting and not displacing capital, and being innovative with a possible demonstration effect in a particularly risky environment seem to apply here. The additional classic of CDC annual reports, of being prepared to be in 'for the long haul', also seems affronted, as Actis exited just four years later in August 2007, when 100 per cent of Flamingo Holdings was sold to James Finlay Ltd, a long-established (colonial plantation) company and wholly owned subsidiary of John Swire and Sons Limited (a UK-originated global conglomerate) (Actis 2008b); hardly a sale likely to promote a deepening of Kenyan capital or ownership. Since Flamingo had tripled in size while Actis was a shareholder, and since John Swire already owned premier tea plantations in Kenya, Uganda and Sri Lanka, the sale tends to support a rather different effect of DFI investment, that it seeks out and then promotes privileged market leaders at great profit to itself and to them, with Actis pocketing the profits and John Swire lengthening its market lead; more a predator behaviour than a developmental one.

Private sector development in action: the British case

The CDC claims that status, experience and worldwide contacts are the basis of its ability to reduce risk. In practice, risk reduction is secured more directly, by institutional oversight at the level of the firm, or its 'parent' national development finance company. Also, throughout the period since the early 1980s the CDC, and the Great Predators in general, have made many references to their relationships with governments which can reduce risk at a higher and potentially more decisive level. For example, the IFC, with its 'long experience with business conditions' in developing countries, assured investors that 'by exercising its latitude to say "no", IFC can influence governments to change policies that impede capital market development' (IFC 1992: 10–11). This ability to say 'no' forms the cornerstone of the power of development finance institutions and has provided the basis for conditionality since their earliest days.

In 1949 the CDC Board reported friendly relations with 'most' of the government and government departments in the colonies, saw their co-operation as 'desirable, to say the least', and then pursued an early assertion of conditionality by remarking that:

> unless a sufficient minimum of consideration and active assistance is forthcoming, the Corporation would hardly feel justified in considering any substantial investment in the area concerned.
>
> (CDC 1949: 46)

The onset of the era of structural adjustment and conditionality provided an extension of this historic power by codifying a more complex set of rules and relationships which governed the likelihood of a DFI saying 'yes'. This was both due to the beneficial effects of adjustment in terms of the institutions' own profitability, a fact which encouraged new investment to be made as a reward, and indirectly due to the effects of adjustment on the macroeconomic climate, thus reducing perceived country risk overall. So, the two types of PSD instrument discussed in chapter 8 – market and investment climate – have been clearly used together for some time.

The CDC itself notes the relationship and asserts that, citing the example of Ghana where its portfolio grew rapidly following the onset of an adjustment programme, its investments 'help to encourage Governments to persist with economic reform, because they are seen as part of the fruits of reform' (CDC 1993: 1). A brief look at the CDC country portfolios in post-adjustment African countries of the 1980s and 1990s confirms this point: there was a general pattern of new investments predominantly following the onset of adjustment programmes. For example, the 1983 IMF-supported Economic Recovery Programme (ERP) in Ghana, was welcomed by the CDC, whose portfolio consequently grew from £4 million in the mid-1980s to more than £29 million at the end of 1992 (CDC 1993: 33). Table 9.5 shows the CDC portfolio in Ghana following structural adjustment, and then the provenance of the investments by 2008. Only the first investment predates adjustment, and while some money assisted the public utilities sector, CDC's involvements are predominantly export-oriented or in the financial sector, illustrating well the role of DFIs in providing institutions and structures for the export, and then recycling, of finance capital from the core states. In Ghana the CDC worked in collaboration with the World Bank-sponsored Financial Sector Reform Programme (to privatise state-owned banks and extend 'financial services'), as a founder shareholder in Continental Acceptances Ltd, a merchant bank which began operations in 1990 as a 30 per cent shareholder in Ghana Leasing Co. Ltd, and with USAID established Ghana's first venture capital fund for 'emerging entrepreneurs', with the CDC providing the general manager. The loan to Ghana Bauxite Co. Ltd involved British-based Alcan Chemicals Ltd, while hotel investment (with IFC) was to Lonrho (CDC 1993: 34–5). Also, the CDC funded British contractors for the rehabilitation of the Tropical Glass factory and the transmission system for the Electricity Corporation of Ghana Ltd (CDC 1993: 32).

Ghana, 25 years on

The CDC summarises that before Ghana's Economic Recovery Programme (ERP), they could only find one 'suitable investment', but that 'activity picked up strongly' once it was in place (CDC 1993: 33). This pattern held for Tanzania, Zimbabwe and Malawi as well (Bracking 1997). By 2008, the claims that DFI money assists the growth and development of the private sector in the long run can begin to be assessed. Tyler (2008) does this for all CDC investments in agriculture from 1948 onward, and overall there is a mixed record across the portfolio. In terms of Ghana, Table 9.5 lists ERP investments and their destinies.[10] Many of these firms have spent much of this time with periodic cash-flow problems which require refinancing, often by other DFIs, which suggests that CDC was correct in their assessment that they were not initially displacing the (competitive) private sector. The electricity projects, still state owned, remain in serious deficit and requiring funds. The private sector projects have mixed results, with the Bauxite company clearly a success and thus sold off to a multinational in Alcan, while the food processing concerns remain troubled. The financial services and capital funds are also successfully functioning in the private sector and with DFI refinancing, illustrating that the Ghana capital market has been a success story in terms of Africa as a whole, warranting an AfDB bond issue in cedi in 2008 (AfDB 2008). However, UK consultants continue to provide technical assistance to the Ghanaian financial sector, and also to financial services across Africa. For example, just for the World Bank, not CDC, from 2000 to 2007, contracts worth $24,644 million were awarded to UK consultants for work in Africa in the financial services sector, of which $2.29 million was for work in Ghana, according to the procurement database, although as explained above, this does not include all contracts the World Bank makes, so the figure is probably higher.[11]

Tanzania, Malawi, Uganda and Zambia

In Tanzania, Malawi, Uganda and Zambia structural adjustment was used to build the strength of the CDC portfolio, but again, not predominantly in cutting edge new projects but to refinance older colonial ventures, often where British companies also had a stake. In Tanzania, after the onset of adjustment CDC invested £40 million in three years as compared to a total portfolio of £69.7 million, such that over 57 per cent of their portfolio in 1992 had been committed in the previous three years (CDC 1993: 18), although this is quite a disingenuous overhead statistic, since if the CDC Annual Report and Accounts for 1992 are interrogated further, it turns out that just under 60 per cent of the whole value of CDC commitments in Tanzania was a rescheduled government loan, while CDC's own managed companies collectively received 33.44 per cent of the total loan investment on the books – East Usambara Tea Co., Karimjee Agriculture, Kilombero Valley Teak and Tanganyika Wattle – meaning that nearly 93 per cent of all the funds went to refinance CDC's own core estates[12] or to the Tanzanian Government (CDC 1993: 40). Similarly, in 1992, of the total loan investments listed as having been extended to Malawi, 63.2 per cent was

Table 9.5 CDC's investments in Ghana, 31 December 1992 and 2008 destinies

	Details (1992)	Equity %	Total £'000	2008 destiny
Twifo Oil Palm Plantations Ltd [a]	Established 1978, palm oil production		1,900	Existing, still DFI active with Unilever applying for recent funds (2005). CDC held debt in 1999.
*Volta River Authority	Electricity		10,702	State-owned, Akosombo Generating Station refitted. Some community services supplied [c, d]. CDC still held debt in 1999.
*Electricity Corporation of Ghana	Electricity, UK contractor for transmission system		6,043	State-owned. Huge losses 1997–2002. HIPC and IDA loans [d]. CDC still held debt in 1999.
Continental Acceptances Ltd	Founder shareholder, established 1990, merchant banking	15	1,488	No longer exists. Incorporated to CAL Merchant Bank. Equity stake for CDC in CAL merchant bank listed for 1999.
*Ghana Leasing Co Ltd 2004.	Equipment leasing	30	294	Existing. Eximbank application, where GLC end-user, refused in 1999.

CDC lists debt and equity holding in 1999. |
*Venture Fund Management Co Ltd	Management company [b]	45		Existing, manages funds
Ghana Venture Capital Fund	Small enterprise development finance	45	155	Managed by Venture Fund Management. USAID and UNIDO involvement. Refinanced periodically.
Ghana Bauxite Co Ltd	With UK Alcan Chemicals Ltd		2,906	Controlled and owned by Alcan Inc. Headquartered in Montreal [e]
Tropical Glass Co Ltd	Glassworks, UK contractor		650	Existing
Hotel Investments Ghana Ltd	Lonrho, IFC, hotel opened 1991		2,125	Refinanced by IFC, 1995. CDC still held debt in 1999.

Table 9.5 continued

	Details (1992)	Equity %	Total £'000	2008 destiny
*Forest Resources Industries Ltd	Pineapple and mango production		450	Debt held by CDC in 1999
Ghana Aluminium Products Ltd	Aluminium extrusion	11	434	Existing
*Millicom Ghana Ltd	Cellular telephone network		1,150	Existing
*Divine Seafoods Ltd	Seafood processing	16	22	Troubled history, subsequent Danish aid involvement (f). CDC held debt in 1999.
Astek Fruit Processing Ltd	Production, packaging of fruit juices		770	Troubled history. Subsequent UNIDO involvement (g). CDC held debt in 1999.
Total			29,089	

Notes:

* Indicates that in addition to total investments shown undisbursed commitments remained outstanding at 31 December 1992. Total is for combined equity and loans in 1992.

(a) Only pre-ERP project.

(b) Established with USAID, CDC-managed project, provides general manager.

(c) University of Ghana, Guide to Electric Power in Ghana (2005), pp. 37–8, at: www.beg.utexas.edu/energyecon/IDA/USAID/RC/Guide_to_Electric%20Power_in_Ghana.pdf

(d) VRA company website, August 2006, at: www.vra.com

(e) BizGuides, 2007, at: www.ebizguides.com/guides/sponsors/alone.php?sponsor=231&country=2

(f) http://www.business.aau.dk/ivo/publications/working/wp30.pdf

(g) UNIDO, February 2003, at: www.unido.org/fileadmin/import/11791_GHA002ASTEKLTD.pdf
CDC Report and Accounts 1999, at: www.cdcgroup.com/files/Report/UploadlReport/CDC_1999_annualreview.pdf. After 1999 the historic portfolio of loans, as apposed to ongoing equity stakes, stopped appearing in annual reports.

Sources: Compiled from CDC Development Report: Britain Investing in Development, (CDC 1993), p. 35, and CDC Report and Accounts 1992 (CDC 1993), p. 44; the latter providing column five.

on-lent to the CDC-managed Sable Farming Co Ltd, in which CDC had a 75 per cent equity stake, while a further loan to Stagecoach Malawi Ltd was to finance the importation of double-decker buses and chassis from the UK (CDC 1993: 30, 41). Commitments in Uganda were to a development finance company and to rehabilitate tea estates with a UK company, while in Kenya too a UK company was involved in a transport project (CDC 1993: 29). In Zambia, two-thirds of investments were in the renewable natural resources sector in 1992, the bulk of which was to two managed projects (MMC 1992: 126).

Zimbabwe, 15 years on, and prime investments in dispute

Of the projects in Zimbabwe that received funding from the CDC at the time of the structural adjustment programme in the early 1990s, a few have seemingly disappeared altogether, while the electricity parastatal remains in financial trouble, and is additionally periodically mired in corruption scandals (see Bracking 2009). Some new capital for the Hwange colliery and power station has reportedly arrived from the Chinese. The agribusiness ventures are under new indigenous ownership or sold out to South African firms (to Tongaat Hulett from Tate & Lyle), or are contested by land squatters (Southdown Holdings). Rusitu Valley Development Corporation was privatised, according to the World Bank privatisation database in 1994, after Zimbabwean Industrial Development Corporation involvement. In 1999 CDC held equity in Ariston Holdings Ltd, an agriculture and horticulture cultivation (for which it swapped its prior investment in Southdown Holdings); while debt in the Cold Storage Commission for wholesale beef supply and abattoir facilities, equity in Lake Harvest Aquaculture, equity and debt in Rusitu Valley Development, and equity in Zimchem Refiners for benzol and tar production, remained from the Economic Structural Adjustment Programme (ESAP) era of 1991–95.[13] Four other ESAP investments in the manufacturing sector also apparently still exist, but without CDC involvement, although there is subsequent evidence of refinancing from other DFIs and private sector companies: Mat-Tools & Forging (Pvt.) Ltd in a joint venture with a Swedish company in 2003 (The Zimbabwe Situation 2003); Retrofit, still listed as a division of Plateau Investments (Pvt.) Ltd in Harare in 2008; COPRO (Pvt.) Ltd, an ostrich farm; and Tropico Zimbabwe (Pvt.) Ltd, which was also financed by the IFC's Africa Enterprise Fund in 1993 and was a subsidiary of a UK firm of the same name (IFC 1993). In sum, the sustainability of these interventions is patchy and thin, although a proportion of the remaining British companies have enjoyed IFI assistance at some point since 1980.

According to Dianna Games, Anglo has had problems with the Government of Zimbabwe over the seizure of large tracts of its commercial farmland at Hippo Valley Estates and Triangle Sugar, which the company jointly owns with South Africa's sugar 'giant' Tongaat Hulett (Games 2006: 107). Anglo American Corporation and Tongaat Hullet own the two estates (*Zimbabwe Independent* 2005). These two, combined with Anglo's Mkwasine Estate, still produce all of Zimbabwe's sugar, mostly for export (Games 2006: 107). In fact, the shareholding is complex but more concentrated than it appears due to cross-holdings, since Tongaat is then 50.6 per cent owned by Anglo South Africa Capital (Pty) back in South Africa: in other words, Anglo sold a controlling stake of Hippo Valley to Tongatt, which it has a majority stake in through another company in its group, although this did serve to 'ring-fence' its Zimbabwean investments (see *Business Report* 2006). The British company Tate & Lyle retains a 10 per cent stake. In 2007, Triangle and Hippo Valley formed a joint venture company – Triangle Sugar Corporation – to assist farmers as it planned to boost sugarcane production among 'new farmers' (*Herald* 2008), despite Anglo remaining in dispute with the Government over the Mkwasine Estate, since subsistence farmers have settled on 90 per cent of the estate without permission (*Business Report* 2006). These estates remain prime assets targeted for ownership by the current elite in Zimbabwe (*Zimbabwe Independent* 2005). The dispute can't be too bad however, or at least accommodation with the Government seems to be ongoing, since in June 2008 Anglo, now a UK-listed company, and in the context of extreme election violence, announced a $400 million investment to develop a platinum mine at Unki (*The Times* 2008).

This concentration of foreign investment in sugar had been supported through ESAP as borrowed aid money was channelled to Triangle and Hippo under the auspices of drought relief in 1993 by both CDC and IFC. The CDC loaned the estates $75.6 million and $63 million, respectively (*Business Herald*, 27 January 1994). A senior CDC official in Harare argued that because of the capital intensity of the sugar industry, large companies were automatically required, in fact were the only companies suitable, since their size was necessary to accommodate the risk associated with investment in an 'underdeveloped' country (interview, Harare, 1994).[14] The representative did not see supporting an oligopoly as a critical problem, but argued that it was easier to deal with large companies, since their financial reporting was better and it was 'obviously' a more efficient way of investing money (interview, Harare, 1994). The cost of appraisal would not, for the CDC, justify involvement of less than £1 million at that time (interview, Harare, 1994). The viability of these investments was underwritten by quotas to both the United States and the European markets, the latter through the Lomé Convention.[15] The CDC representative explained that while the US and EC quotas were national property, and would therefore need to be shared with any other miller, the Zimbabwe Sugar Refinery (which was 51 per cent owned by Tate & Lyle at the time) effectively controlled the quota (interview, Harare, 1994). He ranked the guaranteed export market as paramount to investment decisions in sugar refining, but with the CDC 'still cautious' due to the 'small size' of the ACP quota of 35,000 tonnes (interview, Harare, 1994). In short, enclave structures of grafted-on export sectors, dependent on EU quotas which would change, were the principal result of an adjustment advertised as steering Zimbabwe to a 'free market' system. In hindsight, they helped to build up potentially plum spoils for the future kleptocracy and were vulnerable to policy change in Europe.

However, the investment climate effect may still have sponsored a more significant legacy than the individual firm-level interventions. Overall, by June 2008, over 200 UK and South African companies remained substantially invested in Zimbabwe, many of whom received a boost in the ESAP years. However, the newly passed Indigenisation and Economic Empowerment Act 2008 aims to force them to hand over majority ownership to Zimbabweans, or at least Government cronies. These companies include Lever Brothers, Barclays Bank, Standard Chartered Bank, Standard Bank, Stanbic Bank, Impala Platinum, Angloplat, Mettalon Gold, Rio Tinto, Edcon, Merchant Bank of Central Africa and several enterprises owned by Anglo American (Peta 2008).

Conclusion

The Great Predators have lent against a wide portfolio of large enclave-based firms in Anglophone Africa, and the British frontier institutions, the ECGD and CDC, have had a leading role in shaping the extractive agricultural and mineral industries in the countries covered here. That there is a 'missing middle' is thus not a surprise: without the privileged market access, the supply chains, the equity and connections to Northern governments and the BWI development banks these investments would not have been profitable. In short, they were profitable only in so far as the inequalities on which their profits relied were sustained. As markets have changed, and resistance has grown to this type of enclave growth, many of these loans went bad and became debt that sovereign governments had underwritten. After years of servicing these, they were eventually written off in a fanfare of supposed benevolence.

Notes

1. CSO and ONS is the same institution, but a change in name occurred between these two citations.
2. Direct investment 'refers to investment that adds to, deducts from or acquires a lasting interest in an enterprise', operating elsewhere, where the company owns a holding of 10 per cent or more. A lesser stake is not counted here, but is seen as portfolio investment. The figures are net, in that they measure investments net of disinvestments by a company into its subsidiaries, associate companies and branches (ONS 2008: 5).
3. The investment flow went down by £5.5 billion, while the book-value level dropped by £5.3 billion. These do not exactly match, because 'the levels estimate takes account of revaluation of foreign assets and movements in exchange rates as well as actual flows of investment. The local funding of investment deals also affects stock levels but not flows.' First Release: *Foreign Direct Investment 2006*, Ps 2 (ONS 2008a).
4. A helpful official at the ONS explained that ' '..' indicates data that may allow the returned survey value of a single respondent to be identified by other knowledgeable parties, this is used to comply with the obligations of the Statistics of Trade Act 1947 which ensures such confidentiality for published data obtained from respondents under the Act in exchange for compulsory and legally enforceable data collection by ONS. This is used to protect potentially commercially sensitive data where a respondent is a major or dominant contributor to a published data value'. My sincere thanks to Simon Harrington, of the ONS, FDI Surveys for this explanation, although the underlying logic would benefit from reform.
5. Net earnings equal profits of foreign branches plus UK companies' receipts of interest and their share of profits of foreign subsidiaries and associates. Earnings are after deduction of provisions for depreciation and foreign taxes on profits, dividends and interest. Source: MA4 4.1.
6. The bilateral aid figure is for sub-Saharan Africa rather than Africa as a whole, but it is in the former that most DfID assistance is concentrated.
7. I realise that the figures for 2003–07 are not all debt relief granted by the government (as this is not the first or only time debt has been written down), but I am taking them to be a representative sample thereof, at a high profile time for debt relief, to illustrate a problem of scale in public versus private sector development intervention.
8. Burma and Zimbabwe were the only low-income countries excluded because they 'have not been making debt payments' (HC 2007: 25).
9. Citing HC Debate 19 April 2007: c 778-9WA for the 90 per cent figure.
10. Thanks to Sojin Lim, who assisted with this research.
11. Thanks to Sithembiso Myeni who researched these figures.
12. It would not be surprising, although difficult to research, if a large proportion of the debt rescheduling given to the Government was not also returned to the CDC, since the CDC related new commitments to the ability of a government to provide forex for the purpose of paying dividends and interest on loans previously extended.
13. There were also outstanding debts across a wider portfolio from the 1990s recorded in 1999, debts owed by Wankie Colliery Company for gas processing and transmission, ZESA and Victoria Falls Safari Lodge (in

which CDC also recorded equity). Also, CDC had private equity funds in Commonwealth Africa Investments Ltd, Takura Ventures (Pty) Ltd, Venture Capital Company of Zimbabwe Ltd, plus development finance in the Zimbabwe Development Bank, whose name was changed by an Act of Parliament in March 2006 to the Infrastructure Zimbabwe Development Bank, in addition to debt financing for housing and mortgage finance in the Low Cost Housing Project, Zimbabwe and the Zimbabwe Agriculture Trust for agribusiness debt financing (CDC 1999).

14. Portfolio executive, CDC, regional office for Botswana, Mozambique, Namibia and Zimbabwe, in Harare, March 1994.

15. A quota which was carried forward from the drought year of 1992 to 1993, when there was a record crop (interview, Harare, 1994).

10 Aid effectiveness: what are we measuring?

In the last three chapters we have examined profitability within the political economy of aid, both in and of itself in chapter 7 (through direct contracts), and then in terms of the market structures it facilitates in chapters 8 and 9. In this chapter the more mainstream debate on aid effectiveness will be reviewed, to see how the political economy of development is represented within it. We conclude that the debate on aid is generally inconclusive, since the things that are being measured are generally abstracted and rarefied, such as growth, or 'good governance'. Therefore, it is not a surprise that a large debate can be held which says relatively little about the contribution of aid to wellbeing. Quite simply, the wrong things are being measured, proceeding from a misleading representation of the benevolence of aid. The mainstream focus is not on the social relationships and institutions this book has explored. This matters because it obscures class, social inequality and power in the global order.

A big and largely inconclusive debate

Much aid evaluation is carried out with a version of cost-benefit analysis and seeks to find associations between macroeconomic policy and aid effectiveness, ubiquitously measured in terms of economic growth. However, associations between aspects of development, including growth, and aid processes are difficult to find and quantify, particularly over the long term (see Lancaster 2007; Dalgaard et al. 2004). One problem is that mainstream economics tends to a 'pick and mix' approach to historical causation, along the lines of building bigger and bigger quantitative models, whereby factors are stylised, such as 'bad governance' or 'good policy', and then added into databases alongside economic measurements such as growth and income. The economists then run a regression analysis and end up with propositions on causation which generally hold across a basket of countries (the details of these are discussed in Morrissey 2004). This approach can yield some interesting results when the factors included are obviously pertinent to the question, and where outliers are treated effectively, but can become contaminated by the quality of the inputs or by historical patterns that change. In fact, as a methodology, it does not lend itself well to historical understanding at all. So when economists are asked what effect aid has on growth, they are divided. On the relationship between governance and growth, again they split, although this last time this is more to do with how 'governance' is modelled (see Morrissey 2004). A central problem is that because aid has been so ubiquitous, with most developing countries depending on aid as their central source of external finance for about 40 years, assessing its impact is difficult as it involves the counterfactual of what would have happened if they hadn't been. In short, assessing aid effectiveness is complicated (see reviews in Lancaster 2007 and Riddell 2007), because there are a diverse set of aid instruments or types of aid; they are given to different constituencies, such as NGOs, the private sector and governments; and because they are given for different purposes, such as food relief, school books, roads and so forth. And then, to cap it all, the overall effect (if there is one that's observable in a unity sense) is analysed by people who do not share an epistemology or methodology; that is, by people who do not share the same way of looking at the world, in a philosophical sense, or the same way of assessing it.

Thus, the first aspect of this complexity, as we have seen throughout the book, is that aid instruments vary and are associated with differing objectives and interests. Aid to the private sector is targeted toward meeting both commercial objectives of industrial sectors in the donors' own country, as well as market and growth objectives in the recipient. This contrasts markedly with aid in the form of grants which might be given in support of a vaccination intervention or feeding programme, whose effect is much easier to measure in terms of human welfare and not necessarily important in terms of its contribution to growth (although completely growth-obsessed economists might do such a calculation), or commercial interests in the aid-giving country. Aid for the latter purpose is more likely to be in grant form, while in the former, in loan form.

When these types of aid are all added together some calculations seem fairly uncontested on their overall effect. For example, most people are relieved to learn that aid as a form of liquidity injection is more developmental than foreign earnings per se, say from a mineral extraction industry, since the transparency of such flows already exceeds that pertaining to other external earnings, such as those from oil (Collier 2007: 101–2). In other words, productive plans on how it is to be used, which can be imposed through conditionality of one type or another, or are adhered to by governments voluntarily, actually do lead to it being spent on 'development' more so than money which just arrives as earnings, or in some cases, more accurately, as rents. Whether these 'developmental' effects are offset by the consequences of conditionality in terms of political resentment, the encouragement of profligacy and associated drop in national savings is less understood.

Thus, aid tends to raise growth, whereas oil earnings tend to lower it, at least in the 'bottom billion' who are the particular subject of Collier's recent book. Overall, Collier estimates that aid has added around one percentage point to the annual growth rate of the bottom billion in the last 30 years (2007: 100), although his method is contested by others and is of the large-scale 'pick and mix' variety. Sachs (2005), another heavyweight in the field, argues that aid has been successful in terms of poverty reduction, and should be made much larger and more consistent. Burnside and Dollar (1997 and 2000) find that aid is effective only where countries have good policies, while Hansen and Tarp (2000 and 2001) find it to be effective independently of policies.

However, there are also a powerful group of authors who question whether the aggregate positive growth effect of aid exists and indeed argue that it doesn't or can't be proved: historically by Bauer (1972) and now most prominently represented by Easterly (2001 and 2006; Easterly et al. 2004; also Boone 1994). Roodman (2007) has argued that some effects of a lesser magnitude can be proved, such as increased school attendance or the prevention of famine, but due to poor quality 'noisy' data, the link between aid and growth will remain elusive. In his recent book, *The White Man's Burden*, Easterly explains that the reason $2.3 trillion in aid over five decades has failed to help the very poor is because of a wrong approach which erroneously depends on a 'Big Plan' (2006: 4–5). Easterly's position is that aid doesn't work, a stronger position than it just cannot be proved whether it does or not. He attributes a top-down planners' approach to problem solving, often through a 'Big Push', as a problem relative to a preferred 'searchers' approach, where people seek to respond to contextual features on the grounds: 'The right plan is to have no plan' (2006: 5). Other authors point to different aspects of coordination, delivery, implementation and project-level problems which undermine aid effectiveness, such as lack of ownership, insufficient synchronisation or harmonisation, and lack of coherence around objectives, programmes and policies (Kanbur and Sandler 1999, reviewed in Riddell 2007). A lack of basic equality between donors and recipients is also seen as a problem (Sogge 2002). Some of these more technical aspects were addressed in the Paris Declaration on Aid Effectiveness in 2005, which promotes a deepened harmonisation among donors, and better alignment to the strategies and priorities of recipients, to increase the efficacy of foreign aid. We can add to this list a whole range of insufficiencies which have been posited and discussed around delivery and capacity, although at this level, in this book, this might miss the point. It is not the efficiency of delivery per se that makes aid a good or bad thing for human welfare – this is too crude – but whether the system can be normatively justified. In short, either aid is an extension of democratic solidarity or can be made into such a system, or it is predominantly a central carrier of a deepened capital relation with all the contradictions that that entails. If it is the latter, we must consider dissembling the system.

Other economic effects of international aid can be adverse at an economy-wide level. When aid flows are large relative to a recipient's national product relative prices are distorted, which can result in an appreciation of the real exchange rate, which in turn discourages the production of export goods and undermines import substitution (Killick and Foster 2007). In other words, a windfall of money makes it uneconomic to work to produce exports, which is called 'Dutch Disease', a term coined in 1977 by *The Economist*, to describe the effects of oil and gas discovery on the economy of the Netherlands through the 1970s (see also Tan 1997; Langhammer 2004). The adverse effect on export competitiveness is the critical factor which offsets the benefits of more aid (Collier 2007: 121). Similarly, other authors have found that increasing the availability of foreign aid has made it easier for governments to cut taxation and increase unproductive expenditure, such as military budgets (Hayter and Watson 1985; Boone 1996). Collier estimates that around 40 per cent of Africa's military spending is inadvertently financed by aid (2007: 103). Aid, in essence, does not have to be spent productively by governments, but is fungible and can free up resources in other areas, be spent on consumption or provide a disincentive for national saving. This is a significant problem for the population at large when the original aid came in the form of loans and needs to be paid back on the basis of future earnings. 'Odious' debt is the name of 'aid' which is spent by dictators but which donors nonetheless have expected back. Bond provides some staggering figures for this, such as Nigeria under Buhari and Abacha (1984–98, $30 billion); South Africa under apartheid (1948–93, $22 billion); Democratic Republic of Congo under Mobutu Sese Seko (1965–97, $13 billion) and so forth (2006: 40). Currently, however, the problem of aid fungibility, sometimes alongside these examples from the past, is used by the Right to argue against increasing aid budgets, on the grounds that the money is wasted by corruption.

For example, aid for budget support and debt relief can have the same effect as oil on the economies of the bottom billion, according to Collier. Taking the case of the latest boom in the oil price as a natural experiment for increasing unconditional aid, it tends to exacerbate problems of Dutch Disease and patronage politics, with little or no growth effect (Collier 2007: 101–2). Similarly, aid for projects in failing states was unlikely to have succeeded before they had reached 'turnaround' in their politics (Collier 2007: 118). Indeed, Collier asserts from the economic data that aid is more effective where governance and policies 'are already reasonable' (2007: 102); where it is given in the circumstances of a country where improvements in these areas already has some momentum; and in the form of technical assistance in societies which have already undertaken some incipient reform to their bad governance status (Collier 2007: 111–12). This adds quantitative support to the much-quoted work of Burnside and Dollar (2000) and their followers, which asserts a positive relationship between good policy environments and aid effectiveness (see also World Bank 1998; Dollar and Easterly 1999). There were many studies which denied this association, arguing that aid effectiveness was not related to policy (reviewed in Addison et al. 2005), but much of the confusion has probably been due to the differences in the way 'good' policy environments have been modelled. The group with the most convincing case are those who argue in favour of the association between aid effectiveness and 'good' policy environments (see for example Schabbel 2007).

Translating mainstream research

When an example of this type of analysis is scrutinised it becomes clearer why causal association at this level of aggregation – between growth and aid, or between policy and aid – is so difficult: it is like doing equations with apples, oranges and pears, and assuming that because they are all fruit you can tell how many children will like each sort. For example, consider a study by Clemens et al. (2004), IMF economists, on the relationship between the type of Bretton Woods institutions (BWI) aid and its effect on growth. The authors analysed aid flows to 67 countries from 1974 to 2001, which they sorted into three categories of aid: humanitarian; late impact aid, such as intervention for democratic reform, health or conservation; and early impact aid, which is overhead capital, infrastructure and cash: almost half of all aid. They found a 'strong, positive, and causal effect of early impact aid on economic growth', but didn't find the same positive effect for the other types. This result, for early impact aid, corresponded to 'a project-level rate of return of around 13 percent' (Radelet et al. 2005: 6). Moreover, in sub-Saharan Africa:

> higher-than-average early impact aid raised per capita growth rates by about 1 percentage point over the growth that would have been achieved by average aid flows.
>
> (2005: 6)

Thus, these authors show clearly that (translated): early impact aid (investment), which we can assume is predominantly given to the private sector (capital owners), works better at inducing growth (a measurement of the expansion of capitalism), than aid spent on welfare (poor Africans who do not matter to growth in these terms).

This is not surprising: the neoclassical economic analysis they offer for the relationship between aid and growth indirectly illustrates the legacy of post-coloniality; that is, capitalism works profitably in sub-Saharan Africa, in terms at least of how we are measuring it, when it is the privileged, political, economic elite and international capital who are investing the money, dependent as their profitability is on the historically inherited post-colonial market structures.[1] This 'profitable aid' then contributes to a pattern of externally oriented extractive growth, a financing of the institutional status quo, with all its path dependencies. Politics and the social location of firms are not, as the regression analysis no doubt assumed, exogenous, but are critical to the outcome. The outcome, indeed, may depend on these types of social inequalities. Radelet et al. (2005) use only proxies, which then hide the social agency of those actually involved in the process, where, for example, 'accommodating institutions' and 'good governed' companies are invariably Northern-based multinational companies in countries 'liberalised' to provide full profit repatriation. We return to this issue of aid and capitalist accumulation in the concluding chapter when we return to the overriding narratives of the political economy of development, suffice to say that this 'data' works well to support the 'salvation through external intervention' motif in our first narrative, the BWI narrative (see also Bracking 2006). Translated, however, it can equally illustrate the resilience of the second narrative, the 'resistance but subordination' story, where countries are bound by legacies of dispossession to be subordinate to powerful interests who are rooted externally.[2]

The domestically oriented interests of donors, whether or not their aid in the private sector encourages growth or not, has lead to criticism from some authors (Van Belle et al. 2004: 9–16), while others have argued that their interests prevail over those of recipients (Burnell 1997; Thérien and Lloyd 2000: 31). This 'domestic' interest can be commercial or political. This was certainly the case when Cold War dictators were bankrolled or when aid, such as export credits through the ECGD, is used to support military exports. Tarp and Hjertholm argue that 'the development objectives of aid programmes have been distorted by the use of aid for donor commercial and political advantage' (2000: 80, cited in Riddell 2007: 92). Similarly, Sogge asserts that the allocation of foreign aid is determined by 'ideology and the pursuit of commercial advantage' (2002: 43). White (1999: 517), in particular, argues that donor commercial interests have outweighed recipients' development interests, for example, in their interest in modern highway construction rather than, say, rural roads. Similarly, Browne has recently argued that the expansion of aid from 2005 is primarily due to geopolitical and commercial interests, rather than to altruism, and continues that since aid has been allocated for the 'wrong' reasons, measuring its effectiveness is largely a 'vain pursuit' (2006: 9, cited in Riddell 2007: 92).

When the issue is disaggregated by donor, different combinations and emphases on what motivates ODA can be observed. For example, Tarp notes that US aid is generally directed according to strategic considerations, Japanese aid by commercial objectives, and Dutch and Nordic aid on recipients' needs (Tarp 2000: 92–3), although the association of one country donor with a single pattern of objective is probably simplistic, since all donors use different aid channels and instruments to meet different objectives, perhaps only with differing emphases. The mainstream discussion normally concludes, as Riddell does, with the conclusion that it is a combination of these motivations which persist, although he argues that 'the precise way in which this influence [commercial and national self-interest] is manifested remains contested' (2007: 92). We saw in chapter 7 how aid for infrastructure and the private sector, channelled through DFIs, was affected by different national motivations and commercial interests. This data showed that donors invest in aid instruments and institutions where their domestic and commercial strengths are best matched.

However, this empirical data has more than one normative interpretation. For those who see growth as the best means to meet development objectives, and correspondingly view aid as a poor substitute, these correlations between aid donations and derivative business benefit could be viewed as a type of efficiency, perhaps even as a welcome and surprising one, commensurate with a type of comparative advantage. For these pro-growth economists who have no quandaries about capitalism, to know that aid produces more capitalism would be a good thing. For others, critical realists in particular, correlations between rich states who pay in and their firms who collect the business, might be unsurprising, since it is somewhat axiomatic in Marxism and related realist paradigms that economic processes and outcomes are centrally organised under capitalism by those who have power, and then tend to benefit those same people with power. It is this inequality of power which reflects itself in the ambiguity of the aid debate, since efficiency, growth, productivity and so forth, are only abstracted measurements taken at brief moments in the capitalist race, by the racing cars' technicians (economists!): a cost-benefit analysis of this type is insufficient to a democratic socialist since concerns over growth are normatively of secondary consequence relative to concerns over equity and democratic process. This is not to say, as Collier (2007) does, that the Left are irrationally suspicious of growth, demonstrating a 'headless heart'; rather that they can be agnostic for good reason.

Collier (2007), in fact, makes a powerful case that more capitalism, and thus more growth, in the bottom billion would be a good thing, ironically echoing a previous generation of social theorists on the Left, who may be on the resurgence, who also thought that a vibrant imperialism was (eventually) good for development, in a functionalist and stagist characterisation of history. This is the classic debate between dependency theory (global capitalism traps and oppresses the poor countries without hope of escape) (Munck 1984) and the Bill Warren reiteration of classical Marxism (imperialism builds up the forces and relations of production, building physical infrastructure, and is a necessary bridge to capitalism, socialism and a better future) (Warren 1980). Collier straddles these two traditions of the Left somewhat uncomfortably for anyone who wants to find a purist position, arguing (persuasively) as he does, that there is little hope that the bottom billion can escape since their markets and economies are irrelevant to global capitalism (which also echoes Ferguson's (2006) hypothesis), unless deepened intervention to kick-start these transformative powers of capital can be purposively provided. However, for those of a more qualitative and less economistic persuasion there is another view: it is not capitalism per se that is needed or abhorred, but a more benign type of social relationship than the capital relation, a democratically regulated market based in mutual responsibilities and co-operative economic organisation. This type of social and economic organisation would replace the current focus on 'early impact capital' with a socially responsible pattern of investment, which, not uncoincidently, would be a good idea in the North as well.

Representation of the poorest

An interesting aspect of this debate is how the poorest countries are represented in political economy discourses around inclusion and exclusion. This in turn impacts on whether 'aid intervention' 'goes in' to countries seen as excluded (generally a conservative representation), or 'goes across' a horizontal set of globally conceived practices such as trade and debt, which affect countries 'included' in the world system (historically, the more radical position). Until recently, critical discourse has stressed poorer countries' intimate inclusion, putting the exploitation of workers in the South and the structural oppression of their states at the centre of global accumulation, even though that might be by processes of adverse incorporation (see Bush 2006). Only more recently have there emerged narratives of social exclusion, which instead depict them as set aside, ignored, abjected and forgotten (Ferguson 1999), or in a 'poverty trap' (famously by Sachs 2005; see also Azariadis and Stachurski 2006), bypassed by capitalist accumulation except in the notable exception of extractive industries.[3] It is the history of slavery, colonialism and market capitalism on a global scale that actively produces poverty for one-fifth of the global population, by skewing markets and imposing relationships of power, which, for various reasons – most often due to the burden of more localised compradors such as their own governments – populations find too hard to resist. It is participation within the capitalist global system which has thrown these countries to the edges in the first and perpetuating instance. But it is also true that this global exploitation has consigned the poorest countries to a life of primary commodity production, wherein they have been largely bypassed by industrial manufacturing, such that resident populations have missed out on the critical solidarity of other people organised as workers in trade unions, arguably the most efficient way historically that people have improved their wellbeing. Trade unions reflect that shared 'consciousness of being', referred to in chapter 1, manifested in solidaristic institutions, since the experience of working in industry tends to reduce human distance and breed collective and mutual understanding. These human organisations of the firm and trade union are not as powerful in the poorest countries generally, and other types of social organisation don't seem to have such an effective voice, and thus people are distant from those who could critically provide solidarity. We also saw in chapter 6 how ideas of culture in representations of the African poor can contribute to placing distance between people, which also undermines solidarity.

Critical distance notwithstanding, the moral case for the rich to help the poor certainly remains in tact (Collier 2007), and is so strong that it does not need to be 'proved' by the insult of empirical testing of whether aid contributes to economic growth.[4] Instead the concern here is that in the process of 'giving aid' in the system we have at the moment, the opportunities to do these types of things may be foreclosed, or the effect of doing them be constantly overpowered by the (re)production of yet more vulnerable people. That is the principal reason why it is worth empirically examining the activities of the errant twin of social development – private sector development – as we have done here, since many of the accumulation processes set in train by the 'twin' throw people into poverty, just as quickly as social development is picking them up again, and perhaps more so. This is not because the system is designed to do that necessarily – it is not – or because the people who staff the system are inherently bad – they are not – but because the overall systemic effects of the private sector development system are to endorse and enforce the social relations of capital, which work over time to produce inequality, a proximate cause of poverty. It is the consequences of the capitalist form of economic and social relationship – the one between a capital owner and a non-capital owner or worker – which the political economy of development sponsors. This is a toxic relationship historically, and there is no reason why the 'one in five' of people alive today – the 'bottom billion' – should be thrown into the ring with some of the ugliest predator firms globally, particularly when we have so much historical experience and human ingenuity to draw up in their defence, and with which to find an alternative. The public sector should not be authorising and largely underwriting this unequal contest, when other options, such as social democratic markets and co-operative ownership are available.

A moral case

Pogge put it much better than I could when he outlined two types of responsibility which are invoked by the affront of radical inequality and the severity of global poverty: positive duty, 'to help persons in acute distress', and:

> [a] negative duty not to uphold injustice, not to contribute to or profit from the unjust impoverishment of others.
>
> (2001: 60)

In his essay, Pogge goes on to explain admirably how the existence of radical global inequality means that the rich have violated their negative duty (2001). For our purposes here it is suffice to say that in terms of aid and poverty reduction, many campaigners think they are doing the first – meeting their positive duty to help others – while actually omitting to recognise their affront in terms of the second – that extending capital from the creditor states in the form of ODA, in the current system at least, is indeed deepening injustice and contributing to the unjust impoverishment or prolonged impoverishment of others: profits come home while assets are privatised; CEO salaries inexorably rise, along with preventable deaths from disease and malnutrition. In this sense, the discourse of aid is a hypocritical smokescreen, since it embodies features of an avowed benevolence which actually obscure the use of the aid industry to further the goals of capital export and shore up profitability in modern imperialisms' heartlands.

Pogge argues that radical inequality involves violation of a negative duty by the better off because of:

> the effects of shared institutions, the uncompensated exclusion from the use of natural resources and the effects of a common and violent history.
>
> (2001: 61)

The disproportionate use of natural resources by the rich, and the common history of slavery and colonialism, and its effects, should be known to most readers. In terms of shared institutions, Pogge continues that these were, and are, shaped by the better off and imposed on the worse off, and that this:

> institutional order is implicated in the reproduction of radical inequality in that there is a feasible institutional alternative under which so severe and extensive poverty would not persist.
>
> (ibid.)

In short, the continuation of poverty and suffering is directly related to the actions of the rich in shaping global institutional arrangements, and, we argue here, the Great Predators are foremost in the shaping of the lives of the poor in particular. While Pogge is discussing ethics deriving from the global system, we can apply his analysis to our smaller part of it, the political economy of development or the bespoke economy of the poor. In this economy of the 'publicly aided', so-called shared institutions are imposed – the IMF, World Bank, RDBs and so forth – which then, under an avowed benevolent intent, do the 'positive' duty of development; all the while ignorant of, or ignoring the evidence of, their effect on reproducing structural poverty – thus implicating themselves in a violation of Pogge's negative duty – when better alternatives, which they seldom bother to research, exist. For example, global social movements have produced replete evidence since the days of structural adjustment that neoliberalism assists the production of poverty. Current examples would pertain to countless instances of privatisation, particularly in the utilities sector, where, for example, privatising water systems into the hands of Western multinationals produces profit as its central intent and clean water as a by-product, and countless users cut off from the mains to boot. Whereas, as an alternative, reforming institutional public access to water under a co-operative ownership model ensures that, first and foremost, poor people get some, while the 'profitability' of the system can be forgone in favour of a 'not-for-profit' bottom line. In this case, the latter has rarely been tried, such that starting off on the wrong road means you invariably get to the wrong destination.

The political economy of aid, whatever the quantifiable metrics of aid effectiveness, is systemically guilty of violating Pogge's negative duty. While Pogge doesn't argue this directly, he is critical of development aid on a related level, that it has 'an aura of hand-outs and dependence' (2001: 68). Pogge's resistance to the current global order is found in the introduction of a Global Resources Dividend (GRD),[5] which, unlike ODA:

avoids any appearance of arrogant generosity: it merely incor-
porates into our global institutional order the moral claim of
the poor to partake in the benefits from the use of planetary
resources.

(2001: 68–9)

This type of strengthened moral claim could shore up the poorest from
the worst aspects of abuse. However, remaining with the current
system, even with a GRD, arguably still undermines economic solidarity. Most of the Northern public believe uncritically that aid really
does mean 'help'. In this, they have been recruited to a wider ideology
of 'capitalist ethics', summarised proficiently by Žižek, where 'the
ruthless pursuit of profit is counteracted by charity' (Žižek 2004: 503),
which:

serves as a humanitarian mask hiding the underlying economic
exploitation. In a superego blackmail of gigantic proportions,the
developed countries are constantly "helping" the undeveloped
(with aid, credits, and so on), thereby avoiding the key issue,
namely, their complicity in and co-responsibility for the
miserable situation of the undeveloped.

(Žižek 2004: 504)

For such an important job the relatively low cost of development
grants can be seen as an efficient advertising budget for the greater
public relations job for capitalism that they perform.

There are also other costs to the poorest which pertain to this system
of public relations, since it causes unquantifiable psychological
damage to those who are forced into the receipt of apparent charity,
rather than entitlement as a consequence of their intrinsic humanity
and global citizenship. This feature must be added to the uninspiring
economic balance sheet: the credo of development aid remains 'we are
doing this to help you (because you cannot help yourselves)' (Bernstein 2007: 18). While the human rights agenda and 'rights-based
development' has ameliorated the symbolic violence of charity somewhat, it is still only a palliative to the myriad images and discourses of
'benevolence' which affect the pride and sense of worth of the subject
peoples of the aid chain. For example, consider the inevitable symbolic
violence suffered by the mother whose child is 'adopted' by a 'well-
meaning' NGO, who must then encourage her child to write 'thank
you' letters to her 'sponsors'; or the cleaner in Zimbabwe who once
asked the author whether she had 'come to make money or to give
things away', these being the singular activities she associated with
white residents of this particular hotel; or the micro-credit scheme

home workers paying usurious interest rates for their loans, while being told they are 'lucky beneficiaries'. All of these people, and multitudes alongside them, are living on a stomach-churning discursive paradigm of 'West is Best and Most Benevolent', which still encodes the message of indigenous insufficiency within global social structures which remain largely racialised and highly economically exploitative. The everyday examples are all part of the bigger picture of national pride compromised to the national 'Big Plan' sent from outside in the form of a PRSP.[6]

In summary, mainstream critics of aid, usefully summarised here by Riddell, have asserted that:

> the very process of giving aid sets up perverse incentives which undermine or, at the extreme, completely eclipse the intended beneficial outcomes. Government aid has also long been criticised because of the way that decisions about who to give it to, and for how long, have been influenced by the political, strategic and commercial interests of the donors, rather than being driven and shaped by the urgent needs of the recipients.
>
> (Riddell 2007: 2)

In terms of this book, it has not been assumed that there were beneficial outcomes intended in the first instance, which were singularly calibrated by the needs of recipients. Rather, we have modelled a triple motivation of developmental, commercial and geostrategic factors, in chapter 6, as the framework of analysis for aid to the private sector. All three were seen as fundamentally bound together by their part in the transmission of a relationship of power within political economy. In other words, the needs of recipients could not be undermined by contamination by other prerogatives within the aid relationship, such as commercial interests, since the pursuit of these was seen as part and parcel of that relationship in the first instance. It is a given that in the export of the capital relation a discursive battle of ideas will ensue about the normative motivation and effect of the money. We are also not concerned with the mainstream growth argument per se, although the debate here is set to become increasingly fashionable in the coming years, since growth is of ambiguous benefit to the poor in a class system of accumulation. (Consider, for example, a hypothetical environmental disaster, an oil spill which destroys fishers' livelihoods but causes a growth spurt nonetheless as damaged tankers are retrieved, families are relocated, more oil is drilled and so forth.) In unequal societies growth is regularly captured by the rich and used to shore up their position relative to the poor, as they build more electric fences, employ more guards and set loose more dogs in their efforts to prevent ethical wealth redistribution.

Conclusion

This chapter has reviewed some key writers in the ongoing debate about aid effectiveness, and then examined how far this literature impacts on the argument of this book. Riddell posed the 'dilemma', which is causing the shift in emphasis from poverty reduction of a welfarist variety to more interest in growth, that while more aid is used to address immediate poverty problems, such as health and education, less has been channelled into projects and programmes to address more systemic structural problems, to 'contribute to accelerating the wealth-creating potential of recipient country economies' (Riddell 2007: 7–8). In short, he wants more private sector development. However, these are not contending objectives, since they have always coexisted: even if the fashion of commentators has changed, the empirics of intervention remain, and they show that the latter has been pursued with alacrity even in the poverty reduction era. Indeed, a very traditional answer to Riddell's problem has been aid given directly to the private sector, or PSD instruments: aid designed to improve the operating environment of the private sector in terms of both soft and hard infrastructure. That is, technical assistance to redesign tax, customs and financial regimes, and so forth, as well as to directly purchase the means of production and exploitation.

Investments in 'hard' infrastructure such as electricity generators, dams, roads and ports is thought to improve long-run economic efficiency and cause growth much more efficiently, in the eyes of neoliberal economists, than aid for short-run social protection, or saving today's lives. If this book has a single by-line for this wider economists' debate it would be that aid to the private sector does not provide a better life for Africans, at least, because in the closed oligopoly that is the international aid industry there are too few leakages to 'trickle down' to them. They just pick up the bill for their own exploiters. Meanwhile, the costs of the accumulation the system authors, in lost biodiversity, lost resources and lives, in environmental pillage and lost opportunity costs to do something else, all while we pretend that the West is 'helping', is too great. The balance sheet is a negative, as the South Durban Community Environmental Alliance (SDCEA) and its friends in Oil Watch have recognised with their 'keep the oil in the soil' campaign (see also Bond et al. 2007). Riddell doesn't list the environment as one of his changes of the last two decades which have prompted him to write his new assessment of foreign aid, but when so much aid has historically helped large MNCs do their dirty work of hoovering up resources, questions of environmental sustainability are the proverbial elephant in the room. The achievements of trade unions, NGOs and social movements in the South and North, who have been providing consistent and comprehensive evidence of the costs of the development industry, largely to deaf official ears, must now also be recognised and acted upon to forge a new system of solidarity which does not bear the insult of being assessed by its impact on growth alone.

Notes

1. Needless to say Radelet et al. (2005) is significantly different in its normative and purposive conclusions. As a neoclassical economics paper it goes on to encourage financing of the status quo.
2. The beneficial effects of aid on the private sector per se are not so clear in other research, while Birdsall also cautions other effects of rising aid to the private sector (2007).
3. I was rebuked by a colleague recently for talking in the second narrative, and thus 'selling out' on the first, where it was axiomatic that capitalism was exploiting each and every rural African and a central cause of their problems. I think both are equally true.
4. I would not care if it didn't, so long as children get fed, babies are vaccinated and so forth.
5. A dividend taken as a small tax, say 1 per cent, of the value of a natural resource which is used or sold by governments, which would have raised $300 billion annually in 2000, against an ODA figure (from UNDP 2000: 218) of $52 billion that he cites for that year (Pogge 2001: 66–7).
6. This might partly explain why Robert Mugabe has been applauded in the UN for his little polemical pops at the West, despite his own atrocious record of political torture, stolen elections and government-induced starvation: 'your enemy is my friend'.

11 Conclusion

In this book we have examined the market structures which confront developing countries wishing to enhance wellbeing in their societies. It has explained how the closure of development opportunities for many African countries occurred in the briefest period of historical time, after possibilities were opened on independence, providing only the shortest interregnum in which the development dream could be wrought and then reigned in again by the Great Predators of global capitalism. The argument has been that power exercised through the Northern states by the wealthy, since around 1982, has increasingly wrought those 'developmental' frontiers of the core creditor states more fully into the logics of private wealth accumulation, and closer to the financial centres of capitalism. It is this process which has been illustrated and explored in this book.[1]

The brief institutional interregnum of post-war Keynesian interventionism in global affairs was reigned in, after a symbolic moment of resistance in the United Nations in 1973, when calls for a new international economic order (NIEO) rang out. The majority of countries of the South were demanding their right and equal opportunity to have a welfare state. It wasn't to be. Instead, beginning symbolically with the coup in Chile in 1972, and then systemically after the onset of the 'debt crisis', a neoliberal future began. Dates do not, in fact, fix this process absolutely since events are only salient in a permanent social struggle. In other words, a purposive reform of the development finance structure took place as a consequence of a liquidity crunch from 1982, which became a conduit for a rebalancing of class power. The illustration of this argument has come by discussing the motivations, destinations and effects of development finance. These are that the development finance institutions (DFIs) fund a highly profitable industry in itself (chapter 7), but also, critically, sponsor exclusionary types of social and economic structures in other countries (chapters 8 and 9), which assist the profitability of the Northern cores of capitalism through their frontier institutions and companies (illustrated by a case study in chapter 9). In the process, it is hard to find evidence of social benefit, such as would be evidenced by human development indices or poverty reduction, or more problematically suggested by economic growth (chapter 10). Instead, it can be shown that enclaves of privilege have been created with embedded vertical linkages to the firms, markets and capital-owners of the North (chapters 8, 9 and 10).

An international financial elite sits in the boardroom of the 'house of trade' with the power to direct liquidity to the hands of the preferred centres for production and 'development' (see Arrighi 1994; Braudel 1981). This global elite has the power to deny the essential fuel of accumulation, money capital, to undermine those states of which it disapproves. The 'boardroom' directs a whole apparatus of supporting and interlocked financial regulatory institutions, some grafted on to the formal nation state, and others reinvented from colonial roles into semi-autonomous supranational and intergovernmental institutions. This institutional web is a hybrid form that defies the public–private classification. It exists in an unaccountable realm of pseudo-privatised activity, yet remains underwritten economically and authored institutionally and politically by those creditor states which head the Bretton Woods system. The global elite reward the national elites who stay 'on message' and in line with the neoliberal developmentalist transcript, despite the economic abjection of their wider societies by international financial institution (IFI) austerity measures. The reward is often a liquidating of national investment funds, or 'country funds', for the collective use of the national elite.

Thus, the apparent political equality of universal membership of Bretton Woods is compromised in practice by the binary divide between those that lend, who monopolise the voting quota, and those that borrow, who have only a nominal vote – some 5 per cent for sub-Saharan Africa as compared to the United States' 17 per cent – which buys little influence. In short, unequal power is at the core of world economic governance. A core cabal of the representatives of rich states controls these pseudo-public institutions to provide an oligarchic managed market largely for the benefit of their own 'national' and joint companies.[2] The missing element in this governance regime is consideration of politics as embodying and affecting real livelihoods for people who have a right to participation and popular control. The issue at stake is a traditional one for politics: how are resources owned, used and distributed, and how democratic is the procedure which makes these decisions?

These conclusions echo other work. It has been generally established that economic neoliberalism, from its first generation economic programming within structural adjustment programmes, through the Poverty Reduction Strategy Papers (PRSP) reformation, does not lead to economic deregulation but the construction of (more) regulating institutions. It sometimes also produces political illiberalism in Southern states (see Bush 2002; Hibou 2006). While neoliberal economic orthodoxy advocates less intervention in markets, policy in practice often leads to more, and of a different type, as a necessity arises to reform and replace regulatory institutions and processes (Snyder 2001; Bernstein 2007). Markets require regulation, a role authored by the state, such that intervention does not reduce, but changes its type under neoliberal processes (Harvey 2005).

Core nation states also dominate global power relations, not least because of their control over credit and financial resources. In Klein's more recent treatise on the 'shock doctrine' (2007) the corporation and the state – the United States and companies like Halliburton – are depicted as joined and purposive, where they use shock therapy to create countries anew, and in a 'free market' image, through the destruction wrought by shock and trauma. Since capitalism can morph and root itself in many different and unlikely soils, however, it remains doubtful whether the instance of shock has to be a central or necessary part of modern accumulation, as seems to be implied by Klein's exposition (2007). A system, such as the one described in this book, could equally well do such work in countries where trauma is everyday and persistent in the lives of the forgotten poor. That being said, her conclusion that a people's reconstruction is needed is apposite, although how far this model can be expected in Africa remains an open question, as Harrison recently asserted (2008).

The analysis of the political economy of development in this book is no exception to the general argument of these authors. Here we find a regulatory regime which is directed at managing and containing the aspirations and relationships of states to the global order. Its avowed objective is the same neoliberal free market society that is pursued in richer countries (excepting China), to be attained once 'development' has succeeded. Development interventions in the pursuit of that end, however, are not accompanied by a sequential reduction in the scope of supranational management, as you might logically expect on a road to free market capitalism and democratic society. Instead, states only 'graduate' to a space which replicates the same contradictions as the road toward it: all countries exist in a highly regulated political economy of neoliberalism, where that fact is consistently obscured and denied by its architects. In short, the power in the 'political economy' actually works to ensnare poor people into lives that are brutish and short, particularly those living in non-industrialised and post-colonial states.

The current financial crisis

The precedents outlined in this book do not bode well for the outcome and distribution of costs associated with the current financial crisis (2007–08). The 'market competition' of new creditors such as China, India and the Asian sovereign wealth funds, is principally serving to recapitalise the same system for another onslaught on the global poor. For example, it was sovereign wealth funds, meaning pools of dollars earned by successful exporting, which largely bailed out iconic US banks, such as Citigroup and Merrill Lynch, to avert the prospect of total market failure at the height of the credit crunch.[3] The rise of Asia merely puts the anti-democratic character of the current Westphalian system and its rather weak claims to 'internationalism' into sharper relief. It may also offer the prospect of a financially reinvigorated, but even less democratic reincarnation of the same system.

Moreover, the global credit crunch is still working its way through the global economy and social hierarchy, revaluing assets and bankrupting banks and firms where there is no slack to cut costs in production. In the short term the problems in the core may make the emerging markets look slightly more attractive for floating investment, portfolio and sovereign wealth funds. In the medium term this might look more like moving the proverbial deck-chairs on the *Titanic* when the iceberg has already been hit. For one thing there is a historical pattern which suggests that within capitalism the poor people will end up paying disproportionately for a crisis – eventually – it may just take a while for the full tally to emerge. This is because the rich are generally more powerful, and thus have the means to pass on their economic woes to more vulnerable people.

This might be, for example, because they can put up prices on commodities that they know the poor have to buy, called goods with 'inelastic demand', such as gas for heating. This causes inflation, and inflation shifts the burden of adjustment, experienced through a decline in real income, to the most vulnerable. The poor are those people least likely to be able to negotiate a rise in their incomes to accommodate the rising prices associated with inflation, such as pensioners and casual workers. At the time of writing, the largest banks have already written-off or written-down some part of their losses, the medium-size banks and smaller building societies have done the same, and in the process a few have gone under, but most have effectively handed on their liabilities to customers through higher charges and interest rates. Firms too, in the North at least, are in the process of adjusting to higher borrowing costs and higher raw material costs by hiking up prices, particularly in the energy and fuel sectors, while resisting workers' claims for more wages. The workers in the North are paying higher overheads and have less to spend in household budgets. In countries such as Britain, where a property bubble accompanied the expansion of credit through the boom years, many people may be forced into repossession of homes. More widely across Europe, there is a higher rate of unemployment and a lower average wage in real terms.

It is in the South, however, and in general, that a larger part of the bill will fall for capitalism's expansionist folly, both absolutely and relatively, as is the historical lot of the economically vulnerable. The core banks find it difficult to pass on the true costs of crisis to Northern workers as the governments of Europe and North America regulate the global banking system, and don't like too much trouble in their own back yards, where their electorates live. Those who will pick up the bill are countries that still need to borrow at higher interest rates, countries who have a large debt stock at flexible interest rates, and those countries whose demand for higher priced commodities, in particular oil, is inelastic in the face of soaring prices. The non-oil producing countries with the lowest incomes will pay most, and the poorest people within them are the last in line. For these people there are no luxuries in their budgets, the purchase of which can be postponed or avoided until the crunch is over; no elasticity with which to ride out the storm, since they only buy food, fuel (for heating, not cars) and some limited consumer durables now. In global terms, it is these two items which have been most subject to inflation recently.

Why this is so is complex, and not all to do with the credit crunch, since the economies of fuel and food are also part of the reason why that particular boom and bust in the money market occurred in the first place, and are also partly separate from it. But we can probably safely speculate that the rise in oil prices is related to devaluation in the US economy and to a drop in the supply of safe investment locations in the United States. This causes excess supply of dollars globally, a reduction in their value, global inflation and rising oil prices since the oil-producing countries' elites and the US oil companies have a shared interest in clawing back their profit margin as the value of the dollar drops. The precedent here is events in the early 1970s, after the Bretton Woods system of fixing the value of the dollar was abandoned unilaterally by the United States in 1971 and the dollar was allowed to free float. The dollar dropped in value, as did all the debts the United States owed in dollars, and the value of other people's dollar holdings in the petrodollar and eurodollar markets. Powerful agents clawed back earnings and the value of their chips in the global money markets by hiking the price of the commodities they sold. Oil price rises, quadrupling in 1973–74, can be seen as an example of this process. But since oil is an example of a commodity with relatively inelastic demand (where people cannot easily find substitutes, and for which their consumption is pretty necessary and not reducible), more inflation ensued. However, in the contemporary period, some of the rising prices of food and fuel may also be because of demographics; because, for example, China and India are becoming relatively richer, and increasing their demands in global meat and petrol markets. That being said, there is still an intuitively powerful alternative explanation, that industrial conglomerates and finance houses at the top of the system, the Great Predators, are busy passing the buck. It is the poorest for whom the impact of rising prices of commodities is the most extreme and harsh. Meals will be missed and grates will be cold.

In sum, immanent processes at work make democratic reform of the regulation of money and its institutional system of supply all the more urgent. This is because it is the global monetary system which passes a rich person's problem to a poor person, and which spreads the diseases of Northern capitalism to those who can least afford to bear the cost. But the conclusion that democratic reform is required of current institutions would contradict the politics adopted by the largely Northern-dominated social movementism at a global level (represented, for example, by the anti-globalisers of Seattle, with their blend of culture jamming and situationism), in terms of the characterisation of the corporate firm and the global public sphere. But this might not be a problem, since this type of opposition can be improved upon.

First, opposition to the firm from this type of social movement resistance has had only marginal effect, since it has a cultural focus on brands and reputation, rather than workers and quality of living. For example, under pressure from its opponents, the firm subcontracts to local production companies to avoid attention, as has happened in the Nigerian oil industry, while keeping its most profitable assets – the intellectual property, licenses and natural resource agreements – to itself. The regulation of the Indian clothing industry also illustrates this point, where Northern companies are put under pressure through the reputation of their brands, and desiring to avoid a direct association with child labour, they merely lengthen supply chains. The corporate firm becomes the invisible financial controller, the puppeteer of a plethora of other more domesticated companies. In short, the firm and the brand prove amorphous when opposed, and as shape-shifting as the most energetic spirit. As Hoogvelt explained (2001), in the twentieth-century history of capital, the division of labour within firms became increasingly more complex, and processes of fragmentation and internalisation served to shift ownership and responsibility both out and in, depending on the expediency of the issue the firm was confronting. An extension and acceleration of these processes has been the most common corporate response to opposition concentrated at firm level, resulting in ever shifting and more abstracted corporate ownership relations, and little social change.

The anti-globalisation movement has also adopted a relatively uncritical oppositionism towards the public IFIs. The World Bank, IMF and WTO are understood as undemocratic, unaccountable and responsible for globalised poverty through the imposition of financial discipline, austerity and markets which favour the rich. These charges are broadly correct. However, these criticisms also warrant an historical examination of the counterfactual argument: what if they were closed down or hadn't been created? This question suggests that a certain level of pure oppositionalism may be counter-productive. As public regulators of sorts these institutions have a proper and legitimate role to play, and without rules-based systems peripheral economies would arguably be even poorer. These institutions are children, first and foremost, of Keynesian ideology which demanded a regulating influence in world markets to protect against the economic brutality of the unpredictable business cycle. Their construction was prompted by the devastating depression of the 1930s, and the experience of the Second World War in resisting fascism and Nazism. The problem for radical change should not be how to destroy international financial regulators per se, but more how to enable these institutions to properly do the job in an accountable and democratic way. In other words, the World Social Forum demand for IFI closure would be only a pyrrhic victory, if an alternative mutualist form of co-operative regulator were not instantly constructed and embedded from within the democratic social movement. An entirely unregulated market, as Polanyi (2001 [1994]) showed a long time ago, and the recent history of marketisation in the former Soviet Union and Eastern Europe attests to, is a worse option (Stiglitz 2001). In sum, without endorsing the more popular call to shut down the IFIs entirely, of the World Social Forum, the reform being advocated here would be so far-reaching that they would be unrecognisable, like closing them down and instantly opening them up again, but with a different operating logic.

The problem of politics

This book has illuminated the cruel irony which confronts those seeking radical change in that the institutional superstructure of the global economy does regulate capitalism, but not in a way which leads to the outcome of increased economic equity or redistribution. In this sense, the many authors who have urged that the public sphere should be reinvigorated as a centre for democratic values, and to counter corporate power (beginning from Klein 2000; Hertz 2001; Monbiot 2000), have often failed to see how 'public' regulation already is. The problem is not that the liberal divide of public and private is not being respected, it is that it doesn't exist in the liberal sense at all. Instead, financial managers in the supposed 'public' regulators do not seek social equity or reduced inequality, or share the normative values of worker and social movements. So given this political economy and distribution of power, what political theory can inform social change?

One possibility is to re-engage with theories of imperialism. In one important definition of imperialism, associated with Lenin and Hilferding, imperialism was equated with the export of capital from the centre to the periphery of the global economy (reviewed in Weeks 1983: 223–7; Spence 1985: 118–26; Brewer 1990; Bracking and Harrison 2003). This economic process was accompanied by brute force and political oppression (Luxemburg 1968 [1923]); a process of looting resources (Rodney 1972; Zeleza 1993, reviewed in Bond 2006). This book has shown how a similar process of export is still a functional business of Northern states through their activities in support of their domiciled companies. They conduct business promotion, the supply of export and investment insurance for trade and exchange; 'aid projects' for companies to invest in; and underwrite consortia through participation in the IMF and IFC in order to facilitate their companies' participation in the larger and more lucrative private sector projects in the South. Additionally, the hoary debate in early Marxist theories of imperialism about the meaning of competitiveness within a 'monopoly stage', where finance capital dominates trade and investment, can be seen as partially solved here. Committees to 'manage the common affairs of the bourgeoisie' have been developed at the global level to manage the competition between both national firms and national DFIs. And they are part of the development industry. Moreover, the global bodies of the IFC and IMF are joint ventures in the sense that they are jointly owned by the most powerful states, who extend credit. They have been referred to here as creditor states. In other words, national elites still compete in terms of capital export, but have developed a coordinated system to manage the 'rules of the game' within the marketplace, as we saw in chapters 3 and 4.

Another important definition of imperialism, associated with Kautsky, equates it with unequal state power (see Weeks 1983: 223–7; Brewer 1990) and the continuous remaking of this inequality in the modern global order. We can observe the symptoms of such a system in the undoubtedly iniquitous global trading and investment systems and the arbitrary, if not racialised, basis of modern risk and investment calculations (Haufler 1997; Maurer 2002; De Goede 2004; Mkandawire 2005, reviewed in Bracking 2006). The remaking of this inequality is also a key job of the modern nation state, through its departments of foreign affairs, trade, exporting regulation and export and investment insurance (see Payne 2005). More obviously, although not covered here, we see unequal power in the military misadventures of our age (on the United States see Chomsky 1993 and 2007; Pilger 2007). In this book, the deployment of financial and business assets, under the organisational auspices of the state and multilateral organisations, has been outlined in relation to how unequal power and differential economic outcomes are organised. The DFIs, alongside other international institutions such as the WTO, restructure economic inequality and manage the duopoly of the majority poor world and the minority rich.

Thus, theories of imperialism describe the political economy of development well. But they are not so good at telling us why it has turned out this way, or how to change it. References to historical materialism, class struggle or the falling rate of profit seem to be entirely too abstract. Instead, theories of power may be more helpful. But power, as any political sociologist will attest, is a complicated and multidimensional affair (see Haugaard 2002), having both discursive and material elements. While the author identifies with post-structural analysis, in the sense that power and inequality are quite clearly a product of discursive practice, historiography, sociological representation and so forth, power is also concrete and material in its effects and practice. In this book power has been discussed unashamedly in terms of who has the money and the resources, in an instrumental sense of who does what to whom. This is a concrete, empirical and critical realist context in which to discuss power. It is often called 'power over', as opposed to other ways of looking at power, such as 'power within' or 'among' or 'to do (something)' (types of power are reviewed in Mosedale 2008: 222–4). The book has focused on institutions which are simultaneously both the product of history and working in contemporary affairs, to recreate themselves and inequality and power more widely, through their control over money and resources. They are shaping the possibilities and life contexts of future generations of African people, in an international political system otherwise bereft of democratically authored authority, as voting in the UN so clearly demonstrates.

Marx wrote two iconic truths about power and ideology, that:

1. real power is hidden, occluded, mystified and that it must be critically and metaphorically 'unveiled' to be seen and understood; and that
2. ideology exists as a battle between the hegemonic or dominant ideas of the age and the opposition to these ideas arising from the everyday consciousness 'arising from being' of the majority peoples (see Giddens and Held 1982, Larrain 1983).

In other words people have positionality or standpoint, although he didn't use those words, which at best can form into class consciousness. But elite power is arraigned against them.

Dominant ideas are generally perpetuated and promoted by elite people (reviewed in Therborn 1982).[4] Meanwhile, the everyday lives of people give rise to many experiences which contradict the 'common sense' of the dominant discourse (reviewed in Giddens 1982).[5] For example, neoliberals promote the view that capitalism works to help the poor because free markets are the best and/or only way to promote economic development. However, many people experience economic and social exclusion, and sometimes violent abjection, from the markets of capitalism. Consequently, they understand that this is an ideological statement representing the ability of the powerful and wealthy to persuade everybody else that their wealth is legitimate and 'fair', dependent though it may be on grotesque global inequality and increasing environmental destruction. It has been the purpose of this book to unmask the concrete power which is instrumentally wrought by institutions in the global economy, according to 1. above; while also exploring this contradictory thesis about the meaning of power, in 2. The experience of the poor has contradicted the discursive meanings given to DFIs within the dominant ideology of the age; that is, the discourse of modernist development. It has called them 'aid' institutions, but they have exploited people. These financial institutions have (re)produced economic inequality, within a system which simultaneously depicts them as benevolent and 'aid-giving'.

Marx also wrote an iconic truth about institutions, years before it was reinvented in a more nebulous form by the 'new economic institutionalists' of right-minded academic cadre or by the post-war discursive writings of the new Marxists. The first of these modern groups outlined a theory of 'new economic institutionalism', which argues that institutions underpin economic exchange (see Coase 1988; Williamson 1985; North 1990), and that the influence of institutions could have a hundred to a thousand years worth of vintage on the way economic transactions are carried out (Williamson 2000: 597; see also North 1971). Meanwhile, the second group, the post-war structuralists and Marxists, wrote that power and struggle were made up from collective understandings of everyday action and organisation (most importantly, in the work of Bourdieu, Habermas and Foucault). But Marx preceded these contributions with a very neat formulation: that institutions represent and embody concretisations – or ossifications – of past struggles, like the high water marks left by tides (see Marx 1971).

Thus, when Marx writes that the 'tradition of all the dead generations weighs like a nightmare on the brain of the living' (Marx 1963 [1852]: 15) he points out that we are constrained by the results of past struggles. They shape our present. Moreover, in terms of this book, our institutions are understood to have been created at the height of social conflict or at an interregnum where lines are drawn and dust settles. These institutions then perpetuate particular spheres of manoeuvre, habituated activities, born of the worldview of those times. They continue to use the language and behaviours of the time in which they were born, when struggle paused at a salient. We can use this insight to look at the nation state in contemporary times, and note that many of the ways it functions seem anachronistic. Globalisation has added new ways of doing things. Thus, Polanyi (2001 [1944]) underscored the critical importance of state institutions to the nurturing of market economy in the first half of the last century, but now they are joined in this role by international organisations. Our nation states are ossified and inept in relation to some of their past functionalities, such as balancing the national accounts, as capital becomes globally and strategically organised and commanded. Similarly, welfare states, which often represented the high water mark of the social struggle of the 1960s, are now notoriously hard to create or defend.

This book has illustrated that the Bretton Woods institutions are a particularly good example of Marx's hypothesis. For much of the last 60 years they have operated using the 1940s post-war mindset of Keynesianism and state-led intervention. More critically, they have reflected and reinforced the structure of power which prevailed then. They have privileged, for the subsequent development age, the winners of the Second World War in terms of power, boardroom representation, ownership and votes. They stand at the helm of a Keynesian system of public underwriting and sponsorship of private accumulation, using the peoples of the South as a vast reservoir of surplus producing labour, and their natural resources as an unlocked storeroom to loot on behalf of the North. In terms of the new social theorists, they are thus contained in a field, and internalise a 'habitus' from development discourse (see Bourdieu 1977); or in Foucault's world they act (only) on an ensemble of possible actions derived from the last ensemble of possible actions, or in a particular 'field of action' (Foucault 1983: 221). In this they have recurring policy fashions, which often fail, and use the same blunt interventionist tools, such as adjustment, despite their problems. In short, they are habituated and rarely come up with new ideas which would fall outside their inherited ways of thinking and doing. Because of this, and because of what they do, the institutions of the development age have become critically constrained in their ability to sell the development project as a benevolent gift to the poor, while simultaneously pursuing the export of capital from the North and the reconstruction of Northern power and privilege. The nightmare of the past in the everyday lives of the poor has caused strategic resistance from within the 'lifeworld' (see Habermas 1986) of the majority poor. Or, in other words, the divergence of everyday consciousness and the dominant ideology looks increasingly like a chasm! As a consequence Bretton Woods has little legitimacy.

In sum, the underlying problem is one of unequal social and economic power, which causes states to have unequal power and financial systems to reflect it. The theory of imperialism described well the global political economy that results. This analysis implies, deductively, that radical change demands a political revolution in national and international institutions, which can only be constructed from the people and their democratic organisations. This would involve a deliberative attempt to use the technologies developed by financial managers themselves, to 'structurally adjust' the nature of global markets in favour of the poor and excluded, at the second tier of Braudel's model. Markets are managed, so how that is done both shapes social and economic outcomes, and can be the subject of change. Moreover, this reform of the Westphalian system is made more urgent because of immanent processes already at work, as outlined above. The challenge is a political one, so what political resources can we bring to bear on it?

A tale of two narratives

The first is a discursive and moral resource, which can critique the current narratives of the political economy of development as introduced in chapter 1. We can start that process here. We termed the dominant development narrative, *'crisis but salvation'*. This is promoted by the Bretton Woods institutions (BWIs), the governments of core creditor states, and the epistemic academic community and policy lobby which support incremental change to the current system. In this discourse, the development of the poorer countries for the benefit of their citizens is depicted as a complex task for experts to do, but nonetheless a technically possible one. Those with an uncritical view of what development does are situated here, as described at the beginning of the book. Around this narrative is a permanent rose tint of respectability: of responsible, right-minded people busying themselves with reform initiatives, learning from past mistakes and getting the new policy prescriptions 'right'. It is a story of a capitalist economy which is known to have flaws and not be perfect, but nonetheless which constitutes the only show in town and the least worst option. Detractors from the narrative are seen as not policy relevant, 'off message', and at worst irresponsible, since they will lead the poor into experiments with other social systems which are 'known' to be hazardous, repressive and totalitarian. Thus, mention co-operatives or mutual societies and pretty quickly you will be countered with references to Stalin's Gulags, Nicolae Ceauşescu, Pol Pot and so forth.

Against the ogres and demons of development alternatives are arraigned the good forces of globalisation, whose messages of necessary adjustment and austerity are rarely liked, but who are, nonetheless, proved right by economic theory, scientific calculation and the lessons of history. The depiction of capitalist economy is of a sometimes flawed system which can be a bit slow to deliver, but which can be hurried along by good policy to deliver predictable and incremental changes for the better. Thus, there might be a 'crisis' in everyday wellbeing, sometimes explained by rising population, natural disasters and human nature, but salvation is available in the form of neoclassical economics, which creates intelligibility in an abstracted historical manner, and suggests a rosier future in the form of an inevitably upwardly rising graph. In this genre, and the World Development Indicators are a good example, progress is represented year on year (without mentioning any shocking aggregates or set backs); there is a direct relationship posited between rationality and a masculinised individualism; and politics is always exogenous, a 'problem' for the rational reformer who is inevitably an economist in the *crisis but salvation* narrative.

Needless to say, that the actual institutions and agents that 'do' the 'development', as outlined in this book, are obscured by this mode of representation. Also, the practice of institutions in constantly remaking post-colonial structures is measured somewhat accidentally, as we saw in the example of the research by Radelet et al. (2005) on the relationship between aid and growth. Always, the language and practice of benevolence hides the underlying capitalist profitability and privatised extraction of wealth within the political economy of development. In this narrative there is no space for poverty reduction to be anything other than derivative of capitalist growth; indeed synonymous with it. This is proven by the evidence of labour force and value of stocks rising in 'good performers' (the inevitably rising graph); and increased private sector growth. We just need to (keep on) wait(ing) for the temporally inconsistent and contradictory existence of destitution to resolve itself through the continued institutionalisation of neoliberalism. This will hasten 'The Market', measured through economic growth, in its good work of human salvation.

This dominant narrative fatally, and that can be read literally for many people, confuses the measurement of the incremental accumulation of the rich – in such indicators as GDP, growth, capital stock, share values and so forth – with an indicator of wellbeing for the rest of us. When economies grow, and development happens, the global class system readjusts, and there are important ways in which costs are borne by the poorest, as Harvey outlined in his description of accumulation by dispossession. It can be a zero-sum game of wealth for some at the expense of impoverishment for others. At an intuitive level this association can be seen, for example, in the Marxist concept of use values which are finite, where one person having or consuming the thing would inevitably mean someone else not doing so. But somehow modern economics works to hide the finite nature of things, and also works to effectively silence those critics who point out the obvious – that too much consumption by the rich is bad for the poor – treating them like spoilers at the party. The romantic age of development must be ended by contesting its avowed, but flawed, intellectual authority.

But there are also important problems with the narrative of resistance, our second narrative, which can be characterised as *'resistance but subordination'*. In this the noble and often romanticised poor are pitted in a relentless battle against the evil forces of an anthropomorphised imperialism or capitalism, in a duel in which they are always expected to lose. In fact many radical critics of the system seem to be so convinced by the discourse of necessary economics that they spend whole books wriggling around it, trying to suggest reform at the edges only because they have decided a priori that nothing else is possible. Another weakness of this narrative, which reduces its effectiveness as a discourse of social change, is that resistance is often not depicted in class terms, but in popular or nationalist frames, which unrealistically expects elites in Southern countries to be a central part of the solution. African reality is multiconditioned by the past, and its continuing structural inheritance within the present, but this does not mean that the heroic leaders of the national liberation struggles, and the inheritors of their structural position, will remain nobly resistant. The popular front of intellectuals, workers and peasants has long disintegrated. The leaders of modern Africa do not, in most circumstances and at most moments, align themselves with the poor. What they often do is pretend: the signification of the 'poor, subordinate and oppressed' category can be useful strategically in global clubs. It allows leaders leverage to acquire bigger aid budgets, and can activate 'White Guilt' that prevents global action against their own often violent and tortuous modes of governance. Post-colonial reality has been wrought in complex patterns. The new elites have often used the legacy of conquest, dispossession and slavery to fill their own tables. The majority population still toil under the yoke of a neo-imperialism, some of the coordinates of which have been described in this book.

The political leaders of Africa are not inevitably bad news, just as liberation movements do not have to inevitably become authoritarian. But there are powerful structural incentives to make them that way. Not least among these is the political economy of development, because in important ways it sponsors elite accumulation and popular economic exclusion. Inherited economic enclaves (Mhone 2001) in many African countries subjected to occupation have subsequently shaped exclusionary technologies of power. Since aid budgets often support these enclaves through private sector development (PSD) funds, they provide perverse incentives for political elites in sub-Saharan Africa to effect a form of politics which is anti-developmental, and which increases their global incorporation and consumptive power at the expense of the poor (see Ferguson 1999). They do not wish to share national resources from which they are claiming a 'developmental rent'. The type of anti-developmental politics sponsored by exclusionary accumulation uses abjection and political violence as social discipline. It only partially de-racialises models of dispossession. It also, perhaps most critically, paralyses an alternative to capitalism by reworking discursive logics of territorial subordination, within the signification of the 'poor, subordinate and oppressed'. This powerful cultural representation obscures modern patterns of accumulation of class-based power and wealth, and is strategically used by people to increase their wealth who do not easily fall within the parameters of that which they invoke.

Social inequality is also increased by economic systems which incorporate a critical financial dualism. Foreign exchange holders, who are often beneficiaries of the political economy of development, have access to a lucrative parallel economy, while the 'official' economy is prone to periodic devaluations. Development finance is the predominant source of country-based liquidity for the poorest countries. Their political elites must negotiate with the Great Predators for 'overhead capital', and enforce the discipline of capital accumulation in order to get it. In the process, they become members of a globalised financial class and become culturally and socially distant from their own country people, growing to share instead the opulence and wealth of their global counterparts. In short, the *'resistance but subordination'* narrative romanticises post-colonial governmentality, since elite power is situated, and is not necessarily or even predominantly counter-hegemonic. The current rulers of Africa often borrow and reuse the discursive tropes of the nationalist and liberationist past, and then repackage them in a patriotic and racial nationalism, while all the time forging Faustian pacts with Northern businesses and the Great Predators which further disempower the masses. The 'consciousness arising from being' of the poor is countered and dissembled in at least three ways: by the generalising disciplines of neoclassical economics found in the policy advice of the IFIs; by the pretended benevolence of the development paradigm; and by the romanticised agency and avowed class positionality of their own rulers. Confused? – you will be! The intellectual project here is to restore value to the knowledge and consciousness of the dispossessed, in order to counter the opposite tendency of the powerful to try and disorganise and disregard it.

Where next for the political economy of development?

The political economy of development as outlined here can also be depicted in concepts borrowed from social theorists, such as Habermas and Foucault. In this tradition, it is a material example of an assemblage of governing technologies at a global level which create fields of action in poorer countries. In these 'development fields of action' opportunities for the rich elites are enhanced by adherence to 'development discipline' and tropes of governmentality; to the 'development speak' so accurately parodied in Holman's *Last Orders at Harrods* (2007). This is the language of 'capacity building', 'empowerment', 'participation', 'country ownership' and 'necessary and unavoidable adjustment', whose use can garner more money from Bretton Woods representatives. At a global level this process of negotiation for working overhead capital has become codified in the poverty reduction process, at least for African countries negotiating with the Westphalian system, in a way that conditions and continuously reshapes inherited patterns of subjectivity and economic location in sub-Saharan Africa. More particularly this book has shown how this negotiation is concerned with a market for development finance which is culturally, politically and racially embedded, and expressed in risk calculations derived from investors' perceptions and life worlds. Markets then condition livelihoods, with access to development finance acting systemically to sponsor profits for the privileged. But this field of action is not immutable, and can be reordered.

Development is also a 'political technology', a constructed collective discourse which aligns and subjects individuals to capitalist discipline and compromised political sovereignty. But as a narrative it can also be purposive and counter-hegemonic, with solidarity expressed through reforms in aid paradigms. Many people also use 'development' to express their opposition to capitalism and as a discursive tool in their demands for social justice. While the current aid paradigm is shaped by neoliberalism, where development and capitalist growth are used virtually interchangeably in mainstream discourse, this is contested everywhere. Moreover, this book has illustrated that the whole institutional architecture is populated and managed by a directive human agency; in other words, another future is not only possible but foreseeable. Civic action and trade union resistance, sometimes through social movements is evident, but is not often recorded or seen in the elite global village. This may change as inclusive modes of technology and communication are more widely used. Organic intellectuals of the Gramscian type can help by augmenting voice from the generally dispossessed.

In a wider sense, changes in the political economy of development would also fundamentally alter power relations within capitalist economic processes. Capitalism is an historically embedded political economy which has historically relied on unequal and unaccountable power. However, already the progress of liberal democracy and social democracy have shown that demands for political and economic equality and popular control fundamentally conflict with the discourses that make capitalism the 'common sense' of our age. The externalities of capitalism, such as pollution, have been reduced in particular instances and over time. Not enough, but a start. Workers' welfare has improved in some democracies as a result of persistent pressure from workers and social movements for democratic reforms and social welfare. Again, there is more to do. What needs to be done next is to take the managing structures of capitalism, starting with the ones most pertinent to the economic futures of the poorer majority as outlined in this book, and shift their 'fields of action' once and for all. In short, it should no longer be possible to privatise wealth in the face of poverty, particularly when the vehicle of the process is an institution ostensibly set up to help the disadvantaged. The 'public good' at issue is social welfare for all, and public management of money can make that happen.

In other words, instead of funding big, profitable, environmentally damaging projects in the private sector, the Great Predators could fund small, worker- and community-run projects in the public, community and mutual sector. They would become instead, the 'Great Providers'. There is no need to liquidate economies with venture capital and pools of equity, when the same money could be delivered to burial societies, mutual insurance funds, workers' co-operatives and trade unions. This would help shift the balance of power in favour of the poor. Capital would then be raised locally for infrastructural projects, collectively and democratically. The entrepreneurs and small- and medium-sized enterprises, the 'SMEs' of development speak, can be funded at savings clubs rates of 2 to 3 per cent, not the usurious rates of current micro-credit schemes. Prebisch's well-founded faith in the mass of small traders and entrepreneurs would finally be translated into policy, and their energies unleashed (Prebisch 2003).[6] However, for development to be driven by the poor, unchallenged, means disarming the spoilers, and in this case that means the already rich. Most importantly, the global regulatory architecture, which was built to benefit the historically rich, must be dismantled and reformed, including the institutions regulating trade and investment, immigration and development, as discussed here. The Great Predators, in particular, must be managed in a new incarnation by the borrowers, not the creditors.

Many of the social structures that could deliver a better quality of life have been tried before, and many of them have been given a bad reputation by the authoritarianism of the Soviet system, Eastern Europe, China and 'African Socialism'. However, localised, community-centred, small-scale, economic co-operatives with a low environmental impact still hold out the best chance of economic renewal. Where large-scale units are necessary and smaller ones impractical for technical reasons, such as in some energy and utilities infrastructure, democratic and popular control of the budgets should be a condition of the project: donor conditionality cannot do this job effectively, and cannot substitute for proper democratic accountability. Worker and social movement histories have their skeletons in the cupboards to be sure, but these demons must be faced off, since the alternative system, which is the one described in this book, is also flawed in at least two respects: its politics and its economics. We can do better.

Notes

1. By default of the author's own class positioning, nationality and other sociological attributes, a disproportionate volume of the evidence has been from the British institutional network, although where data and ability permits, a global case has been made. In that sense the claim to global scope is, in parts, made in the correspondence between a British case study and the assumed likeness to other bilateral equivalents, a method which inevitably carries the normal caveats of a problematic generalisability. None the less, it is for the reader to decide whether the case has been 'proved'.

2. While China, India and so forth are entering the key markets as 'big' players, they are not, at the time of writing, having a decisive role in (re)setting the rules of the game (yet).

3. According to the *Economist* (2008), the governments of Singapore, Kuwait and South Korea provided much of the $21 billion lifeline to these banks on 15 January 2008, making a $69 billion running total of recapitalisation from sovereign funds, the surplus savings of developing countries, to the worlds biggest banks since the sub-prime crisis began.

4. This is not entirely tautological since dominant ideas and those of dominant people can diverge. An idea largely found in Marx and Engels, *The German Ideology* (1970: 64–6) and commonly referred to as the 'dominant ideology thesis' (see Abercrombie and Turner 1982).

5. Most notably in Marx (1971) *Preface to A Contribution to the Critique of Political Economy*, pp. 20–2.

6. Raúl Prebisch (1901–1986) was a renowned development economist.

Bibliography

Abdul-Raheem, T. (2008) '15% is not just a number, it is a choice between life or death', Tajudeen's Thursday Postcard, Justice Africa (17 April), at: www.justiceafrica.org/blog/2008/04/17/choose-life-and-dont-let-them-take-away-the-15-pledge/

Abercrombie, N. and Turner, B. S. (1982) 'The Dominant Ideology Thesis'. In A. Giddens and D. Held (eds), *Classes, Power, and Conflict: Classical and Contemporary Debates*. Basingstoke: Macmillan.

Actis (2008) 'Portfolio', at: www.act.is/portfolio/index.asp, accessed 4 June 2008.

―――― (2008a) 'CDC buys a 14% stake in Flamingo Holdings, a fully integrated horticultural business', at: www.act.is/press/releases/cdc-buys-a-14-stake-in-flamingo-holdings-a-fully-integrated-horticultural-business.asp

―――― (2008b) 'Actis and Helios exit Flamingo Holdings', at: www.act.is/press/releases/actis-and-helios-exit-flamingo-holdings.asp

―――― (2008c) 'Michael Turner, Partner, Agribusiness', at: www.act.is/press/pdf/michael_turner.pdf

Addison, T., Mavrotas, G. and McGillivray, M. (2005) 'Aid to Africa: An Unfinished Agenda', *Journal of International Development*, 17, pp. 989–1001.

African Development Bank (AfDB) (2008) *Group Financial Presentation: Operational and Financial Analysis* (May).

―――― (2008a) 'Procurement Statistics, Procurement Summary by Country from 2003 to 2008' (April), at: www.afdb.org/portal/page?_pageid=473,969665&_dad=portal&_schema=PORTAL, accessed 13 June 2008.

Altenburg, T. (2005) 'The Private Sector and Development Agencies: How to Form Successful Alliances'. Discussion Paper to the DIE-GDI Working Group, Tenth International Business Forum, New York (August).

Amnesty International (2000) *UK Foreign and Asylum Policy: Human Rights Audit*. London: Amnesty International.

Andresen, S. (2000) 'The Financial Stability Forum', *CESifo Forum*, 1(4), pp. 18–20.

Arrighi, G. (1994) *The Long Twentieth Century*. London: Verso.

―――― (2002) 'The African Crisis: World Systemic and Regional Aspects', *New Left Review*, 15, pp. 5–36.

Ashley, C., Warner, M. and Romano, J. (2005) *Directions for Private Sector Development Instruments in Africa: 8 Strategies for the Policy*

Maker, Overseas Development Institution (ODI) (June), at: www.odi.org.uk/iedg/Business_Development_Performance/Pape rs/ODI_PSDInstruments_Africa.pdf, accessed 3 June 2008.

Asian Development Bank (ADB) (2006) 'Proposed Loan and Political Risk Guarantee Islamic Republic of Afghanistan: Roshan Phase II Expansion Project, Report and Recommendation of the President to the Board of Directors, Asian Development Bank', at: www.adb.org/Documents/RRPs/AFG/40918-AFG-RRP.pdf, accessed 14 July 2008.

—— (2007) *Asian Development Bank & United Kingdom: A Fact Sheet.* ADB (31 December), at: www.adb.org/documents/fact_sheets/ ukg.pdf

Azariadis, C. and Stachurski, J. (2006) 'Poverty Traps'. In P. Aghion and S. N. Durlauf (eds), *The Handbook of Economic Growth, Vol. 1A*, pp. 295–384. Amsterdam: Elsevier Science.

Bairoch, P. (1997) *Victoires and deboires*, 3 vols. Paris: Gallimard.

Bauer, P. T. (1972) *Dissent on Development*. Cambridge, Mass.: Harvard University Press.

Bayart, J.-P. (1993) *The State in Africa: The Politics of the Belly*. London: Longman Group UK.

Bebbington, A. J., Dani, A. A., de Haan, A. and Walton, M. (eds) (2008) *Institutional Pathways to Equity: addressing inequality traps*. London and Washington D.C.: Palgrave and World Bank.

Beckman, B. and Sachikonye, L. M. (eds) (2001) *Labour Regimes and Liberalization*. Harare: UZ Press.

Bennell, P. (1990) 'British Industrial Investment in Sub-Saharan Africa: Corporate Responses to Economic Crisis in the 1980s', *Development Policy Review*, 8(2).

—— (1994) *British Manufacturing Investment in sub-Saharan Africa: Corporate Responses During Structural Adjustment*. Institute of Development Studies, Sussex University, Working Paper 13 (December).

Benuri, T. (1990) 'Modernisation and its Discontent: A Cultural Perspective on the Theories of Development'. In F. A. Marglin and S. A. Marglin (eds), *Dominating Knowledge: Development, Culture and Resistance*. Oxford: Clarendon Press.

Bernstein, H. (2005) 'Development Studies and the Marxists'. In U. Kothari (ed.), *A Radical History of Development Studies*. London: Zed Books.

—— (2007) 'The Antinomies of Development Studies', *Austrian Journal of Development Studies – Perspectives on Development Studies*, 23(2), pp. 12–27.

Berthelemy, J.-C., Kauffmann, C., Valfort, M.-A. and Wegner, L. (2004) *Privatisation in Sub-Saharan Africa: Where do we stand?* Paris: OECD.

Best, J. (2003) 'From the Top-Down: The New Financial Architecture and the Reembedding of Global Finance', *New Political Economy*, 8(3), pp. 363–84.

Bhinda, N., Leape, J., Martin, M. and Griffith-Jones, S. (1999) *Private Capital Flows to Africa: Perception and Reality*. The Hague: Forum on Debt and Development.

Birdsall, N. (2007) 'Do No Harm: Aid, Weak Institutions and the Missing Middle in Africa'. Centre for Global Development, Working Paper No. 113, available from: http://ideas.repec.org/p/cgd/wpaper/113.html, accessed 16 July 2008.

Bisley, N. (2007) *Rethinking Globalisation*. Basingstoke: Palgrave Macmillan.

Blitzer, C. R. (1986) 'Financing the World Bank'. In R. E. Feinberg and contributors (eds), *Between Two Worlds: The World Bank's Next Decade*. U.S.-Third World Policy Perspectives No. 7. New Brunswick and Washington D.C: Transaction Books for the Overseas Development Council.

Bond, P. (2002) *Unsustainable South Africa: Environment, Development and Social Protest*. Scottsville, SA: University of KwaZulu-Natal Press.

—— (2005) 'Dispossessing Africa's Wealth', *Pambazuka News*, at: www.pambazuka.org/en/category/features/30074

—— (2006) *Looting Africa: The Economics of Exploitation*. London: Zed Books.

Bond, P., Dada, R. and Erion, G. (eds) (2007) *Climate Change, Carbon Trading and Civil Society: Negative Returns on South African Investments*. Scottsville, SA: University of KwaZulu Natal Press.

Bonefeld, W. and Holloway, J. (eds) (1995) *Global Capital, National State and the Politics of Money*. New York: St. Martin's Press.

Boone, P. (1994) 'The Impact of Aid on Savings and Growth'. Centre for Economic Performance, Working Paper No. 677, London School of Economics.

—— (1996) 'Politics and the Effectiveness of Foreign Aid', *European Economic Review*, 40(2), pp. 289–329.

Bourdieu, P. (1977) *Outline of a Theory of Practice*. Cambridge: Cambridge University Press.

Bracking, S. (1997) *Expanding markets and regulating dependency through structural adjustment: business and the case of Zimbabwe since 1989*. University of Leeds, PhD, mimeo.

—— (1999) 'Structural adjustment: why it wasn't necessary and why it did work', *Review of African Political Economy*, 26(80) (June), pp. 207–26.

—— (2003) 'Regulating Capital in Accumulation: Negotiating the Imperial "Frontier"', *Review of African Political Economy*, 30(95), pp. 11–32.

———— (2005) 'Guided Miscreants: Liberalism, Myopias, and the Politics of Representation', *World Development*, 33(6), pp. 1011–24.

———— (2006) 'Contemporary political economies of sub-Saharan Africa: the post-colonial legacy of multiple narratives', *Afriche e Orienti*, Special Issue II, Occidente e Africa: Democrazia e nazionalismo dalla prima alla seconda transizione, pp. 85–102.

———— (2007) *Corruption and Development: The anticorruption campaigns.* Basingstoke: Palgrave Macmillan.

———— (2009) 'Political Economies of Corruption beyond liberalism: an interpretative view of Zimbabwe', *Singapore Journal of Tropical Geography* (forthcoming).

Bracking, S. and Harrison, G. (2003) 'Africa: Imperialism goes naked', *Monthly Review* (November), pp. 12–18.

Braudel, F. (1981) *The Structures of Everyday Life.* New York: Harper & Row.

———— (1982) *The Wheels of Commerce.* New York: Harper & Row.

Brewer, A. (1990) *Marxist Theories of Imperialism*, 2nd edn. London: Routledge.

Brown, B. M., George, S. and Tiffen, P. (1992) *Short Changed: Africa and World Trade.* London: Pluto Press with the Transnational Institute.

Browne, S. (2006) *Aid and Influence: Do Donors Help or Hinder?* London: Earthscan.

———— (2007) 'From Demiurge to Midwife: Changing Donor Roles in Kenya's Democratisation Process'. In G. R. Murunga and S. W. Nasong'o (eds), *Kenya: The Struggle for Democracy*, pp. 301–29. Dakar: CODESRIA Books and London: Zed Books.

Burnell, P. (1997) *Foreign Aid in a Changing World.* Buckingham: Open University Press.

Burnside, C. and Dollar, D. (1997) *Aid, Policies, and Growth.* World Bank, Policy Research Working Paper no. 1777, Washington D.C.: World Bank.

———— (2000) 'Aid, Policies and Growth', *American Economic Review*, 90(4), pp. 847–68.

Bush, R. (2002) *Counter-revolution in Egypt's Countryside: Land and Farmers in the Era of Economic Reform.* London: Zed Books.

———— (2007) *Poverty and Neoliberalism: Persistence and Reproduction in the Global South.* London: Pluto.

Bush, R. and Szeftel, M. (1994) 'Commentary: States, Markets and Africa's Crisis', *Review of African Political Economy*, 60, pp.147–56.

Business Report (2006) 'Anglo sells stake in Zimbabwe sugar business' at: www.busrep.co.za/index.php?from=rss_&fArticleId=3583391 (8 December).

Calderisi, R. (2006) *The Trouble with Africa: Why Foreign Aid Isn't Working.* New Haven, CT, and London: Yale University Press.

Cammack, P. (2001) 'Making the Poor Work for Globalisation?', *New Political Economy*, 6(3), pp. 397–408.

———— (2002) 'The Mother of All Governments: The World Bank's Matrix for Global Governance'. In R. Wilkinson and S. Hughes (eds), *Global Governance: Critical Perspectives*, pp. 36–53. London: Routledge.

Central Statistical Office (CSO) (1996) *Business Monitor, MA4 Overseas Direct Investment*, S. Harrington (ed.), Table 1.4, p.7. London: HMSO.

Chipika, J. T., Chibanda, S. and Kadenge, P. G. (2000) *Effects of Structural Adjustment in Southern Africa: The Case of Zimbabwe's Manufacturing Sector during Phase 1 of ESAP, 1991–1995*. Harare: SAPES Books.

Chomsky, N. (1993) *Year 501: The Conquest Continues*. London: Verso.

———— (2007) *Failed States: The Abuse of Power and the Assault on Democracy*. Harmondsworth: Penguin Books.

Chronic Poverty Research Centre (CPRC) (2004) *The Chronic Poverty Report: 2004–5*. Manchester: CPRC.

Clarke, S. (1991) *The State Debate*. Basingstoke: Macmillan.

Clemens, M., Radelet, S. and Bhavnani, R. (2004) *Counting Chickens When They Hatch: The Short-term Effect of Aid on Growth*. Centre for Global Development, Working Paper no. 44, at: www.cgdev.org/content/publications/detail/2744, accessed 14 July 2008.

Coase, R. H. (1988) *The Firm, the Market and the Law*. Chicago: University of Chicago Press.

Cockcroft, L. and Riddell, R. C. (1990) *Foreign Direct Investment in Sub-Saharan Africa*. London: Overseas Development Institute.

Collier, P. (2007) *The Bottom Billion*. Oxford: Oxford University Press.

Commonwealth Development Corporation (CDC) (1949) *Annual Report*. London: CDC.

———— (1950) *Annual Report*. London: CDC.

———— (1971) *Annual Report*. London: CDC.

———— (1972) *Annual Report*. London: CDC.

———— (1973) *Annual Report*. London: CDC.

———— (1982) *Annual Report*. London: CDC.

———— (1983) *Annual Report*. London: CDC.

———— (1991) *Annual Report*. London: CDC.

———— (1993) *Development Report: Britain Investing in Development*. London: CDC.

———— (1997) 'About Us', at: www.cdcgroup.com, accessed November 1997.

———— (1999) 'Annual Report and Accounts' at: www.cdcgroup.com/files/Report/UploadlReport/CDC_1999_annualreview.pdf

———— (2008) 'Press Release: Financial results for the 12 months to 31 December 2007', at: www.cdcgroup.com/files/PressRelease/UploadPDF/Annual-results-14-April-2008.pdf

—— (2008a) 'What We Do', at: www.cdcgroup.com, accessed 18 April 2008.

—— (2008b) 'Code of Business Principles and Prohibited Activities', at: www.cdcgroup.com/pdfs/CDC%20Business%20Principles.pdf

Cook, R. (1997) Speech, Socialist Environmental Resources Association, London (25 January).

Cowen, M. and Shenton, R. (1995) 'The Invention of Development'. In J. Crush (ed.), *The Power of Development*. London and New York: Routledge.

Craig, C. (2008) 'CDC reports record emerging markets results amid sale discussions', *Financial News: Private Equity News, Dow Jones* (14 April), at: http://www.penews.com/archive/content/2350356821, accessed 3 June 2008.

Craig, J. (2000) 'Evaluating Privatisation in Zambia: A Tale of Two Processes' *Review of African Political Economy*, 27(85), pp. 357–66.

Crick, B. (1980) *Orwell: A Life*. Harmondsworth: Penguin Books.

Crown Agents (2001) website at: www.crownagents.com, accessed 24 April 2001.

—— (2008a) 'Our story begins in the middle of the 18th century, a period of British expansion', at: www.crownagents.com/includes/historyTimeline/popups/1749.htm

—— (2008b) 'Building the empire's infrastructure' at: www.crown agents.com/includes/historyTimeline/popups/1869.htm

—— (2008c) 'The first *Joint Agents General for Crown Colonies* are appointed – forerunners of today's Crown Agents', at: www.crown agents.com/includes/historyTimeline/popups/1833.htm

—— (2008d) 'War brings about the opening of Crown Agents' first international office' at: www.crownagents.com/includes/historyTimeline/popups/1940.htm

—— (2008e) 'Our Work with Japan' at: www.crownagents.com/countries.asp?languageID=1&contentID=138

—— (2008f) 'Crown Agents wins award as Large Consultancy Firm of the Year 2006' at: www.crownagents.com/includes/history Timeline/popups/2006.htm

Dalgaard, C.-J., Hansen, H. and Tarp, F. (2004) 'On the Empirics of Foreign Aid and Growth', *The Economic Journal*, Royal Economic Society, 114(496), pp. F191–F216.

De Goede, M. (2004) 'Repoliticizing financial risk', *Economy and Society*, 33(2), pp. 197–217.

Dembele, Demba Moussa (2005) 'Aid dependence and the MDGs', *Pambazuka News*, at: www.pambazuka.org/en/category/features/29376

Demery, L. (1994) 'Structural Adjustment: Its Origins, Rationale and Achievements'. In G. A. Cornia and G. K. Helleiner (eds), *From*

Adjustment to Development in Africa: Conflict, Controversy, Convergence, Consensus? Basingstoke: Macmillan.

Department for International Development (DfID) (1999) 'Statistics', at: www.dfid.gov.uk/public/what/what_frame.html

—— (2005) 'Niger latest news and situation reports', at: www.dfid.gov.uk/news/files/niger-sitrep0108.asp (August 2005)

—— (2006) *Statistics on International Development 2001/02–2005/06*, October.

—— (2007) *Statistics on International Development 2002/03– 2006/07.*

—— (2008) 'Statistics', at: www.dfid.gov.uk/aboutdfid/statistics. asp, accessed 24 April 2008.

Dollar, D. and Easterly, W. (1999) 'The Search for the Key: Aid, Investment and Policies in Africa', *Journal of African Economies*, 8(4), pp. 546–77.

Dornbusch, R. (1989) 'Debt Problems and the World Macroeconomy'. In J. D. Sachs (ed.), *Developing Country Debt and the World Economy.* Chicago: Chicago University Press.

Easterly, W. (2001) *The Elusive Quest for Growth: Economists' Adventures and Misadventures in the Tropics.* Cambridge, Mass.: MIT Press.

—— (2006) *The White Man's Burden: Why the West's Efforts to Aid the Rest have done so much ill and so little good.* Oxford: Oxford University Press.

Easterly, W., Levine, R. and Roodman, D. (2004) 'Aid, Policies and Growth: Comment', *The American Economic Review*, 94(3), pp. 774–80.

ECA Watch (2001) at: www.eca-watch.org/worldtrade.html

—— (2001a) at: www.eca-watch.org/index1.html

—— (2008) 'Export Credit Agencies Explained', at: www. eca-watch.org/eca/ecas_explained.html, accessed 3 June 2008.

Economist (2008) 'The invasion of the sovereign-wealth funds'(19 January), p. 11.

Eiteman, D. K., Stonehill, A. I. and Moffett, M. H. (1992) *Multinational Business Finance*, 6th edn. New York: Addison-Wesley.

Elliott, L. and Atkinson, D. (2008) *The Gods That Failed: How Blind Faith in Markets Has Cost Us Our Future.* London: The Bodley Head, Random House Books.

European Development Finance Institutions (EDFI) (2006) *European Development Finance Institutions Activities 2006.*

—— (2007) *European Development Finance Institutions Activities 2007*, at: www.edfi.be/EDFI-Report-2007.pdf

European Investment Bank (EIB) (1992) *Financing Europe's Future.* Luxembourg: EIB. Leaflet.

Export Credit Guarantee Department (ECGD) (1999) *Annual Report and Trading Accounts 1998/99.* London: TSO.

Fafchamps, M. (2006) 'Development and Social Capital', *Journal of Development Studies*, 42(7), pp. 1180–98.

Ferguson, J. (1990) *The Anti-Politics Machine: 'Development', Depoliticization and Bureaucratic Power in Lesotho.* Cambridge: Cambridge University Press.
——— (1999) *Expectations of Modernity: Myths and Meanings of Urban Life on the Zambian Copperbelt.* Berkeley: University of California Press.
——— (2005) 'Seeing Like an Oil Company: Space, Security, and Global Capital in Neoliberal Africa', *American Anthropologist* (September), 107(3), pp. 377–82.
——— (2006) *Global Shadows: Africa in the Neoliberal World Order.* Durham, NC, and London: Duke University Press.
Financial Action Task Force (FATF) (2008) 'About the FATF', at: www.fatf-gafi.org/pages/0,2987,en_32250379_32235720_1_1_1_1_1,00.html
Financial Times (2002) 'CDC edges toward a private life', Simon Targett, 21 April, at: http://specials.ft.com/ftfm/FT3CNIKG80D.html, accessed 3 June 2008.
Folkerts-Landau, D. (1985) 'The Changing Role of International Bank Lending in Development Finance', *IMF Staff Papers*, 32(2), pp. 517–63.
Foucault, M. (1983) 'Afterword: The Subject and Power'. In Hubert Dreyfus and Paul Rabinow, *Michel Foucault: Beyond Structuralism and Hermeneutics*, pp. 208–39. Chicago: University of Chicago Press.
Gallagher, J. and Robinson, R. (1953) 'The imperialism of free trade', *Economic History Review*, 6.
Games, D. (2006) *A Nation in Turmoil: The Experience of South African Firms Doing Business in Zimbabwe.* The South African Institute of International Affairs, Business in Africa, Report no. 8, Pretoria.
Gélinas, J. B. (2003) *Juggernaut Politics.* London: Zed Books.
George, S. (1991) *The Debt Boomerang: How Third World Debt Harms Us All.* London: Pluto Press.
Germain, R. D. (2002) 'Reforming the International Financial Architecture: The New Political Agenda'. In R. Wilkinson and S. Hughes (eds), *Global Governance: Critical Perspectives*, pp. 17–35. London: Routledge.
Gianturco, D. E. (2001) *Export Credit Agencies: The Unsung Giants of International Trade and Finance.* Westport, CT: Greenwood Publishing Group.
Giddens, A. (1982) 'Class Structuration and Class Consciousness'. In A. Giddens and D. Held (eds), *Classes, Power, and Conflict: Classical and Contemporary Debates*, Basingstoke: Macmillan.
Giddens, A. and Held, D. (eds) (1982), *Classes, Power, and Conflict: Classical and Contemporary Debates*, Basingstoke: Macmillan.
Girvan, N., Bernal, R. and Hughes, W. (1980) 'The IMF and the Third World: the case of Jamaica, 1974–80', *Development Dialogue*, 2.
Global Witness (1999) *A Crude Awakening: The Role of the Oil and Banking*

Industries in Angola's Civil War and the Plunder of State Assets. Global Witness: London.

Green, M. and Hulme, D. (2005) 'From Correlates and Characteristics to Causes: Thinking about Poverty from a Chronic Poverty Perspective', *World Development*, 33(6), pp. 867–80.

Habermas, J. (1986), *The Theory of Communicative Action: Reason and the Rationalization of Society, Vol. 1*. Cambridge: Polity Press.

Hall, D. J. (2007) *Energy Privatisation and Reform in East Africa*, a report commissioned by Public Services International (PSI), Research Unit, University of Greenwich, UK, at: www.psiru.org/reports/2006-11-E-Eafrica.doc, accessed 12 June 2008.

Hansen, H. and Tarp, F. (2000) 'Aid Effectiveness Disputed', *Journal of International Development*, 12, pp. 375–98.

———— (2001) 'Aid and Growth Regressions', *Journal of Development Economics*, 64, pp. 547–70.

Harrison, G. (1999) 'Corruption as "boundary politics": the state, democratisation, and Mozambique's unstable liberalisation', *Third World Quarterly*, 20(3), pp. 537–50.

———— (2005) 'Economic Faith, Social Project, and a Misreading of African Society: the Travails of Neoliberalism in Africa', *Third World Quarterly*, 26(8), pp. 1303–20.

———— (2008) Review of *The Shock Doctrine: The Rise of Disaster Capitalism* by Naomi Klein, *Review of African Political Economy*, 35(116), pp. 353–6.

Harvey, D. (1982) *The Limits to Capital*. Oxford: Basil Blackwell.

———— (2005) *Spaces of neoliberalization: towards a theory of uneven geographical development*. Stuttgart: Franz Steiner Verlag.

Haufler, V. (1997) *Dangerous Commerce: Insurance and the Management of International Risk*. Ithaca: Cornell University Press.

Haugaard, M. (ed) (2002) *Power: A Reader*. Manchester: Manchester University Press.

Hayter, T. (1972) *Aid as Imperialism*. Harmondsworth: Penguin Books.

Hayter, T. and Watson, C. (1985) *Aid: Rhetoric and Reality*. London: Pluto Press.

Held, D. and Krieger, J. (1983) 'Accumulation, Legitimation and the State: the Ideas of Claus Offe and Jurgen Habermas'. In D. Held et al. (eds), *States and Societies*. Oxford: Martin Robertson.

Herald (2008) 'Sugar Producer to Boost Output', 27 February 2008, at: www.herald.co.zw/inside.aspx?sectid=31353&cat=8&livedate=2/27/2008, accessed 16 July 2008.

Hertz, N. (2001) *The Silent Takeover*. London: Heinemann.

Hibou, B. (2006) 'Domination and Control in Tunisia: Economic Levers for the Exercise of Authoritarian Power', *Review of African Political Economy*, 33(108), pp. 185–206.

Hickey, S. and Bracking, S. (2005) 'Exploring the politics of poverty reduction: from representation to a politics of justice?', *World Development*, 33(6), pp. 851–66.

High Level Panel Report (2007), *Investing in Africa's Future: The ADB in the 21st Century*. Report of the High Level Panel for the African Development Bank.

Hildyard, N. (2008) 'A (Crumbling) Wall of Money: Financial Bricolage, Derivatives and Power', The Cornerhouse, UK (October), at: www.thecornerhouse.org.uk/pdf/document/WallMoneyOct08.pdf, accessed 21 October 2008.

Hobson, J. A. (1938 [first published 1902]) *Imperialism: a study*, 3rd edn, pp. 53–4. London: George Allen & Unwin.

Holloway, J. (1995) 'The Abyss Opens: The Rise and Fall of Keynesianism'. In W. Bonefeld and J. Holloway (eds), *Global Capital, National State and the Politics of Money*, pp. 7–33. New York: St. Martin's Press.

Holman, M. (2007) *Last Orders at Harrods: An African Tale*, reprinted edn. London: Abacus.

Hoogvelt, A. (2001) *Globalisation and the Postcolonial World. The New Political Economy of Development*, 2nd edn. London: Macmillan.

Hooke, A. W. (1982) *The IMF, Its Evolution, Organization, and Activities*. Washington D.C.: International Monetary Fund.

House of Commons (HC) (1990) *International Debt Strategy*. Treasury and Civil Service Committee, Third Report, March, no. 138. London: HMSO.

———— (1994) *Trade with Southern Africa, Vol. II: Memoranda of Evidence*. Trade and Industry Committee, Fourth Report, no. 220-II. London: HMSO.

———— (1994a) *Expenditure Plans of the Foreign and Commonwealth Office and the Overseas Development Administration*. Second Report from the Foreign Affairs Committee, Session 1993–4, Observations by the Secretary of State for Foreign and Commonwealth Affairs. Cm 2685. London: HMSO.

———— (1997) *International Monetary Fund*. Treasury Committee, Minutes of Evidence (Wednesday 29 January), HC68-iii. London: TSO.

———— (1999) *The Export Credits Guarantee Department – Development Issues*. International Development Committee, First Report (20 December), HC 73. London: TSO.

———— (2000) *The Future of the Export Credits Guarantee Department*. Trade and Industry Committee, Third Report (January). HC52. London: TSO.

———— (2001) *Corruption*. International Development Committee, Fourth Report (4 April). HC 39-I: Report and Proceedings of the Committee and HC-39 II: Minutes of Evidence and Appendices, at:

www.publications.parliament.uk/pa/cm/cmintdev.htm, accessed 20 June 2001.

—— (2006) *Private Sector Development. Government Response to the Committee's Fourth Report of Session 2005–06*. International Development Committee (10 October). HC 1629. London: TSO.

—— (2008a) *DfID and the African Development Bank: Seventh Report of Session 2007–08, Vol. I*. International Development Committee Report, together with formal minutes (8 May). HC 441-I. London: TSO.

—— (2008b) *DfID and the African Development Bank: Seventh Report of Session 2007–08, Vol. II Oral and written evidence* (8 May). HC 441-II. London: TSO.

House of Commons Library (2007) *Gleneagles G8 commitments on debt relief and aid - two years on*. Janna Jessee, Economic Policy and Statistics Section Research Paper 07/51 (4 June), at: www.parliament.uk/commons/lib/research/rp2007/rp07-051.pdf

International Capital Market Association (ICMA) (2008), at: www.icma-group.org, accessed 4 March 2008.

—— (2008a) 'Market Data', at: www.icma-group.org/market_info/market0.html, accessed 4 March 2008.

International Export Credit Institutes (IECI) (vars dates) *The World's Principal Export Credit Insurance Systems*. New York: IECI.

International Finance Corporation (IFC) (1992) *Contributing to Development*. Washington D.C.: World Bank Group.

—— (1992a) *Basic Facts about IFC, an IFC brief*. Washington D.C.: World Bank Group.

—— (1992b) *IFC Brief: Africa Project Development Facility: Advising African Entrepreneurs (APDF)*. Washington D.C.: IFC.

—— (1993) 'IFC Approves financing for Four Projects in Africa', at: www.ifc.org/ifcext/africa.nsf/Content/SelectedPR?OpenDocument&UNID=26B7123016DE8C8085256961005BC984 (April).

—— (2006) 'IFC's Products and Services: Financing, Technical Assistance, and Advisory Services for Emerging Markets', Washington D.C., at: www.ifc.org/ifcext/about.nsf/AttachmentsByTitle/Products_Services_2006Brochure/$FILE/ProdServices_brochure.pdf

Jones, P. S. (2004) 'When "development" devastates: donor discourses, access to hiv/aids treatment in Africa and rethinking the landscape of development', *Third World Quarterly*, 25(2), pp. 385–404.

Kanbur, R. and Sandler, T. (1999) *The Future of Development Assistance: Common Pools and International Public Goods*. Overseas Development Council (ODC) Policy Essay no. 25. Washington D.C.: ODC.

Kegley, C. W., Jr (2009) *World Politics: Trend and Transformation*, 12th edn. Belmont, CA: Wadsworth Cengage Learning.

Kharas, H. J. and Shishido, H. (1991) 'The Transition from Aid to

Private Capital Flows'. In U. Lele and I. Nabi (eds), *Transitions in Development: The Role of Aid and Commercial Flows*. San Francisco: International Center for Economic Growth.

Kiely, R. (2006) *The New Political Economy of Development*. Basingstoke: Palgrave Macmillan.

Killick, T. and Foster, M. (2007) 'The Macroeconomics of Doubling Aid to Africa and the Centrality of the Supply Side', *Development Policy Review*, 25(2), pp. 167–92.

Klein, N. (2000) *No Logo: Taking Aim at the Brand Bullies*. London: Picador.
———— (2007) *The Shock Doctrine: The Rise of Disaster Capitalism*. London: Penguin Books.

Kristof, L. (1969) 'The nature of frontiers and boundaries'. In C. R. E. Kasperson and J. V. Minghi (eds), *The Structure of Political Geography*. Chicago: Aldison Publishing.

Krueger, A. O. (1974) 'The Political Economy of the Rent-Seeking Society', *American Economic Review*, 64(3), 481–7.
———— (1986) 'Aid in the Development Process', *World Bank Research Observer 1*, no. 1 (January), pp. 57–78.

Lafay, J. D. and Lecaillon, J. (1993) *The Political Dimension of Economic Adjustment*. Political Feasibility of Adjustment series, General Editor: Christian Morrisson. Development Centre of OECD.

Laïdi, Z. (1989) *Enquête sur la Banque mondiale*. Paris: Fayard.

Lancaster, C. (1999) 'Aid Effectiveness in Africa: the Unfinished Agenda', *Journal of African Economies*, 8(4), pp. 487–503.
———— (2007) *Foreign Aid: Diplomacy, Development, Domestic Politics*. Chicago and London: The University of Chicago Press.

Langhammer, R. J. (2004) 'Halving Poverty by Doubling Aid: Is There Reason for Optimism?', *The World Economy*, 27(1), pp. 81–98.

Larrain, J. (1983) 'Ideology' in Bottomore, T. (ed.) *A Dictionary of Marxist Thought*. Oxford: Basil Blackwell Ltd.

Lele, U. and Nabi, I. (1991) 'Concessionary and Commercial Flows in Development'. In U. Lele and I. Nabi (eds), *Transitions in Development: The Role of Aid and Commercial Flows*. San Francisco: International Center for Economic Growth.

Lindert, P. H. and Morton, P. J. (1989) 'How Sovereign Debt Has Worked'. In J. D. Sachs (ed.), *Developing Country Debt and the World Economy*. Chicago: Chicago University Press.

Luxemburg, R. (1968 [first published 1923]) *The Accumulation of Capital*. New York: Monthly Review Press.

Mackintosh, M. (1990) 'Abstract Markets and Real Needs'. In H. Bernstein, B. Crow, M. Mackintosh and C. Martin (eds), *The Food Question*, pp.43–53. London: Earthscan.

Manji, F. (2007) 'Behind the mask of remittances', *Pambazuka News* (12 April), at: www.pambazuka.org/en/category/features/44839

Marx, K. (1963 [first published 1852]) *The Eighteenth Brumaire of Louis Bonaparte.* New York.

——— (1971) 'Preface' to *A Contribution to the Critique of Political Economy,* trans. S. W. Ryazanskaya, ed. M. Dobb. London: Lawrence and Wishart.

Marx, K. and Engels, F. (1970) *The German Ideology,* ed. and intro. C. J. Arthur. London: Lawrence & Wishart.

Maurer, B. (2002) 'Repressed futures: financial derivatives' theological unconscious', *Economy and Society,* 31(1), pp. 15–36.

Mayer, J. D. (2005) 'The geographical understanding of HIV/AIDS in sub-Saharan Africa', *Norsk Geografisk Tidsskrit – Norwegian Journal of Geography,* 59: 1, 6–13

Mbembe, A. (2002) 'African Modes of Self-Writing', *Public Culture,* 14(1), pp. 239–73.

Mellor, J. W. and Masters, W. A. (1991) 'The Changing roles of Multilateral and Bilateral Foreign Assistance'. In U. Lele and I. Nabi (eds), *Transitions in Development The Role of Aid and Commercial Flows.* San Francisco: International Centre for Economic Growth.

Mendez, R. P. (1992) *International Public Finance: A New Perspective on Global Relations.* New York and Oxford: Oxford University Press.

Mhone, G. (2001) *Labour Market Discrimination and its Aftermath.* United Nations Research Institute for Social Development, Conference on Racism and Public Policy, Durban (3–5 September).

Milanovic, B. (2003) 'The Two Faces of Globalization: Against Globalization as We Know It', *World Development,* 31(4), pp. 667–83.

Mkandawire, T. (2005) 'Maladjusted African Economies and Globalization', *Africa Development,* 30, pp. 1–2.

Monbiot, G. (2000) *Captive State,* Palgrave Macmillan Mosley P et al. (1991) *Aid and Power: The World Bank and Policy-based Lending, vol. 1: Analysis and Policy Proposals.* London: Routledge.

Monopolies and Mergers Commission (MMC) (1992) *Commonwealth Development Corporation: A Report on the Efficiency and Costs of, and the Services Provided by, the Commonwealth Development Corporation* (June). London: HMSO.

Morrissey, O. (2004) 'Conditionality and Aid Effectiveness Re-evaluated', *World Economy,* 27(2), pp. 153–71.

Mosedale, S. (2008) *Women's Empowerment in Development Theory and Practice: A Case Study of an International Development Agency.* University of Manchester, PhD Thesis.

Mosley, P. (2001) 'Making Globalisation Work for the Poor', *New Political Economy,* 6(3), 391–7.

Mosley, P., Harrigan, J. and Toye, J. (1991) *Aid and Power: The World Bank and Policy-based Lending, vol. 1: Analysis and Policy Proposals.* London: Routledge.

Munck, R. (1984) *Politics and Dependency in the Third World: The Case of Latin America.* London: Zed Books.

Murunga, G. R. (2007) 'Governance and the Politics of Structural Adjustment in Kenya'. In G. R. Murunga and S. W. Nasong'o, *Kenya: The Struggle for Democracy*, pp. 263–300. Dakar: CODESRIA Books and London: Zed Books.

Murunga, G. R. and Nasong'o, S. W. (2007) *Kenya: The Struggle for Democracy.* Dakar: CODESRIA Books and London: Zed Books.

Mwanza, A. M. (1992) *Structural Adjustment Programmes in SADC: Experience and Lessons from Malawi, Tanzania, Zambia and Zimbabwe.* Harare: SAPES Books.

Naidu, S. (2008) 'India's Growing African Strategy', *Review of African Political Economy*, 35(115), pp. 116–28.

National Audit Office (NAO) (1989) *Report by the Comptroller and Auditor General, on the efficiency and effectiveness of the Commonwealth Development Corporation* (March), report no. 275. London: HMSO.

Nelson, J. (1990) 'Introduction: The Politics of Economic Adjustment in Developing Nations'. In J. Nelson (ed.), *Economic Crisis and Policy Choice.* Princeton, Princeton University Press.

North, D. C. (1971) 'Institutional Change and Economic Growth', *Journal of Economic History*, 31(1), pp. 118–25.

———— (1990) *Institutions, Institutional Change and Economic Performance.* Cambridge: Cambridge University Press.

OECD and AfDB (2005) *African Economic Outlook 2004/05.* Paris: OECD and AfDB.

Offe, C. (1975) 'The Theory of the Capitalist State and the Problem of Policy Formation'. In L. Lindberg et al. (eds), *Stress and Contradiction in Modern Capitalism.* Lexington, Mass.: D. H. Heath.

———— (1984) *Contradictions of the Welfare State.* London: Hutchinson.

Office for National Statistics (ONS) (2008) *Foreign Investment Surveys*, at: http://www.statistics.gov.uk

———— (2008a) *First Release: Foreign Direct Investment 2006.* London: HMSO.

Onimode, B. (1989) *The IMF, the World Bank and the African Debt, Volume 1: The Economic Impact.* London: Zed Books.

Oppong, J. R. (1998) 'A vulnerability interpretation of the geography of HIV/AIDS in Ghana, 1986–1995', *Professional Geographer* 50, pp. 437–48.

Organisation for Economic Co-operation and Development (OECD) (2006) *The Challenge of Capacity Development: Working Towards Good Practice.* Paris: OECD.

———— (2007) *Business for Development: Fostering the Private Sector.* Paris: OECD Development Centre.

———— (2008) 'Glossary of Terms', at: http://stats.oecd.org/glossary/detail.asp?ID=6043

—— (2008a) 'DAC Chair Announces Agreement to Untie Aid to More Countries' at: www.oecd.org/document/24/0,3343,en_2649_18108886_40660248_1_1_1_1,00.html, accessed 5 June 2008.

Orwell, G. (1939) 'Not Counting Niggers', *The Adelphi* (July), at: www.orwell.ru/library/articles/niggers/english/e_ncn

Palan, R. (2000) *Global Political Economy: Contemporary Theories*. London: Routledge.

Payne, A. (2005) *The Global Politics of Unequal Development*. Basingstoke: Palgrave Macmillan.

Peta, B. (2008) 'Mugabe approves indigenous ownership law', *The Star*, at: www.int.iol.co.za/index.php?set_id=1&click_id=68&art_id=vn20080310060143523C439170

Pieterse, J. N. (2002) 'Global inequality: bringing politics back in', *Third World Quarterly*, 23(6), pp. 1023–46.

—— (2004) *Globalization or Empire?* London: Routledge.

Pilger, J. (2007) *Freedom Next Time*. London: Black Swan.

Pogge, T. W. (2001) 'Eradicating Systemic Poverty: brief for a global resources dividend', *Journal of Human Development*, 2(1), pp. 59–77.

—— (2002) *World Poverty and Human Rights: Cosmopolitan Responsibilities and Reforms*. Cambridge: Polity.

Polanyi, K. (2001 [first published 1944]) *The Great Transformation: The Political and Economic Origins of Our Time*. Boston, Mass.: Beacon Press.

Porter, T. and Wood, D. (2002) 'Reform without Representation? The International and Transnational Dialogue on the Global Financial Architecture'. In L. E. Armijo (ed.), *Debating the Global Financial Architecture*, pp. 236–56. Albany, NY: State University of New York Press.

Power, M. and Mohan, G. with Naidu, S. (eds) (2008) 'The "New" Face of China–African Co-operation', special issue of *Review of African Political Economy*, 115.

Prebisch, R. cited at Charlick, R. (2003) 'Voices of the Third World', at: wwwcsuohio.edu/polisci/courses/PSC326/Voices.htm, accessed 9 January 2004.

Radelet, S., Clemens, M. and Bhavnani, R. (2005) 'Aid and Growth', *Finance and Development*, 42(3), pp. 1–9, at: www.imf.org/external/pubs/ft/fandd/2005/09/radelet.htm

Rendell, Sir W. (1976) *The History of the Commonwealth Development Corporation*. London: Heinemann.

Reno, W. (2000) 'Clandestine Economies, Violence and States in Africa', *Journal of International Affairs* 53(2), pp. 433–59.

Riddell, R. C. (2007) *Does Foreign Aid Really Work?* Oxford: Oxford University Press.

Rodney, W. (1972) *How Europe Underdeveloped Africa*. London: Bogle-L'Ouverture Publications and Dar-Es-Salaam: Tanzanian Publishing House.

Rogerson, A., Hewitt, A. and Waldenberg, D. (2004) 'The International Aid System 2005–2010: Forces For and Against Change', Overseas Development Institution (ODI) Working Paper no. 235. London: ODI.

Roodman, D. (2007) 'Macro Aid Effectiveness Research: a Guide for the Perplexed', Centre for Global Development Working Paper no. 135, at: http://ideas.repec.org/p/cgd/wpaper/135.html, accessed 16 July 2008.

Saad-Filho, A. and Johnston, D. (eds) (2004) *Neo-Liberalism: a Critical Reader.* London: Pluto Press.

Sachs, J. (2005) *The End of Poverty: Economic Possibilities for our Time.* New York: Penguin Books.

Sachs, W. (1999) 'The archaeology of the development idea'. In W. Sachs, *Planet Dialectics.* London: Zed Books.

Said, E. W. (1993) *Culture and Imperialism.* London: Chatto and Windus.

Santiso, C. (2007) 'Strengthening checks and balances in financial governance: The evolving role of multilateral banks in Latin America'. In S. Bracking (ed.), *Corruption and Development: The Anti-Corruption Campaigns*, pp. 273–92. Basingstoke: Palgrave Macmillan.

Scammell, W. M. (1987) *The Stability of the International Monetary System.* London: Macmillan.

Schabbel, C. (2007) *The Value Chain of Foreign Aid: Development, Poverty Reduction, and Regional Conditions.* Heidelberg: Physica.

Sidell, S. R. (1988) *The IMF and Third-World Political Instability: Is There a Connection?* London: Macmillan Press.

Skocpol, T. (1990) 'Sustainable Social Policy: fighting poverty without poverty programs', *The American Prospect* 1(2), pp. 58–70.

Smyth, R. (1985) 'Britain's African colonies and British propaganda during the Second World War', *Journal of Imperial and Commonwealth History*, 14, pp. 76.

Snidal, D. (1979) 'Public Goods, Property Rights, and Political Organizations', *International Studies Quarterly*, 23(4) (December), pp. 532–66.

Snyder, R. O. (2001) *Politics after Neoliberalism: Reregulation in Mexico.* Cambridge: Cambridge University Press.

Soederberg, S. (2002) 'On the Contradictions of the New International Financial Architecture: Another Procrustean Bed for Emerging Markets?', *Third World Quarterly*, 23(4), pp. 607–20.

——— (2004) 'American Empire and "Excluded States": the Millennium Challenge Account and the Shift to Pre-emptive Development', *Third World Quarterly*, 25(2), pp. 279–302.

——— (2005) 'Recasting Neoliberal Dominance in the Global South: a Critique of the Monterrey Consensus', *Alternatives*, 30, pp. 325–64.

Sogge, D. (2002) *Give and Take: What's the Matter with Foreign Aid?* New York: St. Martin's Press.

Spence, M. (1985) 'Imperialism and decline: Britain in the 1980s', *Capital and Class*, 25 (spring), pp.117–39.

Spero, J. E. and Hart, J. A. (2003) *The Politics of International Economic Relations*, 6th edn. Toronto: Thomson Wadsworth.

Standard & Poor's (2007) *Supranational Report*, Special Edition (September).

Stiglitz, J. E. (2001) 'Foreword'. In K. Polanyi, *The Great Transformation: The Political and Economic Origins of our Time*. Boston, Mass.: Beacon Press.

Storey, A. and Williams, S. (2006) *An Irish Development Bank?* A Paper Prepared for Dóchas by Andy Storey and Simon Williams, Centre for Development Studies, UCD, at: www.dochas.ie/documents/Irish_Development_bank.pdf, accessed 8 June 2008.

Tan, G. (1997) *The Economic Transformation of Asia*. Singapore: Times Academic Press.

Tarp, F. (ed.) (2000) *Foreign Aid and Development: Lessons Learnt and Directions for the Future*. London: Routledge.

Tarp, F. and Hjertholm, P. (2000) *Foreign Aid and Development: Lessons Learnt and Directions for the Future*. London: Routledge.

Tate's (1992) *Export Briefing*. London: Tate's.

Therborn, G. (1982) 'What Does the Ruling Class Do When it Rules?'. In A. Giddens and D. Held (eds), *Classes, Power, and Conflict: Classical and Contemporary Debates*. Basingstoke: Macmillan.

Thérien, J.-P. (2002) 'Debating Foreign Aid: Right and Left', *Third World Quarterly*, 23(3), pp. 449–66.

Thérien, J.-P. and Lloyd, C. (2000) 'Development assistance on the brink', *Third World Quarterly*, 21(1), pp. 21–38.

Thomas, A. and Crow, B. (1994) *Third World Atlas*, 2nd edn. Open University Press.

Tilly, C. (2000) *Durable Inequalities*. Berkeley, CA: University of California Press.

Times (2008) 'Outrage over £200m UK investment in Zimbabwe', at: www.timesonline.co.uk/tol/news/world/africa/article4207971.ece (25 June).

Tollison, R. D. (1982) 'Rent-Seeking: A Survey,' *Kyklos*, 35(4), pp. 575–602.

Touch Base Africa (2008) 'Nigerian Bank on London Stock Exchange', at: www.touchbaseafrica.co.uk/products/business-news.php, accessed 3 June 2008.

Toussaint, E. (2004) *Your Money or your Life*. Chicago: Haymarket Books.

Tyler, G. (2008). *All-Africa Review of Experience with Commercial Agriculture: The Fall and Rise of the Colonial Development Corporation*. Background Paper for the World Bank Competitive Commercial Agriculture in Sub-Saharan Africa (CCAA) Study, at: http://siteresources.worldbank.org/INTAFRICA/Resources/257994-1215457178567/CCAA_Success_failure.pdf

UK Trade and Investment (2008) 'Talk to Us', at www. uktradeinvest.gov.uk/ukti/appmanager/ukti/ourservices?_nfls= false&_nfpb=true
—— (2008a) 'Doing Business with Aid Organisations', at: www.uktradeinvest.gov.uk/ukti/appmanager/ukti/ourservices?_nfpb=true&_pageLabel=aid_funded_business&_nfls=false
UNAIDS (2008) 'HIV Treatment', at: www.unaids.org/en/PolicyAnd Practice/HIVTreatment/default.asp
UNCTAD (1994) *World Investment Report 1994*. New York and Geneva: United Nations.
UNCTC (1989) *Transnational Corporations in World Development: Trends and Prospects*. New York: UNCTC.
UNDP (2000) *Human Development Report 2000*. New York: Oxford University Press.
USAID (2007) *Global Development Alliance: Expanding the Impact of Foreign Assistance through Public-Private alliances*, Washington D.C., at: http://pdf.usaid.gov/pdf_docs/PDACL196.pdf
Van Belle, D. A., Rioux, J.-S., and Potter, D. M. (2004) *Media, Bureaucracies and Foreign Aid: A Comparative Analysis of the United States, the United Kingdom, Canada, France and Japan*. New York: Palgrave Macmillan.
van de Walle, N. (2001) *African Economies and the Politics of Permanent Crises, 1977–1999*. New York: Cambridge University Press.
War on Want (2006) *Globeleq: The Alternative Report*, at: www.waronwant.org/downloads/WoW%20Globeleq%20report.pdf, accessed 12 June 2008.
Warren, B. (1980) *Imperialism: Pioneer of Capitalism*, John Sender (ed.) London: Verso.
Watkins, K. (2004) 'Africa's Burden of Debt is still Far Too Heavy', *Financial Times* (22 September).
Weeks, J. (1983) 'Imperialism and World Market'. In T. Bottomore (ed.), *A Dictionary of Marxist Thought*, pp. 223–7. Oxford: Blackwell.
White, H. (1999) 'Global poverty reduction: are we heading in the right direction?', *Journal of International Development*, 11(4), pp. 503–19.
Williamson, J. (1990) *The Progress of Policy Reform in Latin America*. Washington D.C.: Institute for International Economic.
Williamson, O. E. (1985) *The Economic Institutions of Capitalism*. New York: Free Press.
—— (2000) 'The new institutional economics: taking stock, looking ahead', *Journal of Economic Literature*, 38(3) (September), pp. 595–613.
Woolcock, M. (2007) 'Toward an Economic Sociology of Chronic Poverty: Enhancing the Rigor and Relevance of Social Theory', Working Paper 104. Manchester: IDPM/Chronic Poverty Research Centre (CPRC).

World Aid Section (WAS) (1991) *EDF 08, European Community-Funded Aid Projects in Developing Countries: Consultancies,* compiled by the UK Permanent Representation to the European Communities (January).

World Bank (1988) *Adjustment Lending. An Evaluation of Ten Years of Experience.* Washington D.C.: World Bank.

———— (1998) *Assessing Aid: What Works, What Doesn't and Why.* Oxford: Oxford University Press.

———— (2005) *World Development Report 2006: Equity and Development.* New York: Oxford University Press.

———— (2005a) 'Projects and Programs' (in Niger), at: web. world bank.org/external/default/main?menuPK=382482&pagePK=1411 55&piPK=141124&theSitePK=382450

———— (2007) *World Bank Annual Report 2007, IBRD Management's Discussion and Analysis, 30ᵗʰ June 2007,* at: http://siteresources. worldbank.org/EXTANNREP2K7/Resources/AR07Financial Statements_Management.pdf, accessed 3 June 2008.

———— (2007a) *Special Purpose Financial Statements and Internal Control Reports of the International Development Association* available from http://siteresources.worldbank.org/EXTANNREP2K7/Resources /AR07FinancialStatements_IDA.pdf, accessed 4 June 2008.

———— (2007b) *IBRD Financial Statements and Internal Control Reports June 30 2007,* at: http://siteresources.worldbank.org/EXTAN-NREP2K7/Resources/AR07FinancialStatements_IBRD.pdf, accessed 4 June 2008.

———— (2008) 'World Bank Launches $1.2 Billion Fast-Track Facility for Food Crisis', Press Release (29 May), at: web.worldbank.org/ WBSITE/EXTERNAL/NEWS/0,,contentMDK:21783685~pagePK:64 257043~piPK:437376~theSitePK:4607,00.html, accessed 4 June 2008.

———— (2008a) 'Procurement Database', at: web.worldbank.org/ WBSITE/EXTERNAL/PROJECTS/0,,menuPK:41389~pagePK:9586 3~piPK:95983~tgDetMenuPK:228424~tgProjDetPK:73230~tg ProjResPK:95917~tgResMenuPK:232168~theSitePK:40941,00.html# ContractAwards

Xtrakter (2007) [ICMA's own data service], at: www.xtrakter.com

Zeleza, P. (1993) *A Modern Economic History of Africa.* Dakar: CODESRIA.

Zimbabwe Independent (2005) 'Triangle Next – Mnangagwa', at: www.thezimbabweindependent.com/index.php?option=com_ content&view=article&id=11365&catid=31:local-zimbabwe-stories& Itemid=66 (January)

Zimbabwe Situation (2003) 'Dabengwa throws hat into the ring', at: www.zimbabwesituation.com/jul12a_2003.html

Žižek, S. (2004) 'From Politics to Biopolitics ... and Back', *The South Atlantic Quarterly,* 103(2/3), pp. 501–21.

Index

Printed and bound by CPI Group (UK) Ltd, Croydon, CR0 4YY

16/04/2025

14658482-0001